LUTHERAN HIGH SCHOOL RELIGION SERIES®

Saved by Grace

A Study of Christian Doctrine

Teachers Guide for Grade 11

By Garth D. Ludwig
   Roger Riggs
   Ronald J. Schlegel

Edited by Board for Parish Services Staff
Editors: Jane L. Fryar
       Arnold E. Schmidt
       Dirk van der Linde

Publishing House
St. Louis

Editorial secretary: Phoebe Wellman
Write to Library for the Blind, 1333 S. Kirkwood Road, St. Louis, MO 63122-7295 to obtain *Saved by Grace* (Teachers Guide) in braille or sightsaving print for the visually impaired.

The quotations from the Large Catechism in sessions 76–90 are from *Luther's Large Catechism: A Contemporary Translation with Study Questions* by F. Samuel Janzow. Copyright © 1988 by Concordia Publishing House.

Unless otherwise stated, the Scripture quotations in this publication are from The Holy Bible: NEW INTERNATIONAL VERSION, copyright © 1973, 1978, 1984 by the International Bible Society. Used by permission of Zondervan Bible Publishers.

Scripture quotations marked RSV are from the Revised Standard Version of the Bible, copyrighted 1946, 1952, © 1971, and 1973 by the Division of Christian Education of the National Council of the Churches of Christ in the U.S.A., and used by permission.

Quotations from the Lutheran Confessions are from *The Book of Concord: The Confessions of the Evangelical Lutheran Church*, ed. by Theodore G. Tappert. Copyright © 1959 by Fortress Press.

The quotations from the Large Catechism in sessions 76–90 are from *Luther's Large Catechism: A Contemporary Translation with Study Questions* by F. Samuel Janzow. Copyright © 1978 by Concordia Publishing House.

Copyright © 1988 Concordia Publishing House
3558 S. Jefferson Avenue, St. Louis, MO 63118-3968
Manufactured in the United States of America

All rights reserved. No part of this publication may be reproduced, stored in a retrieval system, or transmitted, in any form or by any means, electronic, mechanical, photocopying, recording, or otherwise, without the prior written permission of Concordia Publishing House.

Contents

To the Teacher — 5

Unit 1: Salvation, Part 1 — 8
  1 Paul, the Man and His Message (Rom. 1:1–7) — 8
  2 Profile of a Saint (Rom. 1:8–17) — 10
  3 The Wrath of God (Rom. 1:18–32) — 11
  4 The Judgment of God (Rom. 2:1–16) — 13
  5 The People of God (Rom. 2:17–3:8) — 15
  6 We Are All Guilty (Rom. 3:9–20) — 17
  7 Pardoned (Rom. 3:21–31) — 18
  8 Faith and Works (Rom. 4:1–5) — 20
  9 Forgiveness (Rom. 4:6–15) — 22
  10 The Faith of Abraham (Rom. 4:16–22) — 23
  11 *Our* Faith (Rom. 4:23–25; Gal. 3:1–25) — 25
  12 Rejoice (Rom. 5:1–11) — 27
  13 Concluding Activities for Unit 1 — 29

Unit 2: Salvation, Part 2 — 31
  14 Let Christ Reign by Grace! (Rom. 5:12–21) — 31
  15 What Do You Know? (Rom. 6:1–14) — 33
  16 Slavery (Rom. 6:15–23) — 35
  17 Marriage (Rom. 7:1–6) — 36
  18 Our Struggle with Sin (Rom. 7:7–25) — 38
  19 Victory through the Spirit (Rom. 8:1–13) — 40
  20 Children of God (Rom. 8:14–25) — 41
  21 The Power and the Promise (Rom. 8:26–30) — 43
  22 What Shall We Say about All This? (Rom. 8:31a) — 44
  23 Super Conquerors (Rom. 8:31b–39) — 45
  24 Concluding Activities for Unit 2 — 47

Unit 3: The Righteousness of God Rejected — 48
  25 The Tragedy of the Jews (Rom. 9:1–5) — 48
  26 God's Chosen People (Rom. 9:6–21) — 50
  27 "In Wrath, Remember Mercy" (Rom. 9:22–33) — 52
  28 Zeal, Truth, and Knowledge (Rom. 10:1–13) — 54
  29 Evangelism (Rom. 10:14–21) — 55
  30 Cast Away or Set Aside (Rom. 11:1–15) — 57
  31 Baking and Botany (Rom. 11:16–25) — 59
  32 Mercy and Majesty (Rom. 11:26–36) — 60
  33 Concluding Activities for Unit 3 — 61

Unit 4: The Righteousness of God Applied — 62
  34 Therefore . . . (Rom. 12:1–2) — 62
  35 Evaluate and Activate (Rom. 12:3–8) — 64
  36 Love, the Real Thing (Rom. 12:9–13) — 66
  37 Good Swallows Evil (Rom. 12:14–21) — 67
  38 Citizenship (Rom. 13:1–7) — 69
  39 Wake Up (Rom. 13:8–14) — 71
  40 The "Weaker Brother" (Rom. 14:1–12) — 73
  41 The "Stronger Brother" (Rom. 14:13–23) — 75
  42 God-Given Unity (Rom. 15:1–13) — 77
  43 Personal Notes (Rom. 15:14–33) — 79
  44 Warm Regards and a Strong Warning (Rom. 16) — 80

    45 Concluding Activities for Unit 4 — 83

Unit 5: Faith Battles Pride — 84
    46 When Christians Quarrel (1 Cor. 1:10–17) — 84
    47 Trying to Be Wiser Than God (1 Cor. 1:18–2:5) — 85
    48 The Pleasure Principle (1 Cor. 6:1–20) — 87
    49 To Marry or Not to Marry (1 Cor. 7:1–40) — 88
    50 When Temptation Strikes (1 Cor. 10:1–13) — 90
    51 Worship That Does More Harm Than Good (1 Cor. 11:17–34) — 91
    52 Concluding Activities for Unit 5 — 93

Unit 6: Faith Uses God's Gifts — 94
    53 Finding My Spiritual Gift (1 Cor. 12:1–31) — 94
    54 Using My Spiritual Gifts in Love (1 Cor. 13:1–13) — 96
    55 A God of Peace and Order (1 Cor. 14:1–40) — 97
    56 We Shall Be Raised from the Dead (1 Cor. 15:1–34) — 98
    57 We Shall Be Raised with Spiritual Bodies (1 Cor. 15:35–58) — 100
    58 Concluding Activities for Unit 6 — 101

Unit 7: Faith Points Us to Service — 102
    59 The Glory of the New Covenant (2 Cor. 3:1–4:6) — 102
    60 Don't Lose Heart (2 Cor. 4:7–5:10) — 104
    61 Ambassadors to the World (2 Cor. 5:11–6:2) — 105
    62 God Loves a Cheerful Giver (2 Cor. 9:1–15) — 106
    63 When I Am Weak, Then I Am Strong (2 Cor. 12:1–10) — 108
    64 Concluding Activities for Unit 7 — 109

Unit 8: The Joy That Proceeds from Faith — 111
    65 Joy in Advancing the Gospel (Phil. 1:3–29) — 111
    66 The Ultimate Role Model (Phil. 2:1–16) — 112
    67 Strive for the Goal and the Prize (Phil. 3:7–21) — 114
    68 Rejoice in the Lord (Phil. 4:4–13) — 116
    69 Concluding Activities for Unit 8 — 117

Unit 9: Faith Expressed by Hope — 118
    70 Living to Please God (1 Thess. 4:1–12) — 118
    71 The Coming Day of the Lord (1 Thess. 4:13–18) — 119
    72 The Suddenness of That Day (1 Thess. 5:1–18) — 121
    73 The Appearance of the Antichrist (2 Thess. 2:1–17) — 122
    74 In the Meantime Live by Faith (2 Thess. 3:1–16) — 123
    75 Concluding Activities for Unit 9 — 125

Unit 10: Knowing What We Believe: Studies in Luther's Large Catechism — 126
    76 Basic Christian Teachings Revisited (Preface) — 126
    77 What Makes God God? (First Commandment) — 127
    78 How to Serve God (Second and Third Commandments) — 128
    79 Honoring Parents and Other Authorities (Fourth Commandment) — 129
    80 Out among Our Neighbors (Fifth, Sixth, and Seventh Commandments) — 131
    81 Don't Even Think It! (Eighth, Ninth, and Tenth Commandments and Close of the Commandments) — 132
    82 The Father of Us All (First Article) — 134
    83 Jesus Is Lord (Second Article) — 135
    84 The Holy-Maker (Third Article) — 136
    85 Prayer Talk (Introduction to Lord's Prayer) — 137
    86 Prayers of God's Family (First, Second, and Third Petitions) — 138
    87 Prayers for Deliverance (Fourth, Fifth, Sixth, and Last Petitions) — 140
    88 Living In/Out Your Baptism (Sacrament of Holy Baptism) — 141
    89 Bread and Wine, Body and Blood (Sacrament of the Altar) — 142
    90 "I'm Guilty, But . . . " (Confession) — 144

To the Teacher

Saved by Grace offers primarily an inductive approach to the study of Christian doctrine. The first four units provide a verse by verse study of St. Paul's epistle to the Romans. Units 5 through 9 continue the inductive approach with a study of selected portions of Paul's epistles to the Corinthians, Philippians, and Thessalonians. The final unit, however, provides a systematic approach. There students will study Luther's Large Catechism. Note that each student will need a copy of the Large Catechism for this unit.

Saved by Grace is a 90-session course, providing resources for one semester. We recommend class five days per week. However, if the class meets less often, you might (a) extend the material in this course over a longer period of time, (b) assign certain sessions to individuals or small groups for reports in class, or (c) select sessions or units in accordance with class periods available.

Saved by Grace has been designed for 11th grade students, but it may be taught (with adaptations) in grades 9, 10, or 12.

THE LUTHERAN HIGH SCHOOL RELIGION SERIES

This is one of 12 courses for Lutheran high schools. The courses have been designed for a variety of programs. Four courses contain 90 sessions each and provide materials for five sessions per week for one semester. Each of the other eight courses contains 45 sessions and is designed for one quarter.

Following are the 12 courses:

Grade 9

Fitting In: Relationships with God and Others (45 sessions)

For God So Loved . . . :A Study of the Gospel of John (45 sessions)

God's Old Testament People (90 sessions)

Grade 10

God's Plan Unfolds: The Church from Nazareth to Nicaea (90 sessions)

One Body in Christ: A Study of the Church (45 sessions)

Instruments in God's Hands: A Study of Christian Ethics (45 sessions)

Grade 11

Saved by Grace: A Study of Christian Doctrine (90 sessions)

The Church Takes Shape: A Study of Church History (45 sessions)

Which Way Is the Right Way? A Study of Christianity, Cults, and Other Religions (45 sessions)

Grade 12

Personal Christian living (90 sessions)

Engagement and marriage (45 sessions)

The general epistles and Revelation (45 sessions)

This design was prepared after a survey of all high schools affiliated with the Association for Lutheran Secondary Schools and after extensive conversations with high school and college teachers. Thus it reflects both current practices and theory. The Parish Services staff wishes to express a special word of thanks to the ALSS administrators for their cooperation and assistance.

While any course assumes a certain background and maturity of the students, each course can stand alone—a previous course in this series is not an *absolute* prerequisite. The Student Books contain no grade level designations; therefore courses can be adapted to other grade levels.

MATERIALS

In addition to this guide, you will need a copy of the accompanying Student Book, a Bible, and a copy of Luther's Large Catechism. (This course generally quotes the New International Version of the Bible. We recommend that you select a translation commonly used in the congregations of your students.)

The students will need a copy of the Student Book, of Luther's Large Catechism, and a Bible. They will also need access to other resources, such as Bible dictionaries, concordances, and the Book of Concord.

USING THIS GUIDE

Some sessions suggest more activities than can be accomplished in one period. Be selective. You know your students. Use the activities and materials that will be of most value to them.

HOMEWORK

We encourage you to ask your students to read in advance the Scripture or Large Catechism portions suggested for each session. To get them into the text, you might assign selected questions from the sessions as homework. Select questions that deal primarily with facts from the text. Do not ask students to work in advance with questions that require discussion.

If students become familiar with the facts in advance, you can use class time for in depth discussion of the issues. You will probably inhibit discussion of issues if you use class time to correct and grade student answers to factual questions.

If you must give grades for homework, we recommend that you make special assignments. Perhaps after the class discusses a text, you can ask students to prepare a short essay to demonstrate that they can apply the text to their lives.

LAW AND GOSPEL

The plans in this guide help you structure sessions so that students see both Law and Gospel. You will want the Holy Spirit to work in them as they hear God's words of accusation, forgiveness, and guidance. As you begin to plan the course, you might reread *The Proper Distinction between Law and Gospel* by C. F. W. Walther. This is good reading for all who work with youth, especially teachers.

Following are restatements of some of Walther's theses. They were adapted and greatly abridged from his book for use in Law/Gospel workshops designed by the Board for Parish Services of The Lutheran Church—Missouri Synod in connection with the 1987 observation of the centennial of C. F. W. Walther's death.

Thesis 1

The doctrinal contents of the entire Scriptures, both of the Old and the New Testament, are made up of two doctrines differing fundamentally from one another, that is, the Law and the Gospel.

... The true points of difference between the Law and the Gospel are the following: These two doctrines differ as regards the *manner of their being revealed* to man; as regards their *contents*; as regards the *promises* held out by either doctrine; as regards their *threatenings*; as regards the *function* and the *effect* of either doctrine; as regards the *persons* to whom either the one or the other doctrine must be preached.

Thesis 2

Only he is an orthodox teacher who not only presents all the articles of faith in accordance with Scripture, but also rightly distinguishes from each other the Law and the Gospel.

... You may correctly state what the Law says and what the Gospel says. But when you frame your statement so as to commingle both, you produce poison for souls. Remember: Law and Gospel are God's Word, but different kinds of doctrine. A person who does not understand this difference has nothing at all to offer people.

Now to understand this difference is certainly no easy task. The third thesis, therefore, furnishes an opportunity for making this point clear to us.

Thesis 3

Rightly distinguishing the Law and the Gospel is the most difficult and the highest art of Christians in general and of theologians in particular. It is taught only by the Holy Spirit in the school of experience.

Thesis 4

The true knowledge of the distinction between the Law and the Gospel is not only a glorious light, offering the correct understanding of the Holy Scriptures, but without this knowledge Scripture is and remains a sealed book.

Thesis 6

The Word of God is not rightly divided when the Law is not preached in its full sternness and the Gospel not in full sweetness, when, on the contrary, Gospel elements are mingled with the Law and Law elements with the Gospel.

Thesis 9

The Word of God is not rightly divided when sinners who have been struck down and terrified by the Law are directed, not to the Word and Sacraments, but to their own prayers and wrestlings with God in order that they may win their way into a state of grace; in other words, when they are told to keep on praying and struggling until they feel that God has received them into grace.

Thesis 10

The Word of God is not rightly divided when the preacher describes faith in a manner as if the inert acceptance of truths, even while a person is living in mortal sins, renders that person righteous in the sight of God and saves him; or as if faith makes a person righteous and saves him for the reason that it produces in him love and reformation of his mode of living.

Thesis 13

The Word of God is not rightly divided when one makes an appeal to believe in a manner as if a person could make himself believe or at least help toward that end, instead of preaching faith into a person's heart by laying the Gospel promises before him.

Thesis 17

The Word of God is not rightly divided when a description is given of faith, both as regards the consciousness and productiveness of it, that does not fit all believers at all times.

Thesis 23

The Word of God is not rightly divided when an attempt is made by means of the demands or the threats or the promises of the Law to induce the unregenerate to put away their sins and engage in good works and thus become godly; on the other hand, when an endeavor is made, by means of the commands of the Law rather than by the admonitions of the Gospel, to urge the regenerate to do good.

Thesis 25

The Word of God is not rightly divided when the person teaching it does not allow the Gospel to have a general predominance in his teaching.

(The theses statements have been taken from the Walther Centennial Law/Gospel Workshops and are used by permission of the Board for Parish Services.)

We encourage you to participate in a Law/Gospel workshop, perhaps with other members of your faculty and teachers from the Lutheran elementary schools in your area. For information about the workshop materials write to Law/Gospel Workshops, Board for Parish Services, The Lutheran Church—Missouri Synod, 1333 South Kirkwood Road, Saint Louis, MO 63122-7295.

You and others on your faculty may prefer to organize your own workshops. In these workshops you might write paraphrases of the theses, discuss how to apply each thesis to your daily teaching routine, and identify procedures that will help you apply the theses to a specific lesson.

Once **(John 12:20–21)** some Greeks came to Philip and said, **"Sir, we would like to see Jesus."** Your basic goal as you teach each day should be to bring students to "see Jesus." Confront them with their spiritual needs; then lead them to see Jesus their Savior as the Answer to those needs. Let His love permeate all relationships in your classroom as you grow together in grace by the Spirit's power. Set this as your primary goal, and let all other objectives grow within this goal.

We invite you to write the editors about *Saved by Grace*. Share the joys and frustrations you experienced as you taught this course, offer suggestions for other courses, etc. Please send your comments to

Editorial Services Unit
Board for Parish Services
The Lutheran Church—Missouri Synod
1333 South Kirkwood Road
St. Louis, MO 63122-7295

UNIT 1: SALVATION, PART 1

BIBLE BASIS: ROM. 1:1–5:11

I am not ashamed of the gospel, because it is the power of God for the salvation of everyone who believes: first for the Jew, then for the Gentile. For in the gospel a righteousness from God is revealed, a righteousness that is by faith from first to last, just as it is written: "The righteous will live by faith."

These words of Paul in **1:16–17** establish the theme for the entire epistle.

Chapters 1–8 reveal God's plan for saving the entire human race. In the first chapters (unit 1) Paul focuses upon how God saved us from what we *do*. Unit 2 **(5:12–8:39)** will focus upon how God saved us from what we *are*.

In units 3 and 4 students will study the last half of Romans. Unit 3 **(chapters 9–11)** deals with questions of God's righteousness among both Jews and Gentiles, and unit 4 **(chapters 12–16)** touches upon issues related to practicing the new life we have through Christ.

The progression in this unit—and also in units 2–4—follows the progression Paul presents in Romans. You will get a flavor of this progression by reading the session titles in the table of contents. To see the direction more clearly, however, skim the central truth for each session in this unit. You might also look at the objectives to help you give direction to your students.

LAW AND GOSPEL

Virtually the entire Book of Romans deals with issues of Law and Gospel. Therefore you and your students will need to accurately understand and apply those teachings. Don't expect that to be an easy task. Martin Luther was a doctor of theology and over 30 years old before he recognized the Gospel message in Paul's words in **1:16–17**.

Some sections in unit 1 are "heavy." Be careful, for example, as you talk about the wrath and judgment of God in sessions 3 and 4, to place those verses **(1:18–2:16)** into their Gospel context.

Be sure to read the discussion of Law and Gospel in the introduction to this guide before you begin teaching this course. Also read widely, especially from works by C. F. W. Walther and Martin Luther. In addition, you might arrange a few discussion sessions with colleagues on your faculty or with pastors in your area to discuss practices they follow to properly present Law and Gospel in their teaching or preaching.

Session 1: Paul, the Man and His Message

BIBLE BASIS
   Rom. 1:1–7

CENTRAL TRUTH

Christ Jesus called Paul to be His apostle, and empowered him to be His slave, just so the Gospel message could be proclaimed to us. This great message tells us that we are called to belong to Christ and called to be His saints.

OBJECTIVES
By the grace of God the students will
1. describe the office of apostle, and explain that its purpose is to proclaim the Gospel of Christ Jesus as trustworthy;
2. express an understanding of who Jesus is, and what it means to belong to Him;
3. explain that it is God's love that moved Him to call us to Himself.

OUTLINE OF ROM. 1:1–7
A. Paul introduces himself as
   1. A slave of Christ **(v. 1)**
   2. A called apostle, set aside for the Gospel **(v. 1)**
B. Paul introduces his message **(vv. 2–4)**
   1. Not a new message, but one promised by the prophets **(v. 2)**
   2. About Jesus Christ
      a) Fully man, a descendant of David **(v. 3)**
      b) Fully God, the Son of God, and resurrected **(v. 4)**
C. Purpose of Paul's apostolic office **(vv. 5–7)**
   1. To call those among the Gentiles to follow Christ **(v. 6)**
   2. To proclaim that they, too, belong to Christ **(v. 6)**
   3. To announce that they are loved by God and are His saints **(v. 7)**

A WORD FROM THE AUTHOR

Along with leading your students into the Word of God, praying with them could be one of the most important ministries you carry out in your classroom. Be sure to begin each class session with prayer.

At first you will undoubtedly have to lead the way. Soon, however, involve the students. If praying in class is new to your students, begin with written prayers from hymnals or good prayer books. This may remove some of the fear of praying in public for your students.

As the year continues, vary the types of prayer you use. Ask for prayer requests, chain prayers, extemporaneous prayers, or the classic prayers from the church fathers which your students could have researched from the library. Take note of the special holy days of the church. Saints' days are particularly good for reminding us of our own discipleship to Christ Jesus.

Prayer requests may soon become the most popular form of prayer. That form gives you and your students time to think of someone or some special need and to mention that person or need to the throne of grace. As God the Holy Spirit carries these prayers to the throne, He touches our spirit, empowering us through the Gospel to feel the same kind of love and care for people as Christ Jesus has. That is why service to people so often follows our prayers for people.

This caring, this unity of faith, this praying you do in your classroom may help your students see how it is done on the larger scale, both in the local congregation and in the *Una Sancta*—the holy Christian church.

GETTING INTO THE LESSON

Many students in our religion classrooms don't fully realize why they are there. They know they have been baptized, they have been confirmed, and they believe in Christ Jesus. Many, however, have little concept of "belonging to Christ Jesus" and what that means in their daily lives. Discipleship to Christ, being His slave and saint, are, perhaps, alien concepts.

At the very beginning of this course, you can be a great help to your students if you repeatedly speak that Gospel message of Paul's: **"[You] are called to belong to Jesus Christ"** (v. 6). It's closely related to Peter's "priesthood of all believers" **(1 Peter 2:9)**. It's a high privilege, and comes to us **"who are loved by God and called to be saints" (v. 7)**. Those students, of course, have this grace. It just may take some time for them to get used to it!

Part of the excitement for you this year will be to watch God work through His Word, bringing the joy of believing and the growth of faith to the lives of the young men and women sitting at your feet.

IN THE WORD

Verse 1: Paul, the Man (Objectives 1, 2, 3)

Paul described himself as a servant of Jesus Christ and a called apostle (who is) set apart for the Gospel.

As the Student Book indicates, the Greek word *doulos* really means slave instead of servant. A first-century reader would stop in his tracks, wondering why a free man and Roman citizen would willingly call himself a slave. A slave was bought and paid for (redeemed). A slave belonged to another person. A slave could not call himself his own man (or herself her own woman). A slave not only owed allegiance first to his or her master, but had to account for every minute of every hour of every day of his or her life. The Romans called slaves "living tools."

Here the light bulb could go off in your students' heads. This slavery actually describes our following Jesus. As the Student Book suggests, ask your students to comment. How is belonging to someone sometimes a burden? Sometimes a joy? Love (of course) causes the difference.

Naturally, if our belonging to Christ is a burden, we are lacking in our love for Him. But rather than "preach" to your students, "but you ought to love Jesus!" emphasize how He first loved (and loves) us. We do not come to love God by being ordered to do so. That love comes as a (super)natural response to the Gospel. That love is a fruit of the Holy Spirit's working in us.

Bring out comparisons, then, with being a disciple of Christ Jesus and being a slave. We were bought and ransomed by Him. The price He paid was blood—His own. We do belong to Him, in the greatest sense of the word. And that belonging lasts forever.

Paul was also an apostle. Follow the description offered in the Student Book. Although many today blur the distinction between the apostolic office and the priesthood of all believers, help your students keep the two offices separate. Your students are not called to be apostles. They do not have a direct, immediate calling to serve Christ, and they do not have apostolic authority.

Paul makes a point of his apostolic office to show that the message he proclaims is trustworthy. It really is God's Word (not Paul's, nor any person's, opinion). Therefore, when we hear that we belong to Christ, we can count on it.

Verses 2–5: The Message (Objective 2)

Paul uses his office as apostle to proclaim the Gospel of Jesus Christ. The Student Book asks your class to compose a description of Jesus from this text. Some points to look for include the following:

1. Jesus is true man, a descendant of David.
2. Jesus is true God, the Son of God.
3. Jesus is resurrected from the dead.
4. Jesus is Lord (back to *doulos* again).
5. Jesus sends His Word out through His apostles (which we have in the Scripture).
6. Jesus calls us by the Gospel to belong to Him.
7. Jesus loves us and calls us saints. That's grace!

The *royal we* in **verse 5** shows again that this is not Paul's word, but God's Word. It may sound as though Paul is boasting. He was—but boasting in the Lord, not in himself!

Verses 6–7: Called to Belong;
Called to Be Saints (Objective 3)

Those of us who teach can so easily make the wonderful Gospel back into Law again! Instead of the "easy yoke" which Christ promises His disciples, we can lock our students into ball and chain. We could easily pack our students up and send them on guilt trips by pointing out our (or their!) lack of commitment. But guilt does not drive us into discipleship. That happens when the Holy Spirit calls us by the Gospel (not the Law).

Have one of your students read aloud **Matt. 11:28–30**. Slavery to Christ Jesus is actually freedom—freedom from burdens, guilt, fears, and death! Ask your students to add to the list of freedoms.

Close with prayer.

Session 2: Profile of a Saint

BIBLE BASIS: ROM. 1:8–17

The Gospel is God's power to work salvation in us. In it God reveals how we are saved by faith in Christ Jesus. This Gospel draws Christians closer as they share and spread the Good News of God's love.

OBJECTIVES

By the grace of God the students will
1. discover ways Christians can express their thanks for the Gospel and how God gives success to the sharing and spreading of His Word;
2. explain how God uplifts and encourages us in our faith through the instrumentality of fellow Christians;
3. relate in their own words that the Gospel is God's power to rescue us by the gift of grace and faith in Christ Jesus.

OUTLINE OF ROM. 1:8–17
A. Thankful for the faith of other Christians (vv. 8–11)
   1. Praying as an expression of gratitude to God (vv. 9–10)
   2. Desiring the fellowship and company of Christians with whom we can share the Gospel (vv. 10–11)
B. Encouraging one another in Christ (vv. 12–15)
   1. Christians need one another's caring and sharing of the Gospel for building up in faith (vv. 12–13)
   2. God works through all Christians to accomplish this mutual building up of faith (vv. 14–15)
C. The Gospel as God's power to save us (vv. 16–17)
   1. The Gospel is what God dynamically uses to bring us salvation (v. 16)
   2. (Since it is not "wise" or "strong" to unbelieving hearts,) the Gospel may appear foolish, but we are not ashamed of it (v. 16)
   3. The Gospel is the Good News that we are saved by our faith in Christ Jesus alone; by that Gospel, God declares us righteous (v. 17)

A WORD FROM THE AUTHOR

The advantage that we have as teachers of the Gospel is that we never work alone. When you think about it, in fact, we are only the facilitators; the Holy Spirit is the Teacher (**John 14:26**).

Through the years I have found that my desire to control my classroom sometimes gets in the way of the Holy Spirit and the Word. Perhaps I have placed myself between Him and my students. One of the most difficult lessons I had to learn was simply to trust the Holy Spirit to work (as He promises) in the Word of God.

That is why I consider the Bible as the primary tool in a high school class on the Christian faith. After all, it is the written Word of God. When Scripture is open and the Word is at work, the Holy Spirit is opening hearts and minds to News about Jesus Christ.

Trusting God to work through His Word (**Is. 55:11**)—That may be the biggest challenge to teaching. It's also far better than the alternative: imagining we are the ones responsible for our students' growth of faith. If that were the case, then we would truly have something to worry about!

GETTING INTO THE LESSON

Verses 16–17 provide the focus for this section of Romans. The Gospel is God's power to work salvation for us; the just (or righteous) live by faith in Jesus Christ. (Actually, this is not merely the theme of this one section, it is the theme of the entire Book of Romans and the touchstone of the entire Christian faith.)

In this session the Student Book follows Paul's writings verse by verse. Therefore **verses 8–10** are grouped under the heading "Thankful" and **verses 11–15** under "Encouraging One Another." Because Paul deals with those topics, so shall we.

Paul, however, was simply building up to a crescendo of "righteousness by faith." This powerful Gospel and the faith it produces is what Paul shares with his fellow Christians in Rome: the righteousness of God is ours by faith in Christ Jesus. This, of course, is the same message you will be sharing with your students.

IN THE WORD

Verses 8–10: Thankful (Objective 1)

Lead the students through this section, asking them to imagine some incredible good that happened to them. The examples in the Student Book are listed as starters, so allow a few additions to the list. Quickly proceed to ask students for ways they express their thanks. Write their responses on a chalkboard or on newsprint.

Direct the students to read **verses 8–10**, and have them list how Paul expressed his thanks. Note that Paul expressed thanks with his whole heart, by remembering the people in his prayers, and by asking

God to provide a way that he might visit them.

This Paul is hardly the same man as Saul of Tarsus! He now loves the people of the church he once persecuted; he spreads the Gospel of Jesus which he once tried to suppress; and he shows that the church (wherever it is) is deeply loved by Christ and Christ's servants and that Christ still ministers personally to His church through those He calls as servants.

Verses 11–15: Encouraging One Another
(Objective 2)

As you guide the students through the exercise in this section, keep in mind that all Christians need encouragement. The Christian with dynamic faith, as well as the one weakest in faith, still needs bolstering from Christian friends. No matter who we are, we will have doubts about God and His love for us, especially when we are under trials. At those times we need a Word from God. Coming from a Christian friend, that Word can be most comforting.

Allow the text to show your students how the Roman Christians encouraged Paul and how we today can help encourage missionaries, pastors, teachers, and others who work in Christ's kingdom. Let your students share times when *they* have received encouragement from Christian friends.

Verses 16–17: The Righteous Live by Faith in Christ
(Objectives 2, 3)

What's the Point?

In our lives as Christians, we are not even to pretend we are strong on our own. We need Word and Sacrament to keep our faith built up, and we need the fellowship that the Spirit gives us in the church. Those who feel no need for other Christians are walking into dangerous territory, especially since "the prince of this world," or "the roaring lion" is on the prowl. The encouragement to stay close together is repeated in **Heb. 10**; and the meeting referred to is hardly a voters meeting or a youth board meeting. It is worship—when the people of God are gathered around Word and Sacrament. The "Day" Paul refers to is, of course, Judgment Day, the Day when Christ Jesus returns for His people.

The Gospel: God's Dynamite

As you guide the students through this portion, find ways to point out the uniqueness of the Gospel. No other "religion" speaks of a God who takes it onto Himself to pay for the peoples' guilt, but Jesus Christ did. That is what Paul is proclaiming: God proclaims us righteous on account of Christ.

Dynamite may be a good word for the kind of power of the Gospel Paul mentions. Luther, referring to this doctrine when he found it in Romans, said that it blew the doors of heaven wide open for him.

Be sure to emphasize throughout this discussion that salvation is a free gift from God, given simply out of His love. That is grace. The moment we, or our students, try to qualify God's grace with our own "ifs," "ands," and "buts," we make the Gospel something less than it is, and it is no longer God's power for salvation.

Living under this free grace changes everything, because our relationship with God has been changed by Christ Jesus. For instance, now we can pray freely and with absolute confidence, not afraid to ask God for a thing. Why? Since God declared us righteous, He is the first one to deal with us that way. Sin cannot be considered by God if He has sent it away!

Close the session with a prayer. Include a thanksgiving for the gift of the Gospel.

Session 3: The Wrath of God

BIBLE BASIS
Rom. 1:18–32

CENTRAL TRUTH

Just as the Gospel reveals the righteousness that God imputes to His people, so God also reveals His wrath toward sinful people who reject Him and His purposes for their lives.

OBJECTIVES

By the grace of God students will
1. tell how God's wrath is a just and logical consequence of the godlessness and wickedness in the lives of sinners;
2. explain the relationship between sinners' rejection of God's truth and the moral and spiritual disintegration of society;
3. agree that to understand truth and reality a person must begin with a true knowledge of God;
4. rejoice in the Good News that they no longer live under condemnation, but have been forgiven through the blood of Christ Jesus.

OUTLINE OF ROM. 1:18–32

A. Reasons for the wrath of God **(v. 18)**
   1. Godlessness (impiety—sins against God)
   2. Wickedness (unrighteousness—sins against human beings)
B. Ignorance is no excuse **(vv. 19–20)**
C. Examples of godlessness and wickedness **(vv. 21–25)**
   1. Knowing God, but not glorifying or thanking Him **(v. 21)**
   2. Calling foolishness wisdom **(v. 22)**
   3. Replacing wisdom with emptiness **(vv. 21–23;** see also **Eccl. 2:14)**
   4. Preferring lies to truth **(v. 25;** see also **Gen. 3:4)**

5. Preferring the creature to the Creator (v. 25)
D. Consequences of godlessness and wickedness (vv. 26–32)
   1. Shameful lusts (vv. 26–27)
   2. Depravity (vv. 28–31)
   3. Death (v. 32)
   4. God "giving them over" (vv. 24, 26, and 28)

A WORD FROM THE AUTHOR

God promises His people, **"Then I will give you shepherds after My own heart, who will lead you with knowledge and understanding" (Jer. 3:15).** This passage has brought me to both the depths of despair and the heights of confidence. I despair when I look at myself and realize how inadequate I am to be a shepherd after God's own heart. I feel confident when I remember God's promise—I am His shepherd, and with God all things are possible. I see too many of my colleagues in the religion classroom looking only to themselves and despairing. I have taped the words of **Jer. 3:15** on my lectern. Before each class I read it and utter the simple prayer, "Lord, make it so!"

GETTING INTO THE LESSON

Begin with prayer.

Review **Rom. 1:17–18** with the students. Point out how the righteousness of God is revealed in the Gospel (v. 17). God gives us the righteousness we need, and we receive it by faith. Contrast this with the way God reveals His wrath (v.18). This brief discussion will serve to tie this session with the session from last time.

Then use the opening question from the Student Book—**What makes you angry?** Continue the discussion until students have given examples of each of the three areas mentioned in the Student Book (being ignored, not being believed, and injustice). As you continue to work through this lesson, be prepared to point out how Paul says human society has done these three things to God (ignoring Him—vv. 18–22; unbelief—vv. 23–25; injustice—vv. 29–32).

IN THE WORD

Verse 18: Reasons for God's Wrath (Objective 1)

The class should have no trouble finding the two reasons (ungodliness and wickedness). Help the class arrive at an adequate definition of the words. You may need to point out that ungodliness and impiety are the same thing. Ask, **If impiety is a sin, against whom is it a sin?** (God—vv. 18–27) From the examples given in the text (vv. 29–32), students should have little trouble recognizing wickedness as sin against other people.

Verses 19–20: Ignorance Is No Excuse
(Objectives 1 and 3)

1. Paul's reference to "supressing the truth" indicates that godless people know that God exists. They have the moral law written in their hearts, even though the natural knowledge of God is distorted by sin. Still, knowing these things, the godless choose to ignore the truth. Or they raise intellectual arguments to disprove the truth they have received.

2. It may be helpful to read **Ps. 8** aloud at this point and discuss it. David believed that even young children know enough to recognize and praise God (v. 2). Call attention to the similarities among **Ps. 8:6–8; Gen. 1:26;** and **Rom. 1:23.**

Then share some things that bring home the existence of God for you (e.g., a sunrise, a thunderstorm, a flower, a smile, a baby's laugh, and the smell of freshly cut grass). After you have shared, ask your students to share their own examples with you.

Verses 21–25: Examples of Godlessness and Wickedness (Objectives 1, 2, and 3)

Examples mentioned by students should include the following:

1. Knowing God and not glorifying and thanking Him (v. 21). Use Jesus' words in **Matt. 5:45** to show how unbelievers continually receive blessings from God without acknowledging Him.

2. Calling foolishness wisdom (v. 22). Think of the countless bizarre attempts humans have made to find answers to eternal questions (e.g., astrology, mysticism, cults, reincarnation, philosophies like nihilism and Nietzscheanism which helped produce Nazi Germany—the list is nearly endless). David said it best, **"The fool says in his heart there is no God" (Ps. 14:1).**

3. Replacing God with idols (v. 23). Use **Gen. 1:26** and **Ps. 8:6–8** to generate a discussion focusing upon how humans, who were created in the image of God, have consistently tried to reduce God by creating God in the image of the beings God created—birds, animals, and reptiles. God ordained people to rule over these beings, not to worship them!

4. Preferring lies to the truth (v. 25). You will likely get lots of examples from the class. Give a few to start them out:
"Abortion can't be wrong, because a fetus is not a human being."
"The universe came into being by itself, and humans evolved as a part of that process."
"If something feels good, it can't be wrong."

5. Preferring the creature to the Creator (v. 25). This is a good point at which to bring in a discussion of humanism (humanity is central in the universe). Point out this view of society and creation as being homocentric rather than theocentric. Ask students if they see any evidence of this philosophy in the media, in their secular text books, or in their own thinking. Talk briefly about what makes the philosophy so attractive to sinful people. What makes it so dangerous?

Verses 26–32: Consequences of Godlessness and Wickedness (Objectives 2, 3, and 4)

1. It may be difficult for your students to see the

logic of Paul's argument in these verses. How does Paul explain the progression from human rejection of God to homosexuality? When people reject God, they also reject His regulations and even His right to make them. Then, anything goes.

When a whole society adopts this view, the mindless pursuit of pleasure—including sexual experimentation—becomes a "normal" and expected part of life, even among children. This conduct soon produces boredom rather than fulfillment. Boredom and the desire for sexual gratification will eventually produce all manner of aberrant sexual behavior. In such a society, homosexual behavior is soon accepted as normal or, even worse, as "gay."

Use **verses 28–32** as an opportunity to help your students to discover that the society Paul has described is not only unrepentant but has developed a fatal approval of sinful behavior and of sinners—**verse 32.**

2. Use the final questions of this lesson to discuss the importance of repentance and the relief and freedom we find in God's forgiveness. This final discussion will bring the Gospel to a session that has stressed God's Law quite heavily. Be sure no student leaves class today under the Law's condemnation!

As time permits, have the class read **Rom. 2:1–16** before they leave today.

Session 4: The Judgment of God

BIBLE BASIS
Rom. 2:1–16

CENTRAL TRUTH
God does not base His judgment upon who we are or what we know, but upon whether or not we have faith in Jesus Christ. A right relationship with the Savior will show itself outwardly in acts of obedience toward God and love toward others.

OBJECTIVES
By the grace of God students will
1. explain the difference between judgment (which is God's business) and the loving kind of confrontation God requires of us when we see a brother or sister in sin;
2. describe God's grace in delaying judgment and respond to that grace in repentance;
3. explain the difference between justification and sanctification;
4. grow in appreciation of Jesus as both Savior and judge.

OUTLINE OF ROM. 2:1–16
A. Judgment is God's business (vv. 1–3)
   1. God judges according to truth (**v. 2**)
   2. God's judgment is inescapable (**v. 3**)
B. Judgment delayed to give opportunity for repentance (**vv. 4–5**)
C. Judgment is impartial in God's court (**vv. 6–15**)
D. Jesus Christ as Judge (**v. 16**)
   1. Jesus is both the Judge and the Standard of judgment
   2. Judged according to the Gospel

A WORD FROM THE AUTHOR
The more years I spend in the religion classroom, the more I become convinced that love is the only effective context for communicating spiritual truth. Paul wrote to Timothy about the false teachers in Ephesus, **"The goal of this command is love, which comes from a pure heart and a good conscience and a sincere faith. Some have wandered away from these and turned to meaningless talk" (1 Tim. 1:5–6).**

Some students are very hard to love, but the Lord Jesus has given us no options. If our teaching is to be more than "meaningless talk," we must genuinely care about all the students He has given us. The harder a student is to love, the more we need to pray for grace to love that student. I find it necessary to look at each of my students individually and then resolve to love them—not because of them or in spite of them, but because the Lord commands it. How comforting it is to know that the Holy Spirit then empowers me to carry out that resolution and that He blesses my efforts.

Paul writes that our goal is to produce people who are able to **"speak the truth in love so we will in all things grow up into Him who is the Head, that is Christ" (Eph. 4:15).** To speak the truth without love is ineffective. To speak without knowing the truth is embarrassing and dangerous. To speak the truth in love is teaching.

GETTING INTO THE LESSON
The opening activity in the Student Book will help you open a discussion about legalism. Help your students realize that we can become as legalistic as easily as the Jewish people to whom Paul was writing. We all share a strong tendency to rationalize our own sins while being judgmental about the sins of others.

Ask the class what would be the best way to approach a fellow student who was being overcome by some sin (drugs, alcohol, sex, stealing, cheating, breaking training rules, etc.). Is "live and let live" a good rule to follow?

After allowing time for some discussion, ask someone to read **Gal. 6:1** aloud. Whatever direction your discussion goes, your students will ultimately end up drawing the conclusion that it is hard to obey the command God gives us in **Gal. 6:1.** Talk about why that is (fear of rejection or ridicule, embarrassment, not wanting to seem holier-than-thou). Help the students understand that calling a sin a sin and building up the person being overcome are loving acts. It's unloving to either ignore sin or to be judgmental about the sinner.

Verses 1–3: Judgment Is God's Business
(Objectives 1 and 4)

God is the ultimate and only judge of the human heart. When we leave judgment to Him, we are free to dwell on the other aspects of judgment Paul mentions. God's judgment is based on truth and is inescapable. For the Christian, this is good news. Cleansed as we are by the blood of the Lamb, we already stand acquitted. We need fear nothing.

Ask your students to give examples of human justice gone awry. Newspapers sometimes run stories of confessed criminals being released by the courts because of legal technicalities or of innocent persons unjustly imprisoned. Witnesses sometimes make mistakes, juries sometimes can be fooled, clever lawyers sometimes find loopholes, and judges sometimes are corrupt. Human justice is sometimes miscarried. But someday God will set wrong things right. He will judge based on truth.

Verses 4–5: A Misunderstood Blessing
(Objective 2)

To introduce this section, ask the class how they would evaluate parents who made rules and set punishments for breaking their rules, but never followed through. For example, suppose the parents set a curfew of 11 p.m., but their teenagers rarely come home before 2 a.m. Knowing this, the parents never even talk to the teenagers about it. What would that tell you about the parents?

Probably your class clown will voice the opinion that these parents are perfect. But most of your students will agree that failure to discipline is a serious weakness in parents. It may indicate that the parents just don't care. And, in any case, the children will certainly take advantage of them. This discussion may help your students understand that while God's tolerance and patience are designed to produce repentance, we often treat it as a sign of weakness.

Paul accuses the Jewish nation of mistaking God's tolerance of their sin as tacit approval. They made the tragic mistake of using God's day of grace to sin more, when He had granted it as a chance for repentance. As God's people today, we must clearly understand why God has delayed judgment in our time. And we must preach the message of repentance among ourselves and in the world **(2 Peter 3:9).**

Verses 6–15: Judgment Is Impartial in God's Court (Objective 3)

1. In our eagerness to avoid synergism (work righteousness), we can fall prey to the temptation to play down the importance of sanctification. Paul had no such problem. He has already made it clear that we are justified by faith in the shed blood of Jesus Christ. As God told His Old Testament people, **"When I see the blood, I will pass over you" (Ex. 12:13).** When God looks at us, He sees the blood of Jesus. He is satisfied. God Himself has provided the sacrifice; God Himself has done all the work. That is justification.

2. We cannot see one another's faith. Only through works can our faith be made visible. Have your students read **Matt. 25:31–46** and talk about the difference between the sheep and the goats. The only visible difference lies in what they did and didn't do. Use this account to diagnose your students' understanding of the difference between justification and sanctification. Make sure they see that the sheep are on the right hand of God because they had faith (justification). Their works simply made faith visible (sanctification).

3. The integrity of God's judgment is evident in the way He deals with people. He bases His judgment upon how they respond to what they could know of His will. For the Jew it was the written Word—the Law and the Prophets. For the Gentile it was the natural knowledge of God written in their hearts (conscience).

Have your students read **Matt. 7:21, 24; Luke 6:47–48; and James 1:22.** Discuss the difference between the privilege of possessing the truth and the responsibility of living it. Be sure to remind students that we are sanctified in the same way we are justified—by God's grace! It is God who enables us both **"to will and to act according to His good purpose" (Phil. 2:13).**

Verse 16: Judged by Jesus Christ
(Objective 4)

Have the class read **Heb. 2:5–18.** Discuss what this passage of Scripture tells us about Jesus. Help your students to see that Jesus, our Judge, is also Jesus, our Brother. He understands what it is to be human. He became a little baby. He hurt. He cried. He was tempted in the same way we are. He overcame the tempter. He died. He rose again. And all of this for us! For what better judge could we hope?

Assign **Rom. 2:17–3:8** for the next session.

Session 5: The People of God

BIBLE BASIS
Rom. 2:17–3:8

CENTRAL TRUTH

God has given us many privileges as His people. These all come to us by His grace. Along with our privileges come corresponding responsibilities. To accept the privileges and ignore the responsibilities leads to hypocrisy, arrogance, and offense. Only as God's Spirit empowers us can we use His ability to respond to His saving work for us.

OBJECTIVES

By the grace of God students will

1. understand the relationship of responsibility to privileges;
2. see that they have not (and cannot) fulfill their responsibilities as God's people on their own;
3. thank God for their own privileged position as forgiven children of God by His grace;
4. respond to God's love with a life-style that is dynamically Christlike rather than merely ritual and routine.

OUTLINE OF ROM. 2:17–3:8

A. The privileges and responsibilities of God's people (vv. 17–20)
   1. The privileges (vv. 17–18)
      a) They have the Word (Law) (v. 17)
      b) They have the right to boast of God (v. 17)
      c) They know the will of God (v. 18)
      d) They know how to discern reality (v. 18)
   2. The responsibilities (vv. 19–20)
      a) Guide to the blind (v. 19)
      b) Light in the darkness (v. 19)
      c) Teacher of the ignorant (v. 20)
      d) Instructor of children (v. 20)
B. The dangers facing God's people (vv. 21–29)
   1. Hypocrisy (vv. 21–23)
   2. Offense (v. 24)
   3. Ritual without reality (vv. 25–29)
C. Objections from the outwardly religious (vv. 3:1–8)
   1. What advantage is there in being a Jew? (vv. 1–2)
   2. So what if we are unfaithful? (vv. 3–4)
   3. Doesn't my sin enhance the goodness of God? (vv. 5–6)
   4. Doesn't my weakness increase God's glory? (vv. 7–8)

A WORD FROM THE AUTHOR

Review is important in every ongoing course of study, but in the religion classroom it is vital. You probably find it quite a challenge to get your students actively involved in the study of God's Word each day. But once the students focus their attention on that Word, the Holy Spirit does His work; spiritual growth can then take place. The more quickly this happens, the more impact each class period will have on the students. A review can get your students back to the same point of view and frame of mind with which they left your classroom.

Reviewing serves another purpose too. As they work through a book like Romans, students can easily lose sight of the overall picture. They quickly reach a point where they "can't see the forest for the trees." So you need to provide an overview for them each day. Place each day's pericope in context.

Your review need not be lengthy. Today, for example, you could remind your students of the purpose of the first five chapters of Romans. Point out the main themes discussed so far, and then focus in on the objectives from the preceding lesson. Draw as much of this information as you can from the class. Keep the students involved. It's like spiritually jumpstarting their brains.

You will probably also find it helpful to post a broad outline of the work you have done so far. Use the chalkboard or large pieces of poster paper you can affix to the walls of your classroom. These will serve as a point of reference for the students, and will give you something to point to while leading the review.

GETTING INTO THE LESSON

Begin with prayer.

Use the questions from the opening section of the Student Book to open up a class discussion. Ask your students to think about the privileges they have. Most will probably believe that their lives are all responsibility—with precious few privileges to go along with the obligations. So the class may need a little help from you to get started. Point out to them that a drivers license is a privilege. What responsibilities go along with holding a driver's license?

Listing our privileges is another way of counting our blessings. Guide the discussion in such a way that your students recognize some privileges they hadn't thought about before (e.g., being an American, being able to get an education, being in an upper class, having Christian parents, having a brother or sister). Additionally, point out that class officers, cheerleaders, and athletes all hold positions that involve responsibility. Use this activity as a lead-in to the section that follows—a discussion about the privilege of being a child of God and the implications that flow from that privilege.

IN THE WORD

Verses 17–20: Privileges and Responsibilities (Objectives 1–4)

1. Paul starts by, in effect, challenging his readers, "You call yourselves Jews . . ." What privileges does he say they enjoy as God's people? (God had given them His written Word; they had the privilege of calling the one true God their God; they knew the will of God; because they had God's Word and knew His will, they could make good decisions based upon this revealed knowledge.)

Then talk about their responsibilities (to share God's Word with sinners who are blind because of a lack of revealed knowledge; to share the one true God with those who in their spiritual darkness are worshiping other gods; to share God's will with the ignorant; to share true wisdom with children who will find it nowhere else).

2. Ask the class if anyone has ever challenged them with words similar to Paul's—"You call yourself a Christian." What were they implying? Talk about it for a while.

Then ask about the privileges and responsibilities of being a Christian. If your students answer frankly, you will probably hear a lot about responsibilities and not a lot about privileges—this is how far too many young people perceive Christianity: "Go to church! Contribute money! Witness! Obey your parents! . . ." Your students will likely compile quite a list when given a chance.

3. To the Jewish nation of long ago and to New Testament disciples, God's requirements are clear: Be holy, be perfect. Remind students that Paul's arguments in the first section of Romans all lead his readers to the same conclusion—every human being has failed to fulfill the responsibilities God has given us.

4. The scribes and Pharisees at the time of Christ had become spiritually arrogant. They looked at the Law, which required perfection, and came to the conclusion they had met this requirement. Other people down through the ages have looked at God's demand for a holy life and have despaired, knowing they could never obey perfectly.

A third possible attitude, one all too prevalent today, would be one of indifference—knowing God's requirement but ignoring it or pretending God has no right to make demands on human beings.

No matter which of these attitudes we adopt, God's righteous requirements go unmet and we, thereby, earn His punishment.

5. The only possible way out of this maze lies at the foot of the cross. Had Paul's readers stopped with **3:8**, they would have thrown up their hands in despair. Read **3:21–24** to help students see where Paul is going with the argument they have been studying for several days now. These verses are very *Good News* indeed!

6. The student book has a part of **Rom. 9:25–26** printed out. Have a student read the full text from **Rom.** 9 aloud. Then have someone read **1 Peter 2:9**. Use these verses to help your students see God's view of His children. Point out how dramatically His perception of us differs from our own. We are a chosen people, a royal priesthood, a holy nation with a marvelous purpose to our lives. What privileges!

7. We are sanctified by grace as well as justified by grace. If we are to "be good," we must do so relying *only* on God's empowering Spirit. To think we can sanctify ourselves through our own efforts leads right back down the path of arrogance or despair.

Verses 21–29: Warning! Danger! (Objectives 2, 3, and 4)

The activity for this section might work best if done in conjunction with the last activity. Divide the class into small groups (three or four in each group). Ask them to do all the written work before coming back for a full class discussion.

Character Flaws

1. Hypocrisy (**vv. 21–23**). Jesus talks more about the sin of hypocrisy than any other sin. Its special danger lies in that it hides itself from the sinner. A hypocrite is someone who thinks she is something she is not. Hypocrites destroy both themselves and those whom they offend.

2. Offense (**v. 24**). The sin of offense involves damaging someone's spiritual well-being by word or deed.

3. Ritual without reality (**vv. 25–29**). It is very easy in organized religion to just go through the motions. There is nothing wrong with rituals, but when ritual becomes an end in itself, the reality behind it gets lost. Christianity is not a matter of ritual, but of relationship—relationship with God through the blood of Jesus Christ. See also **Jer. 4:4**.

Verses 1–8: Objections (Objectives 3 and 4)

The following question-answer dialog is an example of what students might develop as they work through the assignment in this section of the lesson:

(**v. 1**) Question 1: "If God has such high expectations of us, then what good does it do to be the people of God? It seems more trouble than it's worth."

(**v. 2**) Answer: "There are more advantages than you can count. Don't forget about all the privileges you have."

(**v. 3**) Question 2: "So what if some of us don't live up to God's expectation? He made a deal with us, and He has to live up to it even if we don't."

(**v. 4**) Answer 2: "That's so ridiculous that I won't even try to argue with you. Just read what King David said in **Ps. 51:4**."

(**v. 5**) Question 3: "If our lousy conduct makes God look good by comparison, then where's the beef? What's He upset about? He can't punish us for that."

(**v. 6**) Answer 3: "You are really confused. If God

overlooked your sin, how could He judge a place like Sodom and Gomorrah?"

(v. 7) Question 4: "If I'm a liar and my lies make God's truthfulness more evident, then in my own way I'm really giving glory to God, am I not?"

(v. 8) Answer 4: "This sounds too much like the false teaching some people have accused me of. It is foolishly sacrilegious. People who think that way deserve what's going to happen to them."

Encourage some of your students to read their versions of **3:1–8.** Point out once again that this entire section of Romans is Law. Paul is building up to the Gospel of the Lord Jesus and His work for us on the cross.

Contemporary examples of questions 1 and 2 may be easiest to elicit from the class. People of all ages throughout time have said to themselves, "What good is it to be a Christian? You miss out on all the fun." Or, "God has promised to forgive all my sins, so why can't I live as I please?" Some of your students may have had these thoughts cross their minds on occasion, too. As you talk about them, be sure to emphasize the grace of God—grace that cost Jesus Christ His life. He will always forgives repentant sinners, no matter what we have done, said, or thought. But with that forgiveness comes the power both to *desire* and to *do* His will.

Conclude with prayer. If possible, give the students time to read **Rom. 3:9–20** before they leave today.

Session 6: We Are All Guilty

BIBLE BASIS
Rom. 3:9–20

CENTRAL TRUTH
Both human logic and Holy Scripture prove that we are all guilty under the law of God. The Law shows us our sin, but not what to do about it.

OBJECTIVES
By the grace of God students will
1. describe the evidence of original sin in their lives;
2. demonstrate their understanding of Paul's logical argument thus far in Romans;
3. articulate a mature understanding of the purpose of the Law in exposing sinful human nature.

OUTLINE OF ROM. 3:9–20
A. We are all under sin (vv. 9–18)
   1. Proven by logic (v. 9)
      a) Gentiles (1:18–32)
      b) Jews (2:1–3; 3:20)
   2. Proven by Scripture (vv. 10–18)
      a) Corrupt in character (vv. 10–12)
      b) Corrupt in conduct (vv. 13–18)
B. We are all under the Law (vv. 19–20)
   1. Guilty (v. 19)
   2. The Law shows us our sin, but not what to do about it (v. 20)

A WORD FROM THE AUTHOR
A cardinal rule in hermeneutics is that Scripture interprets itself. The night before His death, Jesus promised His disciples, **"But the Counselor, the Holy Spirit, whom the Father will send in My name, will teach you all things and will remind you of everything I have said to you" (John 14:26).** As I continue to grow in the Word, I find that happening more and more often. When a student asks a difficult question for which I have no ready answer, I find Bible passages coming to mind, passages that provide an answer.

Likewise, as I ponder over a verse or section of Scripture wondering how to make this come alive for my students, I often find related verses flooding into my consciousness. Each verse would focus more light upon the section of Scripture under study. Each truth the Spirit brings to mind brings out another facet of the text until it sparkles and glistens like a precious gem. I can't wait to get into the classroom to share what God is showing me.

In this lesson your students will do some hermeneutical work as they research Paul's "string of pearls." As they work, remind them of Jesus' words from **John 14:26.** Point out that the Holy Spirit cannot remind us of what we have not learned. Productive Biblical interpretation always begins with personal Bible study.

GETTING INTO THE LESSON
Begin with prayer.

The lesson introduction printed in the Student Book gives no activity, but it directs several questions at the students. Use them to develop a class discussion. Add a few questions of your own to challenge your group. (E.g., **Would you be embarrassed if I played a tape recording of the conversation you were having with your friends during lunch hour today?**)

Unless someone ate alone, your students will all probably agree it would be embarrassing. If you feel particularly brave during the discussion, you might share with them that even most teachers would probably not want their lunchroom conversation made public. Talk about why we wear different masks for different circumstances. What does this tell us about ourselves?

This discussion could take up the entire class period if you let it, so keep moving toward the central truth: though we are Christian, we are often not what we seem to be, even to ourselves, and the purpose of the Law is to make us conscious of our sin.

IN THE WORD
Verses 9–18: All Under Sin
(Objectives 1 and 2)

In the first unit of this course (**Rom. 1:1–5:11**), the singular use of "sin" occurs only three times (**3:9; 3:20; 4:8**). In the second unit (**Rom. 5:12–8:39**), where it is used 39 times, we will deal with the problem of sin more fully.

Students will need help in clarifying the fundamental difference between "sin" and "sins." In this course's first unit we have been studying texts that show how God provides a forgiveness of our "sins." In the second unit, we will deal with the way God delivers us from "sin." Be sure your students do not confuse bad behavior (sins) with the cause of the behavior (indwelling sin).

As you begin this part of today's lesson, give students a brief overview of the last few sessions. Questions 1 and 2 will help your students review.

Paul proved the guilt of the Gentiles in **1:18–32**. Paul's ministry was to the Gentiles, but he had a great concern for his people, the Jews (**Rom. 9:1–5**) also, so he carefully builds his case against them in **2:1–3:20**. He writes out of love, not out of spite.

Question 3 will get your students into Scripture, but you may have to help them apply it in question 4.

The charge **"there is no one righteous"** (v. 10) comes not from Paul but from a holy God, who looks down upon an entire planet full of unholy beings. God sees a world in which He finds no one free of an evil dynamic called *sin*, a domination that so distorts our minds that no one understands God (**v. 11**), and no one by their own reason or senses can seek or come to God (**v. 12**).

Humanity tends to have a highly inflated value of its intrinsic worth (humanism), but God's evaluation (the only one that counts) has found the human race totally worthless (**v. 12**).

This corruption of human character manifests itself in evil conduct. Paul chooses verses from Psalms and Isaiah to illustrate humanity's violent, aggressive tendencies in word (**vv. 13–14**) and in deed (**vv. 15–16**). The two major consequences of this conduct are an ignorance of "the way of peace" and the absence of "the fear of God."

When one has no peace with God, peace will be lacking in other relationships as well. People who are not or will not be reconciled with God have no peace of mind nor will they have peace with other people (**v. 17**).

Prov. 1:7 says, in essence, **"The fear of the Lord is the beginning of ... wisdom and discipline."** When the principle of sin dominates a person's life, there can be no regard for the will of God or respect for His authority. The fear of God is a necessary ingredient for survival. The thief on the cross asked his partner in crime, **"Don't you fear God?"** (**Luke 23:40**). No answer has been recorded from the thief, nor do we need one. He was where he was, acting the way he was acting, because he did not fear God.

Jesus, however, does give a reply: **"Today you will be with Me in paradise."** One thief feared (reverenced) God and survived; the other did not and died. Eternally.

Verses 19–20: All Under the Law (Objective 3)

Many object to this gloomy view of human worth. They base their objection on the fact that they have not committed the sins listed in Paul's "string of pearls." Like the rich young man who told Jesus that he had kept all the laws from little on, they refuse to look inside themselves. They have come to believe their own masquerade.

The question at the end of this section will probably work best as a class discussion, but it can also be assigned as written work or discussed in small groups. Encourage the students to examine motives rather than actions. Greed, lust, hatred, resentment, rebellion, jealousy, and malice are all evidence of the principle of sin in our lives, even though these things cannot be seen outwardly. This the Law calls sin, and we are all under the Law.

Be aware that, once again, this lesson is primarily Law. As we follow Paul's argument, we must be cautious that our students see the condemnation of God's holy law—yet, we must help them see it in proper context. Let students read **Rom. 3:21–31** before they leave today. In your closing prayers, include thanks to God for His grace and forgiveness.

Session 7: Pardoned

BIBLE BASIS
Rom. 3:21–31

CENTRAL TRUTH
Since no one can satisfy God by keeping the Law, we must reject all thought of work righteousness and leave the entire matter of justification in God's hands. God's plan from the beginning was to justify freely all who believe in the Savior, Jesus Christ.

OBJECTIVES
By the grace of God students will
1. rely solely on what God has done for their salvation through Christ Jesus;
2. describe God's plan of justification and the implication it has for their personal lives;
3. Understand *Bible commentary;*

4. express in both words and actions a growing appreciation for God's plan of salvation.

OUTLINE OF ROM. 3:21–31
A. The righteousness from God (vv. 21–26)
   1. Made known (v. 21)
   2. Available through faith (v. 22)
   3. For all (vv. 22–23)
   4. Free (v. 24)
   5. Sacrifice of atonement (v. 25)
   6. God is both just and Justifier (v. 26)
B. Conclusions (vv. 27–32)

A WORD FROM THE AUTHOR

The night before His crucifixion, the Lord Jesus told His disciples, **"If you remain in Me and My words remain in you, ask whatever you wish, and it will be given you" (John 15:7).**

This verse has always fascinated me; it seems to contain the very essence of teaching the Christian faith. "If My words remain in you" presents a challenge that I, as a teacher, struggle with every day. Getting the student into the Word is easy. But how can I get the Word into the student? I tell them to bring a Bible to class, and they do. I ask them to open the Bible to chapter and verse, and they do. I give them a section of Scripture to read, and for the most part, they do. The student has been led into the Word, but will the Word live in the student?

Whether this happens or not and how it happens is, of course, between the student and the Holy Spirit. But I, as a teacher, am the facilitator; and how I lead the student into the Word does make a difference. No one can tell us exactly how to do this. It is partially a matter of style. Personal enthusiasm for the Word is contagious in the classroom. But, whatever we as teachers do, the Word itself remains the one essential. When the students and the Word interact, the Spirit works His wonders. If we remove the Word, we frustrate the work of the Spirit.

The majority of the activities suggested in the Student Book for this course attempt to get the students to interact with the Word. As students grow in understanding, their enthusiasm for God's Word will also increase. When we see before us students who "read, mark, learn, and inwardly digest" the Word of God, we can be sure we have done our job. The Word will live in them. God grant it be so!

GETTING INTO THE LESSON

As you begin this lesson, try to help the students share times in their personal lives when they felt some threat to their safety. Then ask about the feelings of relief and gratitude they experienced when it was over.

Use a discussion based on the introductory material for today's lesson to get into how your students feel about what God has done to remove the threat of sin for them. Do they feel genuine gratitude? Do they feel guilty about taking salvation for granted? Do they believe that emotion has anything to do with religion?

As you lead this discussion, keep in mind that religion students often feel guilty about a number of things. Their attitude toward God's Word causes some of this guilt. Many of them do not like to study the Word, much less do they desire it to the degree that a newborn baby desires milk **(1 Peter 2:2)**. Assure them that this is God's business. If they keep on studying the Word and thus giving the Holy Spirit an opportunity to affect their lives with His Word, He will generate the necessary change in attitude. We can count on Him to do for us what we cannot do for ourselves.

Another source of guilt may be their lack of emotional response to the good news of salvation. They understand intellectually what God has done, but they just can't get as excited about it as they think they should.

Give them some time to think about what they expect from their study of Romans and have them write a prayer, as directed in the Student Book. Have one or more of your students read their prayer before you get into the Word together.

IN THE WORD
Verses 21–26: The Righteousness from God
(Objectives 1, 2, and 3)

1. The Lord Jesus often quoted from the Old Testament to support His teaching. All New Testament writers followed His example, as does Paul. In session 6 we talked about using Scripture to interpret Scripture, and the activity described here will provide a good opportunity to reinforce that principle.

Allow your students some time to read **Ps. 32** and write out their comments. You may wish to involve them in a class discussion, but don't spend too much time on this activity. In session 9 we will deal with **Ps. 32** in some detail, so do just enough work in it to accomplish two things:
a. Fix the psalm in their minds so they will remember it two sessions from now.
b. Establish the method Paul will use to prove justification by faith (i.e., quoting Old Testament proof passages).

2. This activity (writing commentary) will be easier and more enjoyable if you will go through **verses 22–26** with the class and explain any terminology unfamiliar to them.

Verses 22–23: Ask students to consider the importance of the words *all* and *no difference*. God's plan is available to every living soul—young, old, brilliant, slow-witted, male, and female. It has nothing to do with a person's value as society measures value.

Verse 24: Have a student read Jesus' word in **John 15:25: "They hated me without reason."** Point out to the students that the word translated "without reason" in **John 15:25** and the word translated "freely" in **Rom. 3:24** are identical (*dorean*). The grace of God is completely gratuitous. The smartest, brightest, nicest student in the class stands in the same need of God's grace as the rebellious, ill-behaved, disrespectful sinner taking up space in the back of the room. In no way is grace ever a reward. God saves us without our cooperation.

Verse 25: This does not mean that God ignores sin, but rather that God has dealt with sin. The word *redemption* means the *price paid to buy back a hostage.* Unfortunately, we live in an age where hostage-taking and kidnapping are all too familiar; but it does bring a relevance to the word that might be missed in less violent times. The hostage price God paid was **"with the precious blood of Christ, a lamb without blemish or defect" (1 Peter 1:19).**

Verse 26: God remains a God of justice. His grace, freely given, has its foundation in historical fact—the cross. His patience with sin in the time before Christ's sacrifice could come because He had Good Friday in mind. The Law is satisfied; God is just. He now justifies all who have faith in Jesus Christ. He justifies us without the works of the Law. God is both just and our Justifier. God is love!

Verses 27–31: Conclusions
(Objectives 2 and 4)

Grace is costly—not to us, but to God. Redemption comes to us without any effort on our part. What do we conclude from this? We have nothing to brag about! Pride in achievement is a very human, very natural, emotion. As long as it does not turn into arrogance, pride in achievement can be very healthy for society. But when we insist upon bringing it into our relationship with God, we lose all sense of God's sacrifice. God did all the work; we reap all the benefits.

As you discuss questions 1 and 2 in the Student Book, help your students to clarify the uniqueness of salvation.

When we are given something valuable, free and clear, no strings attached, the only possible response is thankfulness. Receiving something you neither earned nor deserved produces gratitude not pride. "God, look at *me* and what *I am doing*" is not the attitude of the redeemed. "God, I thank You from the bottom of my heart for Your marvelous rescue of my ruined life" is the prayer of the people of God.

Ask another student or two to read the prayer each wrote at the beginning of the session.

Session 8: Faith and Works

BIBLE BASIS
Rom. 4:1–5

CENTRAL TRUTH

Despite Abraham's intimacy with God **(Is. 41:8)**, he had nothing to boast about. He, like all sinful human beings, must be given righteousness on the basis of faith, not works. Works do not produce righteousness; they flow from hearts filled with gratitude for the righteousness God gives.

OBJECTIVES

By the grace of God students will
1. tell what is meant by "work righteousness," "righteousness by faith," and the differences between the two;
2. explain the principle of justification by grace through faith as it applied to God's Old Testament people;
3. compare Paul's teaching on faith with James' teaching on works, and explore the implications both have for their lives.

OUTLINE OF ROM. 4:1–5
A. What about Abraham? **(vv. 1–3)**
   1. Nothing to boast about **(v. 2)**
   2. Righteous by faith **(v. 3; Gen. 15:6)**
B. Works do not produce righteousness **(vv. 4–5)**
   1. God justifies the wicked **(v. 5)**
   2. What good are works? **(James 2:11–26)**

A WORD FROM THE AUTHOR

In the daily routine of classroom teaching, I often find myself thinking thoughts that are inconsistent with the Lord's teaching. As I look over a classroom full of students, I am prone to regard them as a group of people brought together by chance, random choice, or computer scheduling. Jesus taught differently. He said, **"For where two or three come together in My name, there am I with them" (Matt. 18:20).**

(Actually, the Greek verb *come together* was written in the passive, not the active, voice. So our Lord's words might be better translated "where two or three are brought together . . . ." This makes an enormous difference both to the Savior's meaning and to my attitude about how my students got there.)

This group of people I call a religion class did not just happen to come together. They have been brought together by the Spirit of God to achieve the purpose of God. Every religion classroom has tremendous potential for the advancement and enlargement of the church of Jesus Christ on earth! This potential can be thwarted by an abuse of free will. Any or all of the students can say no to the movement of the Spirit in their lives; but, if I as their teacher can catch the vision of **Matt. 18:19–20,** and if I'm sensitive to the physical presence of Jesus Christ in that classroom, the students are more likely to perceive it also. The potential is always there! Jesus is always there! How could I ever think of teaching the faith as routine?!

GETTING INTO THE LESSON (Objective 1)

Begin with prayer.

The seductive power of work righteousness is so strong and so appealing that we can't rid ourselves of it, even in the church. So it becomes imperative that our students learn to recognize it clearly when it rears its ugly head. The attraction lies in an appeal to the ego, to our pride. It allows us to think of ourselves as intrinsically good people who get out of line on occasion rather than corrupt people pretending that we are not.

Justification by faith is unique to Christianity. All other religions and philosophies rely upon some form of work righteousness. Buddhism is a good example you may want to share with your students. The Buddhists follow two sets of paths (Magga). The first path is one of abstaining. The second is one of attaining.

The Eightfold Paths of Buddhism

A. *Abstain from*	B. *Attain to*
1. Causing injury to living things	1. Right understanding
2. Stealing	2. Right thought
3. Sexual immorality	3. Right speech
4. Falsehood	4. Right bodily action
5. Alcohol and drugs	5. Right livelihood
6. Food after midday	6. Right moral effort
7. Amusements	7. Right mindfulness
8. Personal adornments	8. Right concentration

Involve the class in a discussion of what is meant by faith. Give them a few minutes of class time to write out definitions of both words. Have some students read their definitions.

Faith: a dependence upon and trust in a valid object. Many, many people live by faith, but they have faith in an invalid object (e.g., themselves, Joseph Smith, Buddha, astrology, Sun Myung Moon). There is only one valid object for our faith, that is, Jesus Christ. Faith makes us totally dependent upon the grace of God who promises to "justify the wicked."

Works: Our dependency upon our own merit to earn God's favor. It is born out of pride and is sustained by the belief that with a good effort one can fulfill all of God's requirements, whatever they are.

Many people place their trust for salvation in a combination of efforts—God and people working together to effect salvation. This is futile because the two are naturally incompatible as a means of salvation. Salvation through faith depends only upon grace; salvation by works depends upon human effort.

IN THE WORD

Verses 1–3: What about Abraham? (Objective 2)

As much as possible, lead your students to discover on their own the answer to the questions posed. God's dealings with His chosen people did not start with Moses and the Law, but with Abraham and grace four centuries before Sinai. The one time Abraham's righteousness is spoken of in **Genesis (15:6),** it mentions his *believing,* not his *doing.*

Abraham did not come to God. God came to Abraham while he was still in Mesopotamia, living in spiritual darkness **(Acts 7:2–3).** God acted; Abraham believed God, and God counted him righteous. In the same fashion, justification was reckoned to all pre-Christian believers. To believe the *word* of God is the equivalent of believing Jesus Christ who said, **"I and the Father are one" (John 10:30). "In the beginning was the Word and the Word was with God and the Word was God" (John 1:1).**

Verses 4–5: Works Do Not Produce Righteousness (Objective 3)

1. The phrase "God who justifies the wicked" implies two things: first, that all people are wicked sinners; and second, that God regards them in this way when He justifies them. He does not justify them because He sees some merit or value in them. If we continue to see some merit in ourselves that God does not see, we block His process of justification.

2. Paul makes no reference to sanctification in these verses. His interest lies in proving that righteousness (right standing) with God can be obtained only through faith (justification). But the question does arise: What value, if any, is there in good works? We do not want to find ourselves so enthusiastic in helping Paul make his point that we leave our students with the impression that good works are bad and to be avoided!

As your students work on their paragraphs, make sure they understand that Paul is talking about justification, and James is talking about sanctification. Romans contrasts faith with nonfaith; James contrasts saving faith with phony faith.

Jesus told His disciples that they would bear much fruit. Apples are the natural products of an apple tree. Works are the natural product of living faith. Faith works! Our works do not earn for us right standing before God, but knowing God's grace in Jesus Christ, we naturally do what pleases God. Our works make our faith visible.

Session 9: Forgiveness

BIBLE BASIS
   Rom. 4:6–15

CENTRAL TRUTH
Forgiveness, given by God to sinners who have done nothing to earn it, produces profound joy in the lives of the redeemed. This joy is available to all who respond to God's Word in the same way our spiritual father, Abraham, did—by believing Him.

OBJECTIVES
By the grace of God students will
1. describe David's joy in forgiveness as expressed in **Ps. 32:1–2;**
2. explain how God has consistently forgiven His people on the basis of faith;
3. recognize and explain how David's joy in forgiveness and Abraham's walk of faith are relevant in their own lives.

OUTLINE OF ROM. 4:6–15
A. The blessedness of forgiveness (vv. 6–8)
   1. Without works (v. 6)
   2. Sins forgiven = sent away (v. 7a)
   3. Sins covered (v. 7b; Ps. 44:22; Micah 7:19)
   4. Sin not counted (v. 8)
B. Forgiveness is for everyone (vv. 9–15)
   1. Forgiveness given 14 years before circumcision (vv. 9–10)
   2. Circumcision an outward sign; faith an inward seal (v. 11)
   3. Abraham, the father of all believers (vv. 12–15)
      a) Trusting the Law negates the promise (vv. 13–14)
      b) Law produces punishment (v. 15)

A WORD FROM THE AUTHOR
The religion teacher should have the easiest job in school. The Holy Spirit Himself does the teaching (**1 John 2:27**), and God promises that His Word sanctifies the students (**John 17:17**). If our job is so easy, then why does it seem so hard?

This is a complex question for which there are no easy or simplistic answers. Over the years, however, one reason has become more and more evident in my classroom. Far too many of my students do not know the Lord Jesus. I don't mean this in a judgmental way. I'm not questioning whether or not they have saving faith. Their problem is they have been told a great deal about the Lord, but have little personal experience with Him. They have a corporate Savior instead of a personal one.

It is very difficult to love and adore someone you have only heard about. This has always been a problem in the church. Even Philip, who lived with the Lord for three years, did not know Him (**John 14:9**). Jesus' solution for Philip applies to us and our students also. He invites us to believe His Word—**"Believe Me when I say that I am in the Father and the Father is in Me; or at least believe on the evidence of the miracles themselves" (John 14:11).** Jesus implies that there is a difference between believing Him and believing what He did.

Most of my students believe in the historical reality of Jesus Christ, and they appreciate at least intellectually what He has done for them. But too few have the intimate personal knowledge of Him that produces enthusiastic love and praise. The only help for them is to get into the Word, particularly the gospels.

Every chance I get, I try to leave them alone with the Lord. Whenever a point can be made by using an episode from Christ's life, I have my students go to the gospels and use them to bring relevance to whatever else we are studying.

The opening portion of the Student Book for this session briefly tells the story of Simon's dinner party. Have the class read the whole account in Luke for themselves so they can draw their own conclusions about the blessedness of forgiveness.

GETTING INTO THE LESSON
Begin with prayer.

Have students read through the introduction in the Student Book.

All of us at times take for granted things that we always enjoy. God's forgiveness, like the air we breath and the water we drink, can become so familiar and expected that we never think much about it.

The profound gratitude the sinful woman showed Jesus in **Luke 7:36–50** may bring our complacency into focus, but like Simon, we have trouble relating to her. She is not "our kind of people." We probably feel much more comfortable with someone like the rich young man in **Mark 10:17–31**. He was so nice that Mark goes out of his way to point out that **"Jesus looked at him and loved him" (Mark 10:21).** The woman, however, was forgiven, and the young man went away sad.

Have the class read both accounts, and allow enough discussion time to explore fully the differences in the attitude of each sinner toward God's forgiveness. What caused these attitudes?

IN THE WORD
Verses 6–8: The Blessedness of Forgiveness (Objectives 1 and 3)

1. Have your students look up **2 Cor. 5:21** before they read the Leviticus text. It will help them to see the

connection between the symbolic scapegoat and the reality of what happened at the cross.

The ritual involving the scapegoat took place after the evening sacrifice on the Day of Atonement (**Ex. 30:10–20**). The high priest laid his hands on the head of the scapegoat, confessing over it all the sins and transgressions of the people during the previous year. The goat was then led away into the wilderness and set free. This ceremony signified the carrying away of Israel's sins, sins which God had forgiven.

Ps. 103:8–12 also expresses David's understanding of forgiveness. As time permits, compare these verses with **Ps. 32**.

2. Encourage the students to use their imagination to bring the expression "sins covered" to life. An example could be the colloquial way we use the word *covered* today. If you ask another teacher to cover your first hour because you are going to be late, you are asking him or her to take your place and assume your responsibilities. Christ covers for us before the judgment seat of God. The examples do not have to correspond exactly to every theological implication. Just be real enough to speak to the students' hearts.

3. This activity should not be difficult. If there is time, have students read the entire good Samaritan parable and discuss how this relates to God's not counting our sins against us.

The class should readily see the relationship among **verse 18** of **Philemon; Luke 10:35;** and **Rom. 4:8.** You might explain that Onesimus was a runaway slave. The penalty he had incurred was death by crucifixion. Paul appealed to Philemon on behalf of Onesimus in the same way Jesus appeals to the Father on our behalf.

Verses 9–15: Forgiveness Is for Everyone
(Objectives 2 and 3)

Paul points out that God declared Abraham righteous before he was circumcised (14 years before), so Abraham obviously could not have been justified by being circumcised (**vv. 9–10**).

Circumcision confirmed the righteousness God had given to Abraham. It was an outward sign of an inward seal (**v. 11**). Here we see the brotherhood of the forgiven. Abraham is the father of all believers, Jew and Gentile alike. We all have the same father, the same faith, the same forgiveness. We are the same family (**vv. 11–12**).

God gave His law 430 years after He justified Abraham through faith. So Paul can state categorically that Abraham and his offspring received the promise not by the Law, but by faith (**vv. 13–15**).

We live in a complex and often confusing world of human religious tradition and ritual. But still today God continues to justify humble believers by His grace through faith in Jesus.

As you close, discuss briefly with the class how we can reduce the rite of Baptism or the celebration of Holy Communion to meaningless activities that differ little from pagan superstitions. Be sure to remind them that God forgives these sins too—again, by His grace.

Pray with the class for the family of believers.

Session 10: The Faith of Abraham

BIBLE BASIS
Rom. 4:16–22

CENTRAL TRUTH
God uses the circumstances and difficulties in our lives for our good as we rely on Him. His Spirit strengthens our faith so we are enabled to praise God for His deliverance even though, at the time, we see that deliverance only with the eyes of faith.

OBJECTIVES
By the grace of God students will
1. recognize the importance Jesus placed in strong faith;
2. describe the qualities of Abraham's faith that made him an example of great faith;
3. identify and share life experiences by which God has tested and strengthened their own faith;
4. repent for the unbelief in their own lives and ask God's power to trust more fully.

OUTLINE OF ROM. 4:16–22
A. Abraham believed God (**vv. 16–18**)
 1. Who brings dead things to life (**v. 17a**)
 2. Who calls things that are not as though they were (**v. 17b**)
 3. Who demands trust before reason (**v. 18**)
B. Abraham understood the problem (**v. 19**)
 1. His age, first promise given at 75 (**Gen. 12:4**)
 2. Sarah past menopause (80 years old) at time of the last promise (**Gen. 17:17**)
C. Abraham strengthened by the problems (**vv. 20–22**)
 1. Believed God had power to do as He promised (**v. 21**)
 2. Righteous by his faith (**v. 22**)

A WORD FROM THE AUTHOR
"**In the beginning was the Word, and the Word was with God, and the Word was God**" (John 1:1).

The first day I stepped into a religion classroom, I made a promise that I would never take the Word out of the hands of the students. The reason for that promise was **John 1:1**. I believe it is the most sublime sentence ever written.

John is the only writer in the Bible who calls Jesus the Word. He does it not once, but four times (**John**

1:1; 1:14; 1 John 1:1; Rev. 19:13). John understood that while he and his fellow disciples saw and lived with God in the flesh, so future generations would have the same opportunity through the living, written Word.

We can know Jesus only by meeting with Him in His Word. Christianity is a relationship. Like all relationships, it must be developed and sustained by personal contact. My job is not so much to tell students about Jesus, as it is to introduce them to Jesus. If I take the Word out of their hands, this is unlikely to happen.

GETTING INTO THE LESSON
(Objectives 1 and 4)

Begin with prayer.

Faith is viable, a living entity. As such, it is subject to change, even to death. The Bible mentions great faith **(Luke 7:9)**, little faith **(Matt. 14:31)**, lack of faith **(Matt. 6:6)**, and increase of faith **(Luke 17:5)**. Scripture also uses the words **"full of faith" (Acts 6:5).**

In view of this, we should not be surprised to find our students confused about faith. They wonder if they have enough faith to be saved. They need constant assurance that even very weak faith in the Lord Jesus as Savior is a saving faith. Such faith is a gift from God. We cannot drum it up inside ourselves. Rather, as Romans clearly teaches, God gives us faith as His gift.

Besides that aspect of faith that trusts in Jesus for eternal life, we also need faith for everyday living here on earth. As we confront challenges and problems, our faith in God's character and concern for us individually can be a tremendous blessing! Living confidently as Christians in this present world depends upon a living and growing personal faith. Jesus concerned Himself about the faith of His disciples. He scolded, encouraged, and challenged them to grow in faith, to rely more and more on God rather than on themselves.

The opening discussion from the Student Book should acquaint your students with Jesus' concern for His disciples' faith. It should help them to think about our Lord's concern for their own faith as well.

When our faith is weak, we
a. worry about the basic necessities of life, rather than trusting God's promise to supply all our needs **(Matt. 6:30–31);**
b. feel so afraid and angry with the Lord in the face of danger that we do not trust Him and His love to protect us **(Matt. 8:26);**
c. doubt the Lord's power to deal with our present circumstances **(Matt. 14:31);**
d. fail to understand our Lord's teachings **(Matt. 16:8);** and
e. find ourselves unable to utilize Christ's power for the good of His kingdom.

1. Spend some time discussing the passages from Matthew listed in the opening section of the Student Book. Help the students see how each episode fits into Jesus' plan for helping his disciples grow in their faith and trust. Do they see a progression from one incident to the next?

2. Then talk about the way the coming of the Holy Spirit at Pentecost affected Jesus' disciples. The changes spelled out in **Acts 2** seem quite astonishing, given the disciples' behavior during Jesus' earthly ministry.

3. Help students identify situations and circumstances in their own lives that tempt them to unbelief. You may want them to jot down answers to the three questions listed here, assuring them that no one will read their answers unless they choose to share them. You will come back to these answers later in the class period.

IN THE WORD
Verses 16–18: Abraham Believed God
(Objectives 2 and 3)

Abraham was the physical father of the Jewish nation, but he is also the spiritual father of all who are righteous because they believe in God.

Abraham believed God who
— brings dead things to life **(v. 17a)**. God waited until it was physically impossible for Abraham and Sarah to be parents. Then He gave them a son. Before the pregnancy, Sarah found the whole idea laughable **(Gen. 18:10–15),** but Abraham believed. This conviction that he had a God who could bring dead things to life was shown clearly in **Gen. 22,** when he was told to sacrifice Isaac. Each of us shares this belief when, with Abraham, we trust God to resurrect us as He did His Son.
— calls things that are not as though they were **(v. 17b)**. Abraham heard God say **"I *have* made you a father of many nations" (Gen. 17:5)**. God did not say, "I *will* make you a father of many nations." In the mind of God, Isaac's birth was an accomplished fact. Sarah had not yet become pregnant, but that was irrelevant to both God, the Doer, and to Abraham, the believer.

As you help your students paraphrase **verse 18**, ask them for examples of times today when people "hope against hope." Help them see that this phrase generally applies to humanly hopeless situations.

Verse 19: Abraham Understood the Problem
(Objectives 2 and 3)

1. Abraham's faith was not a product of naiveté. He was fully conversant with the biological reasons Sarah could not give birth. Though Abraham had no idea how God would accomplish what He promised, Abraham trusted that God would fulfill His promise.

2. Both the references from Romans and from Hebrews focus on Abraham's flawless faith. The Old Testament record, however, carefully notes several lapses in that faith. (See, for example, **Gen. 12:10–20**.)

Gen. 16:1–4a records one instance where Abraham and Sarah clearly conspired to "help God keep His promise." Notice the language used here: "Perhaps I can build a family through her." Even though Sarah suggested that Abraham use this method, he "agreed to what Sarah said." If students have difficulty reconciling the Biblical record, refer them to **Ps. 103:3, 12; Jer. 31:34b;** and **Micah 7:18–19.** God not only forgives our sins of unbelief, but He forgets them! When God saw Abraham, He saw only a man of faith. When God looks at us, He likewise sees only our faith—not our faithlessness.

Be sure your students understand that God is not angry at them for their lack of trust. Rather, He delights in them and anxiously awaits their requests for His help in dealing with whatever situations they face.

Verses 20–22: Abraham Was Strengthened
(Objectives 3 and 4)

Many believers limit the power of God in their lives by expecting too little. They don't give God room to work wonders for them. This final activity is critical. Perhaps some (or many) of your students will have nothing to share. They have not yet learned to trust their problems to God's care; they need to hear from their peers that God does still act for His people today.

Allow as much time as you can for the sharing activity. Encourage reluctant students as they tell ways God has dealt with the problems and crises they committed to Him.

Finally, have each student write a paragraph based on **Matt. 18:28.** You may want to collect these and read them before the next class session. Students often gain wonderful new insights about trusting God as they meditate on this verse. Some of the students who had nothing to share about God's strengthening power will make commitments in writing that they hadn't thought about before.

Close your class period by having students look back over their answers to the questions about situations in which they rely on themselves, others, or on human reasoning rather than relying on God. Give the students time for silent prayers of repentance. Encourage them to be specific as they ask God's power in dealing with difficulties they face. Read **Micah 7:18–20** as an absolution.

Session 11: *Our* Faith

BIBLE BASIS
Rom. 4:23–25; Gal. 3:1–25

CENTRAL TRUTH
God will credit righteousness to those who believe in Jesus Christ as the only Savior from sin. We have no other valid object for our faith.

OBJECTIVES
By the grace of God students will
1. correctly identify the scriptural meaning of justification and articulate clearly the object of their own personal faith;
2. review the theological concepts Paul has used so far in Romans;
3. use their knowledge of Paul's doctrine of justification to interpret and explain a related portion of Scripture—**Gal. 3:1–25.**

OUTLINE OF ROM. 4:23–25; Gal. 3:1–25
A. We believe in Him who raised Jesus, our Lord **(vv. 23–25)**
B. Justification by faith **(Gal. 3:1–25)**
   1. Does the Spirit's power flow based on human effort or on God's grace? **(vv. 1–5)**
   2. Justification by faith illustrated **(vv. 6–9)**
   3. The Law curses; Christ redeems **(vv. 10–14)**
   4. The covenant promise given before the Law **(vv. 15–18)**
   5. The purpose of the Law **(vv. 19–20)**
   6. Law and Gospel—not rival systems! **(vv. 21–25)**

A WORD FROM THE AUTHOR
Early in the year I give my students time in class to write a letter to me. I ask students to share with me whatever they would like me to know about them. I also ask that they indicate how they think they are doing spiritually. I always promise I will keep what they write confidential.

In giving this assignment, I explain that it is difficult to genuinely care for people you don't know. The letter is one way to speed up the process of getting acquainted. Furthermore, it will help me determine how best to go about the important process of teaching them.

The letters I receive amaze me. My students share things that they would never think of sharing in a one-on-one conversation with anyone but their closest friends. The letter-writing project creates a bond between me and my students. They have trusted me, and I share something in common with them.

This is a portion of one letter I have received:

"I'm 15 and have been through a lot the last two years that has pushed my spiritual life way back. My father is the most evil man I know. He's an alcoholic and crazy. He's a liar, a cheat, and he hit my mom and threw things around the house. Well, anyway, they got divorced two years ago in January, but I used to see him every Sunday. Then he ran off to Florida and married some woman.

"My mom has no financial help from him, and we just got kicked out of our house, plus I did not know what school I was going to. The reason I'm here is a blessing of God through the church. I don't have time or room to tell everything else, but I've been praying for help, and I thank God He gave me you as a teacher, and I believe because of that I will regain my faith in Him."

The student writer gave me permission to reprint this part of her letter. The letter is typical. Needless to say, this student has found a place in my heart. A relationship has been formed. This student entrusted me with some very privileged information. I have gained an insight into her life and personality that will help me to be a more patient and understanding teacher. She, in turn, has given me the gift of seeing my value to her as her teacher. By God's grace, I see that God can use me to make a positive difference in her life!

GETTING INTO THE LESSON (Objective 1)

Begin with prayer.

1. Talk together about the italicized statement in the Student Book. Why is the object of our faith so important? Some people say that sincerity (believing with all your heart) is more important than the object of your faith. How would you respond to someone who said to you, "It doesn't matter what you believe as long as you're sincere"?

2. The church has always set a high priority on knowing what we believe. During the time of the early church, Biblical texts were scarce and the rate of illiteracy high. Individual Christians found it difficult to discover Biblical truth on their own. In answer to these problems, the church developed easily memorized symbols. The oldest of these, the Apostles' Creed, dates back to about A.D. 50. You may want to ask your students to use the Apostles' Creed as a model for their own statements of faith. Warn them, however, not to plagiarize the creed. They should put their faith into their own words.

The activity often works best if groups of three or four students work together to develop a joint creed. You know your students and can best judge whether or not to use small groups for this activity.

IN THE WORD

Verses 23–25: We Believe in Him Who Raised Jesus, Our Lord (Objectives 1 and 2)

1. In these verses Paul turns his attention from Abraham to us, his readers. Students should notice this change of emphasis and apply these verses to their own lives. The personal creeds they just wrote can help them do this.

Paul says that Christians must believe three things in order to be considered righteous before God. We believe the following:

a. God raised Jesus, our Lord, from the dead. His death and resurrection provided the basis for our justification. Jesus was proved to be "the Son of God with power" by that resurrection.

b. Jesus was delivered over to death in order to make expiation for our sins. Peter's wonderful sermon in **Acts 2:14–36** covers the same material, particularly **verses 23–24.**

c. Jesus was raised to life to complete the work of justification. His resurrection proved that the Father accepted Christ's work of atonement for us.

2. Talk together about this question. Encourage your students to put words like **justification** and **expiation** into words that a younger brother or sister could easily understaind.

Gal. 3:1–25: Justification by Faith
(Objectives 2 and 3)

This section will acquaint students with the similarities between Paul's message in Romans and Galatians. It will use **Gal. 3** to help students review the doctrines they have learned so far. Don't be overly concerned if your students don't understand every nuance of Paul's meaning. Encourage them to find the main idea in each section, and to express it in their own words. Help them gain confidence that they can deal with difficult sections of Scripture and interpret them correctly.

Verses 1–5

1. Paul preached to the disciples in Galatia (**Acts 18:23**) and may indeed have founded the church there (**Gal. 1:6**). We can be very sure that he preached justification by grace through faith alone. Others after Paul tampered with this doctrine, introducing legalistic Jewish practices. These "Judaizers" taught that Paul's apostleship was inferior to that of other apostles. They also claimed that the Mosaic law still bound Christians. They particularly preached the importance of circumcision. Paul tells the Galatians that going back to these doctrines is indeed "foolish."

2. Paul urges the Galatians to remember his one basic teaching—faith came as a gift of God's grace from the Holy Spirit. God's other gifts, particularly sanctification, come in the same way—by grace—and not by human effort.

Verses 6–9

1. Your students should note that Paul uses the same illustration here as he did in the opening chapters of Romans. He holds out Abraham as the outstanding example of justification by faith.

2. Jewish believers in particular would be swayed by this illustration. Abraham, the one whom they considered the founder of both their religion and their nation, was justified before God by faith. Surely God would not now demand obedience to the Law as the basis for a right relationship with Him.

Verses 10–14

1. The Law can only bring a curse. To be saved by the Law, one must keep all of it. Since no one can do this, to rely on the Law is to be cursed.

2. Jesus kept God's holy law. But He also became a curse in our place so that we might receive the

promise of salvation by faith, and not by works. You might explain that *redemption* means that we have been bought back from sin, death, and Satan.

Verses 15–18

1. Paul compares our relationship with God to a human covenant or legal will. Once a human will is made and witnessed, it cannot be changed by anyone other than the person who made it. Paul points out that God's covenant (will) promised justification by faith to Abraham 430 years before the giving of the Law. God justified Abraham by faith.

2. God gave His law four centuries after He had made His covenant with Abraham. The Law, then, could not set aside God's covenant (will) of grace which went into effect centuries earlier.

Verses 19–20

1. God gave His law to show the true nature of sin, to expose sin for what it was. God never intended that the Law reveal an alternative method of justification.

2. The Seed was, of course, the Savior—Jesus.

Verses 21–25

If we could have obtained righteousness by keeping the Law, then God's awful sacrifice would not have been necessary. Then Jesus' prayer in the garden, **"Father, if it is possible, may this cup be taken from Me" (Matt. 26:39),** God would have done just that. He would not have insisted upon the cross. The Law can only work to expose sin. Christ died so that we might be saved by God's grace through faith. The Law shows us our sin and our need for the Savior.

Session 12: Rejoice

BIBLE BASIS
   Rom. 5:1–11

CENTRAL TRUTH

Since we have been justified by faith, we have peace with God through our Lord Jesus Christ. Knowing this peace, we can rejoice in hope regardless of the circumstances and troubles we face. His joy is our strength **(Neh. 8:10).**

OBJECTIVES
By the grace of God students will
1. identify joy as a blessing God wants His children to have now in this life as well as in our heavenly home;
2. express their joy in possessing God's peace and in being sure of God's promise of future glory;
3. respond in faith when they confront problems, asking God to use their difficulties as "spiritual isometrics" to produce greater strength.

OUTLINE OF ROM. 5:1–11
A. Rejoice in the present—peace with God **(v. 1)**
B. Rejoice in the future—confident hope **(v. 2)**
C. Rejoice in problems that produce:
   1. Patience **(v. 3)**
   2. Character **(v. 4)**
   3. Confidence **(v. 4)**
   4. Courage **(v. 5)**
   5. Love **(v. 5)**
D. Rejoice in the past **(vv. 6–10)**
   1. Christ died for sinners **(vv. 6–8)**
   2. Christ justified us by His blood **(v. 9)**
   3. Christ saved us by His life **(v. 10)**
E. Rejoice in God **(v. 11)**

A WORD FROM THE AUTHOR

Over the years I have interviewed many teacher candidates for our religion department. One question I ask these people is more significant than all the others put together: "Can you accept your students where they are?"

We all have certain expectations of our students. That is fine, but when our students are not where we expect them to be spiritually, can we accept them where they are?

Only this morning a teacher complained to me about a senior boy whose behavior in chapel left something to be desired. The teacher said, "You'd think that as a senior he would have learned a little more respect and reverence for worship." The teacher was right, of course. The senior should have learned, but he hadn't. He had not reached the spiritual level the teacher had every right to expect from him.

Good teachers have expectations. When our students are not developing as we know they should, we need to be concerned. The problem here, though, was that the teacher was not just disappointed—she was angry. Her concern grew out of anger, not love. It expressed itself as anger, not love.

We care about the spiritual needs of each of our students. Our concern is not based on students' good behavior. It is an independent action on our part, as the Holy Spirit empowers us. Even when we must discipline a student, that student must realize that our decision is born of love.

In today's section from Romans, Paul explains God's love by saying, **"While we were still sinners, Christ died for us" (Rom. 5:8).** God has given us this kind of unconditional love to use with our students. That's good news, for we could never drum it up inside ourselves. God accepts us as we are. Because of that, we can love and accept all our students. We can care for them where they are, and God will use us to help them grow into the people He wants them to be.

GETTING INTO THE LESSON (Objective 1)

Begin with prayer.

This session may present a lot of difficulty for some students. They certainly will need your guidance and direction as they answer the questions in the Student Book. So, it might be wise to go over **verses 1–11** orally first. Answer their questions before you ask them to work through the Student Book material.

This passage presents three kinds of rejoicing, each level introducing a greater degree of delight.

1. Rejoicing in the hope of glory (**v. 2**)
2. Rejoicing in our sufferings (**vv. 3–5**)
3. Rejoicing in God (**v. 11**)

The second, rejoicing in suffering, is a concept most students (and adults, too!) would rather not hear too much about. It requires some degree of spiritual maturity just to understand, much less practice this principle; so, you may want to devote most of today's lesson time to **verses 3–5**.

Discuss the introductory paragraphs of the session with the class. Encourage them to talk about how they feel about being a Christian. It should come as no surprise that many students feel a total commitment to Jesus Christ would take all the fun out of life. Joy in life and Christian living are mutually exclusive in many young minds. Use this lesson to identify that idea as one of Satan's more successful lies.

IN THE WORD

Verse 1: Rejoice in the Present (Objective 2)

An immediate benefit of justification is "peace with God." This peace cuts both ways. God's wrath has been appeased. Justice has been done. A holy God no longer charges our sins against us, because His Son has paid the penalty for them. On the other hand, our hostility toward God (**Rom. 8:7**) has been washed away in the flood of His love as by His grace we came to faith in the Savior. Christ has released us from guilt, fear of retribution, and hostility toward both God and ourselves.

Swiss psychiatrist Dr. Carl Jung once remarked that he never had a patient whose basic problem was not rooted in a fear of death and retribution. Whether that's true or not, certainly no one can attain genuine peace with self or others without having peace with God.

Once we see the conflict between God and ourselves has been resolved, we can find peace with ourselves, peace of mind. God is working in us. He is helping us be what He wants us to be. We have a goal, a purpose, a destiny.

Then, being content with what God is doing in us, and armed with the assurance of His complete forgiveness, we can reach out to each other in genuine concern, forgiveness, and love—even as we have experienced God's forgiving love. Peace with God produces peace of mind which, in turn, produces peace with our neighbor.

Verse 2: Rejoice in the Future (Objective 2)

Ask the class to explain what they understand the word *grace* to mean. It is a difficult concept, perhaps one we humans understand the very least. Undeserved favor weakly expresses such a grand reality!

Here Paul presents the very helpful picture of a believer standing in a pool of grace. The idea of being totally surrounded and protected by the approval of our God stunningly portrays our security in the Kingdom.

Equipped with this picture of our present security, we turn our eyes upward and outward as we contemplate the joy of our future glory. As John writes in his first letter, **"Now we are children of God, and what we will be has not yet been made known. But we know that when He appears, we shall be like Him" (1 John 3:2–3).** Being like Jesus—what an exciting basis for joy!

Verses 3–5: Rejoice in Problems
(Objectives 1 and 3)

Encourage your students to think of problems as spiritual isometrics. Ask the weight lifters in your class to explain what happens when they lift: Muscles don't just grow. First the athlete must break down the tissues of the old muscle so that new and larger ones begin to build. This is a painful process. "No pain, no gain," athletes say to encourage each other (but some doctors warn adults not to apply that principle to their exercise programs).

God applies a similar principle. Ask your students to read and explain **Rom. 8:28**. When we believe that everything God allows in our lives as believers will result in good, either for us or for others, we will be able to "rejoice in tribulation."

Work through the following steps with your students.

1. God knows that our well-being depends upon our trust in Him. Our world praises independence. Our society admires the rugged individualist. It's hard for us to give up our control to God's perfect will for our lives. So, in love, God helps us to do what we need to do to reach the happy state of total reliance on Him.

   a. At times God allows us to get into difficulties so severe that trusting Him is the only possible way out. Jesus used this technique often with His disciples (e.g., **Matt. 8:23–27** and **Mark 6:33–52**). As we wait upon the Lord, we learn patience. A Christian counselor might tell students, "Patience! God is teaching you patience (perseverance). Hang in there, trusting God, and He will provide."

   b. And God does provide. As we experience God's power in dealing with human difficulties, we find it easier to expect Him to do it again next time. A student who has had this experience doesn't have to come back for counseling the next time a problem arises. Rather, the student now begins to counsel others—both by word and example. In this way, Christian character grows.

c. As we progress along this path, we develop outrageous confidence. No problem is too big for our God! We no longer believe these words in theory; they have been proven to us in practice.

d. The product of this process is courage. We can look Satan and the world square in the eye and say, "Do your worst! I will continue to rejoice in the greatness of my God, in His love and power."

Of course, this process recurs again and again throughout each believer's life. We continue to grow as we meet situations that challenge us. See God's promise in **1 Cor. 10:13.** Knowing we will encounter difficulties, how do these words comfort us?

2. Everything God does, He does in love. He wants us to grow up in faith until we become like Jesus. Knowing this, we can run *to* Him with our difficulties, not *away from* Him.

Verses 6–11: Rejoice in the Past (Objective 2)

1. If we doubt God's love, one example of that love stands supreme: **Rom. 5:6–8** explains it.

2. The death of Christ on behalf of sinful humanity has made it possible for us to be "justified by His blood." We have been released from the penalty of our sin. We are certain that Christ died for us, but we too often overlook that He also lives. Paul shows us that salvation includes much more than forgiveness for what we have done. "We shall be saved through His life" refers to the truth that Jesus' life at work in us through the power of the Holy Spirit delivers us from the *power* of sin, just as His death delivered us from the *penalty* of sin.

3. Have students use a good Bible dictionary to define the word *reconcile*.

Adam's sin tore apart our relationship with God. We could only feel hostility toward Him. God brought about our reconciliation through Christ. Now He gives us the ministry of reconciliation. This is why Jesus calls us as the children of God "peacemakers" **(Matt. 5:9).**

Session 13: Concluding Activities for Unit 1

CONCLUDING ACTIVITIES FOR UNIT 1

Open the class session with prayer. Thank God for His Word, especially for the truths He has taught you through your study of Romans so far. Ask Him to direct your minds and spirits to grasp the special insights He has given in Romans. And ask Him to help you apply its truths to your life.

God's Word means more to God's people when we not only know it, but also apply it to our lives. Use this review to encourage your students both to organize their knowledge and to recognize the potential for personally applying it. Session 11 gave students the opportunity to review and interpret the material studied so far as they read **Gal. 3:1–25.** This activity laid the groundwork for the full review you will now ask them to do.

You could use this review session as a test, but it has not been designed as such. Your students will need time to work; you may want to set aside some class time for them to at least get a good start. Students will probably need some help from you—some examples of how to write a "central truth" and examples of ways in which a lesson can be applied.

You could use class work time to help and encourage individuals who will find this assignment difficult.

Your students will need to know how you will use their work. If you will grade the assignment as a test, be sure to tell them. On the other hand, you could have them read their central truths and applications aloud to the class. This takes time, but could provoke marvelous class discussion. Be sensitive to your poorer writers if you choose this procedure. It may be best to collect all the papers, read them, write comments on them, and then select a few to read in class for discussion.

1. Central truths, like beauty, are often in the eye of the beholder. Although you will find all 12 central truths spelled out in this teachers guide, also work along with the students to write your own. Then spend some time comparing notes. Help the students see how to step back from the text, to get a general overview, and then say in as few words as possible what the text says.

2. Application can be tricky. What Scripture *says* is knowledge; what it *says to me* is application. Sometimes, we have no idea what God is saying to our students through Scripture until we ask. If the students can't apply Biblical truths to themselves, then Scripture is not having the impact upon their lives it is supposed to have.

If your class seems unsure as to how to go about this, use session 1 as an example. Ask them to think back over the text and its key words:

Slave. Sometimes teenagers know just how slaves must have felt. Adolescents have no authority of their own and must be subject to everyone under the sun—parents, older brothers or sisters, teachers, all adults, state, country, and God. They can relate to slavery in its negative aspects, but they can also see what it implies for Christian living.

Called to be saints. Each of us who believes in the Lord Jesus is both *called* a saint and *called to be* a saint. If we have the name "Christian," we also have the Christian responsibility.

Paul's view of himself (v. 1) and his ministry (vv. 2–5) was remarkably clear and very different from what we might expect. His relationship with Jesus

Christ had given him a new view of himself and his life's work. Each of us needs to step back and see ourselves from the Lord's perspective. What are my gifts? What is my mission? What do I need to do to accomplish the Lord's will for my life?

Encourage your students to relax, to let their thoughts range over the words of Scripture, and in doing so to allow the Spirit of God to direct their thoughts.

UNIT 2
SALVATION, PART 2

BIBLE BASIS: ROM. 5:12–8:39

This unit continues the study of the righteousness we have received from God. Whereas unit 1 focused upon how God saved us from what we *do,* this unit focuses upon how God saved us from what we *are.* As the Student Book points out, what we *do* is *sin,* and what we *are* are *sinners.*

Sin itself—the rebellion that lies deep within the heart of every human born on earth—had a deadly contaminating effect upon our very nature before we became a member of God's family through His miracle of rebirth. **Rom. 5:12–8:39** describes how the Father has provided a deliverance from sin's polluting effect in our lives. As Paul points out elsewhere, **"If anyone is in Christ, he is a new creation; the old has gone, the new has come" (2 Cor. 5:17).**

Romans shouts the miracle of righteousness: God shares His righteousness with all who believe in the redemptive work of His only Son, Jesus Christ. God has declared us "not guilty" through faith in Jesus Christ alone. We have been freed from the penalty of sin. Now we have been enabled by the Holy Spirit to submit to God's will. This process of sanctification results in greater and growing freedom from the power of sin in our lives. We will never be perfect in this world, but God's Spirit helps us grow as He transforms us step by step into the image of Jesus.

You have great news to share in this unit!

Session 14: Let Christ Reign by Grace!

BIBLE BASIS
Rom. 5:12–21

CENTRAL TRUTH

Through Adam's sin, all humankind became subject to the terrible tyranny of sin and death. Through Christ's sacrifice, grace and righteousness are made available to all. When Adam disobeyed God, "the many were made sinners." Through Christ's obedience to God, "the many will be made righteous."

OBJECTIVES

By the grace of God students will
1. identify both similarities between Adam and Christ and the very different consequences of their work;
2. explain the impact of Adam's sin on all human beings;
3. perceive and clearly express the truth that God's grace in Christ has broken the power of sin's reign in our lives.

OUTLINE OF ROM. 5:12–21
A. Sin
   1. Sin entered **(v. 12)**
   2. Sin increased **(v. 20)**
   3. Sin reigned **(v. 20)**
B. Death
   1. Death entered **(v. 12)**
   2. Death increased (all men) **(v. 12)**
   3. Death reigned **(vv. 14 and 17)**
C. Grace and righteousness
   1. Entered **(v. 15)**
   2. Increased **(vv. 17–18, 20)**
   3. Reigned **(vv. 17 and 21)**

A WORD FROM THE AUTHOR

As we delve deeper and deeper into Scripture, it becomes very apparent that what we call the Christian "religion" is really a relationship. Relationships are formed, not taught. That, in essence, is the crux of our problem as Christian teachers. How do we teach what can't be taught?

The apostle Paul described the mission of the church in a nutshell in **2 Tim 2:2: "And the things you have heard me say in the presence of many witnesses entrust to reliable men who will also be qualified to teach others."** In brief, our job is to teach others to teach others.

The Lord never intended His New Testament church to become a levitical institution like Old Testament Israel. Instead, He instituted the priesthood of all believers. He calls us to disciple the saints in our classrooms until they reach the mature faith that embraces them to teach others.

Already in the first century the author of Hebrews complained that the church consisted of people who **"ought to be teachers, [but who] need someone to teach [them] the elementary truths of God's word all over again" (Heb. 5:12).** Nothing much has changed. The majority of my students have attended Christian schools all their lives. Most of my seniors have sat through 13 years of religion classes, and too often we still feed them spiritual baby food. No wonder they find the whole business rather bland and boring, A 17-year-old still living on pablum and warm milk cannot be expected to enjoy coming to the dinner table.

Teaching our students to teach means providing them with the opportunities to do it. Lutheran high schools provide us with the perfect opportunity for this. I ask my students to share with their classmates what the Lord is doing in their lives. Later, they speak from in front of the classroom. Later still, they share in chapel with the whole student body.

We must give our students both the opportunity and the responsibility for sharing the Word of God with others. Suppose a coach would hold regular practice sessions, but never schedule a game. Under those circumstances an athlete's interest in the sport would quickly evaporate. Likewise, Christians who just sit and listen all their lives never learn to participate in the work of Christ's church. They never grow into mature witnesses for the Lord.

Every teacher knows that the best way to learn a subject is to teach it. As we equip our students to teach others, we will find that they learn better, faster, and with greater interest than they have before.

As students share, they bless us, their teachers. I find that as I sit and listen to my students share their faith, I gain insights, understanding, and compassion for individuals in very powerful and unique ways. I would miss all that if I did all the talking. I learn from my students, and I am blessed by them.

IN THE WORD
Verses 5:12–21 Sin and Death Through Adam; Life Through Christ (Objectives 1 and 2)

Discuss the introductory material in the Student Book as you begin today's session. It deals with the concept of *control*. Ask if anyone knows a person like Denise. How can sin be "a bondage"—i.e., how can it put a person into slavery? Talk about these questions. Listen carefully to your students. Their comments now may help you personalize the text later on in the session.

1. Your students may have difficulty understanding this pericope. Acknowledge the challenge it presents. Then as a group work through the outline the students are asked to rank. The verses they list will probably conform closely with those listed in the outline at the beginning of this session.

Adam sinned, and thus sin became a genetic characteristic of human beings, a fatal disease passed on to every child born on earth. Humanity became helplessly subject to the power of sin.

The effects of sin snowballed as sin brought death, the inevitable consequence of sin. When Adam rebelled against God's command, he suffered spiritual death. From that moment on, Adam could not reproduce offsprings who were spiritually alive. Every descendant of Adam for all time would be born spiritually dead, divorced from fellowship with God, and doomed to eternal separation from Him.

In stark contrast to this grim reality stands the gift of God, a Savior, a second Adam, who by His sacrifice brings life and light back to humanity through the reign of grace and righteousness, God's antidote for sin and death. Note that many Christians labor under the vague impression that the evil of sin and the power of God are somehow equal forces. "If God's grace is great, it is only marginally so," they may think. Help your students see the power of salvation and righteousness as infinitely greater than the power of sin and death. This does not negate sin's power but glorifies God's love for all people through Christ.

2. Have the verses the students chose for each heading read aloud, each as a complete unit. Ask individuals to paraphrase each group of verses.

3–4. Ask each student to write the paragraphs suggested in the Student Books. As they work, help individuals who need further help understanding the text.

5. Adam consciously decided to disobey God's direct command. He chose to take the consequences for his act of free will. Eve was deceived by the most diabolical mind in creation. Adam walked right into transgression with his eyes wide open. The enormity of his rebellion shattered the creation and introduced into humanity something previously unknown.

6. Make sure your students understand the difference between sins and sin. We commit individual sins; sin itself is a condition. Even during the time between Adam and Moses, when the Law had not yet been given, people still died. Paul argues that since death comes as a consequence of sin, human death proves the reality and power of sin.

7. A condemned prisoner who lives on death row awaiting the day of his execution may hope for the governor's pardon. If it comes, that prisoner is not going to say, "But how does this relate to me?" But our students often do ask or need to be shown the monumental implications of their faith.

This activity will force students to look more deeply into what God's rescue of the human race means to them personally. We want them to begin to discover meaningful applications. Encourage a few of your students to share orally what life values they have discovered in this difficult lesson. This will serve as a first step into the kind of sharing-teaching experience described in **"A Word from the Author"** above.

Session 15: What Do You Know?

BIBLE BASIS
Rom. 6:1–14

CENTRAL TRUTH
We have been crucified, buried, and resurrected with Jesus through our baptism. That gives us the power to offer ourselves to God "as instruments of righteousness."

OBJECTIVES
By the grace of God students will
1. understand the significance of Baptism for their lives, particularly for their struggle against sin;
2. see themselves as crucified and risen with Christ;
3. use the power of their baptism to defeat sin more and more consistently in their lives.

OUTLINE OF ROM. 6:1–14
A. Shall we go on sinning? (vv. 1–2)
B. Alive in Christ! (vv. 3–5)
 1. Dead (v. 3)
 2. Buried (v. 4)
 3. Resurrected (v. 5)
C. What does this mean? (vv. 6–14)
 1. Free from slavery of sin through death (vv. 6–7)
 2. New life in Christ (vv. 8–11)
 3. We can say no to sin (vv. 12–13)
 4. We live under grace, not Law (v. 14)

A WORD FROM THE AUTHOR
As a young teacher, I often thought about how wonderful this profession of ours would be if all our students were bright and beautiful. As I matured, the Lord showed me what an ungodly thought that was. Gradually the realization dawned on me that God chooses losers:

"But God chose the foolish things of the world to shame the wise; God chose the weak things of the world to shame the strong. He chose the lowly things of this world and the despised things—and the things that are not—to nullify the things that are, so that no one may boast before Him" (1 Cor. 1:27–29).

Both the Samaritan woman and the Gadarene demoniac would be considered losers by people of the world. Yet, God used both of them as effective witnesses after they had known the Lord Jesus for only a brief time. The rich young man, on the other hand, could not be used by God though, by human standards, he was a real winner.

Many of my students are dropouts. Even though they still come to school, they have dropped out of academic competition a long time before they get to my classroom. They have just one goal for their schooling, and that is to get out as soon as possible. Other students cling to the social fringe. They find no acceptance from any group or clique in school. Still other students have such low self-esteem that they wear the label "loser" like a scarlet letter. All of these students need to hear that God chooses losers. They need to be convinced of the reality of God's power to transform them as He renews their mind (Rom. 12:2). When this transformation begins to take place in their lives, they know it is God's doing and not their own—a realization the student-athlete, the class leader, the valedictorian, and the prom queen often fail to attain.

I have come to love my losers. And I often feel genuine sympathy for the talented winners who are so easy to teach, but who sometimes find it so difficult to give God the credit for what they are.

GETTING INTO THE LESSON
Begin with prayer.

Paul has established that the blood of Jesus Christ cleanses the believer of all sins. By the blood of Jesus, God declares us righteous. Now that we have been saved from the penalty of sin, another question arises. How can we be delivered from the power of sin? How can we work out into our everyday life-style the righteousness God has imputed to us? How can we become on the outside what God has already made us in our baptism? The first half of Rom. 6 gives us the basis for sanctified living.

Use the opening section in the Student Book to talk about how important confidence is to performance. Use other areas of school life such as test-taking, band competitions, and cheerleading tryouts as examples.

IN THE WORD
Verses 1–2: Shall We Go On Sinning?
(Objectives 1 and 2)

Use the questions from the Student Book to help the class think about the relationship between the last session and this one. Ask what Paul means when he says, "We died to sin" (v. 2). The rest of the verses in today's pericope will also help students understand this principle. Basically, Paul is arguing that there has been a change of ownership in our lives. Jesus has purchased us by His death and resurrection. He has freed us from sin and death. It would be a perversion of grace to continue to live as though we were still slaves of sin.

Ask, **Do Christians today sometimes pervert God's grace by misusing it?** (E.g., "I know doing this is wrong, but I can always ask God to forgive me. And He will. Right?") Point out the danger in which a person with such an attitude has placed himself or herself. God does indeed forgive, but hardening our hearts in this way can lead back to spiritual bondage and, indeed, spiritual death.

Verses 3–5: Alive in Christ!
(Objectives 1 and 2)

With the change of ownership in our lives comes a change in operation also. We need to understand what happened in us at Baptism, how we became dead to sin and alive to God through Christ. In Baptism we

died with Jesus;
were buried with Jesus; and
rose with Jesus.

When we became a member of the body of Christ, we did more than join a church; we literally became one with Him. Use **John 15:5** to illustrate this reality: **"I am the vine; you are the branches. If a man remains in Me and I in him, he will bear much fruit; apart from Me you can do nothing."** Our roots no longer go back to Adam and the reign of sin and death. Our roots go back to Christ and the cross. We have identified completely with Him. His life-giving power to defeat sin has now become ours.

As time permits, you might explore the imagery of Baptism by immersion suggested by Paul's words "buried with Christ." While Scripture uses the word *baptize* to mean simply "sprinkle" or "wash," in other places this text highlights the spiritual death, burial, and resurrection typified in immersion. The Word of God, though (not our method of applying water), gives Baptism its power. Be sure your students understand this.

Verses 6–14: What Does This Mean?
(Objectives 1, 2 and 3)

1. Our union with Christ on the cross has broken the hold sin had on our lives. We are no longer slaves of sin. Christians do not have to serve sin ever again. We are under new management!

2. **Verse 11** encourages us to **"count [ourselves] dead to sin but alive to God in Christ Jesus."** The Greek word translated *count* means exactly that, to calculate. It is an accounting term which gives this phrase great importance, for the truism "Numbers don't lie" rings absolutely true in this case, too. Numbers always add up the same way; two and two is always four. Numbers are not subjective. Neither is the truth of our being dead to sin. We can count on it; we are alive to God in Jesus Christ!

3. **Verses 12–14** spell out the two steps necessary for righteous living. We are to stop submitting to sin. And we are to start offering ourselves to God as instruments of righteousness.

As you discuss this concept, take care that your students understand these two things can never be done in human strength. They cannot be works of the flesh, accomplished by merely "trying hard."

Rather, recognizing the new life God has given us, we go to Him daily (perhaps even hour by hour or minute by minute), confessing our weakness and failure and receiving from Him the ability to overcome sin's power. We can do nothing to improve ourselves. As His Spirit empowers us, God transforms us to become more and more Christlike. That continual confession, repentance, and renewal are all involved in the daily remembrance of Baptism that Luther so vigorously urged Christians to practice.

The Student Book asks the class to make two lists. These and your class discussion about them should help students think about today's lesson concepts in a concrete, practical way. How we speak to and about one another provides an easy and accurate barometer to determine how we are following Paul's instructions. Consistently we are offering ourselves to God as instruments of righteousness. We *can* stop gossiping and bruising one another with our language. We *can* bless one another and build up one another with our words. **How can that confidence help us?**

What if we slip into gossip (or any other sin) after we know God's power and plan for us in Baptism? Then, our baptism reminds us of God's covenant of peace and forgiveness. He has made us His children, adopted us at Baptism. We can rely on that forgiving love, count ourselves dead to sin, and once again offer ourselves to Him in confession, repentance, and renewed strength.

Note: A thorough discussion of the Sacrament of Holy Baptism could take several days. You will treat Baptism again in session 88 of this course. At that time, students will be asked to read Luther's comments about this Sacrament from his Large Catechism.

The key issue Scripture stresses as it treats Baptism involves the forgiveness of sins, the adoption into God's family, the new life in Christ, and the power to live as God's forgiven children. These are truths Paul emphasizes in **Rom. 6.** As time permits, however, you may want to explain briefly some of the other Scriptural truths about Baptism (e.g., original sin, infant Baptism vs. "believer Baptism," who may administer Baptism, etc.). See *The Book of Concord* (Tappert edition), pp. 211–14 and 436–46. See also Francis Pieper's *Christian Dogmatics* (CPH, 1953), vol. 3, pp. 253–89.

Session 16: Slavery

BIBLE BASIS
Rom. 6:15–23

CENTRAL TRUTH
Christ has broken the bondage of sin in our lives. He gives us His Spirit's power to choose to obey God. Our choice is made evident by our works.

OBJECTIVES
By the grace of God students will
1. understand the process of sanctification and the choices God helps Christians make as they encounter various situations in life;
2. explain the difference between knowing correct doctrines and obeying God from a willing heart;
3. ask for the Holy Spirit's power to help them live in more and more consistent obedience to God.

OUTLINE OF ROM. 6:15–23
A. To sin or not to sin? **(v. 15)**
B. Remember what you were **(vv. 16–21)**
   1. Slaves to sin **(vv. 17 and 20)**
   2. Slaves to impurity and wickedness **(v. 19)**
   3. Unrighteous **(v. 20)**
   4. Ashamed **(v. 21)**
   5. Dead **(v. 21)**
C. Remember what you are **(vv. 16–22)**
   1. Free to choose **(vv. 16–17)**
      a) Taught in the Word **(v. 17—mind)**
      b) Obedient in the heart **(v. 17—spirit)**
   2. Free from the slavery to sin **(v. 18)**
   3. Slaves to righteousness **(v. 18)**
   4. Slaves to God **(v. 22; Rom. 1:1; James 1:1; 2 Peter 1:1)**
   5. Holy **(v. 22)**
   6. Eternally alive **(vv. 22–23)**

A WORD FROM THE AUTHOR

In his *Story of Civilization*, Will Durant wrote, "Great civilizations are never destroyed by barbaric assault from without but by barbaric decay from within." I believe this truism applies to schools as well. For more and more of our students, Christian schools provide an island of stability in a barbaric world. A Christian high school gives students a four-year reprieve from direct confrontation with a world intent upon the total destruction of God's children. Our schools help students develop a spiritual maturity that becomes increasingly necessary for survival as our society becomes increasingly barbaric. We act as a painful thorn in Satan's flesh, and when we do, he takes a special interest in us.

Satan rarely attacks us head on; He loves to get inside of a group of God's people and cause dissension and division. This tactic is nothing new. Even the disciples quarreled with one another right up to the institution of the Lord's Supper.

Whenever conflict occurs, we need to ask God to help us perceive the real reasons that underlie it. If our faculty feuds with the school administration, if teachers bicker with one another, if the classroom becomes an arena for more conflict than teaching, we can place the blame where it belongs. After all the rationalizations and excuses are put to rest, we can see the real culprit—Satan, busy trying to destroy the church from within.

One verse of Scripture has truly helped me in dealing with conflict. Whenever a colleague hurts me, a parent criticizes, or a student sneers, I remember **Col. 1:27**. In this verse Paul shares one of the great mysteries of the Christian faith: **"God has chosen to make known among the Gentiles the glorious riches of this mystery, which is Christ in you, the hope of glory."**

"Christ in you!" What a glorious truth! Wherever sinful human beings interact, we will find conflict. But when Satan begins to stimulate our flesh to produce conflict and to destroy ministry, God gives us a remedy.

Christ is in us, and He is in those with whom we are in conflict. That's the joy of living with fellow Christians. I can look past the external behavior of even my worst critics and see Christ. I can appeal to others to look past my failures and to see Christ in me. When we practice this principle, conflict disappears and our oneness in our Lord becomes apparent. Jesus says this is our best form of witness. **"I in them and You in Me. May they be brought to complete unity to let the world know that You sent Me and have loved loved them even as You have loved Me"** (John 17:23).

GETTING INTO THE LESSON (Objective 1)

Warning!!! Several major doctrinal aberrations can arise from the Biblical teaching on justification. Moralism, for example, has plagued the church down through the ages. Moralists use the teachings of Jesus to correct believers' life-styles, but without adequately emphasizing Jesus Himself as the Source of all help and spiritual power. **Rom. 6** can easily be mishandled so that students derive merely a moralistic understanding rather than being enabled to handle the effective spiritual "power tools" with which the Holy Spirit wants to equip them.

As you work through the lesson, stress particularly the difference between justification and sanctification. Paul has just finished a thorough discussion of justification. He now turns to the question of sanctification, to a concern about behavior. Paul calls believers "living letters" **(2 Cor. 3:2)**. Sometimes the sermon our students "preach" with their behavior can be very disheartening to those of us who teach them. They need a deeper concern for the importance of works, but we need to be certain they understand this has nothing to do with their righteousness, standing before God, through Christ. Pray for special wisdom and insight as you prepare to teach today.

IN THE WORD
Verse 15: To Sin or Not to Sin? (Objective 1)

1. Paul answers his question quite emphatically. Use this section to generate a class discussion as to why Christians continue to sin. Is it because we can't help ourselves? How often is that true? How often we can help it, and we go ahead and sin anyhow! Why do we do it? Are we guilty of thinking that it doesn't make any difference, because God will forgive us no matter what we do? If this is our attitude, we are guilty of abusing God's grace. But so what? What can happen as long as we believe? Try to get across the danger such an attitude places us in. God's grace alone saves us, through faith in Jesus Christ alone.

Verses 16–23: Whose Slave Are You? (Objectives 2 and 3)

1. Use the paraphrase to help students think through a hard reality. Nobody is free! If we are not serving Jesus Christ, we serve sin and death. There is no other option. Paul, James, and Peter all introduce themselves as "slaves of Christ" **(Rom. 1:1; James 1:1; 2 Peter 1:1)**. Sin's mastery brings misery and death. Satan promises his victims freedom, even as sin's manacles grow tighter and tighter. God wants us to be willing to choose to serve righteousness because He loves us. He wants what is best for us. So, while some might argue that serving sin and serving righteousness are both slavery, we Christians recognize quite a difference between the two.

2. See the outline, point B. Remember what you were **(vv. 16–21)**. Know what you are **(vv. 16–22)**.

3. Help your students distinguish between knowledge and obedience. The Roman Christians seem to have impressed Paul, because they practiced the truths they had learned. Take some class time to discuss the importance of knowing the truth. Then talk about why it's so necessary to put the teachings of Jesus into practice. Ask for practical ways this can be applied (e.g., attitude toward parents, language, cheating, grudges).

4. You might ask students to read **1 John 3:7** as you discuss consistently practicing righteousness. God empowers this kind of consistency. It comes as a direct outgrowth of *who we are* as reborn men and women of God. Orange trees produce oranges because they are orange trees. Christians produce the fruit of righteousness because Christ lives inside us. That does not mean we will be perfect this side of heaven. But God has promised to continually transform us into the image of Christ Himself **(2 Cor. 3:10)**.

So, when we fail (and even if we seem to fail quite consistently in some areas), we can claim God's forgiveness and draw on His power to obey even as we trust His promise to sanctify us. **"He who calls [us] is faithful, and He will do it"** (1 Thess. 5:24 RSV).

5. Sin pays dreadful wages to its slaves—death. God gives eternal life as a free gift to His children. What a contrast! Knowing the great love of our Savior motivates us to obey Him, to please Him, to serve Him—but from a heart filled with love, not out of a sense of duty.

Session 17: Marriage

BIBLE BASIS
Rom. 7:1–6

CENTRAL TRUTH

The Law demanded much, but offered no assistance in fulfilling its own demands. The Law has not been set aside, but rather its demands have been met in Christ. He fulfilled all the demands of the Law for us. Now we have God's promise, **"Sin shall not be your master, because you are not under law, but under grace"** (Rom. 6:14).

OBJECTIVES

By the grace of God students will
1. explain Paul's allegory about marriage to the Law, and marriage to Christ;
2. explain the difference between lives under the Law and under grace;
3. list implications our union with Christ has for daily living.

OUTLINE OF ROM. 7:1–6
A. Married to the Law (vv. 1–3)
B. Married to Christ (vv. 4–6)
  1. We belong to one whose resurrection freed us from
      a) The control of our sinful nature **(v. 5)**
      b) Sinful passions which the Law only made worse **(v. 5)**
      c) The fruit of death **(v. 5)**
  2. We belong to one whose resurrection enables us to
      a) Bear fruit to God **(v. 4)**
      b) Serve in the new way of the Spirit **(v. 6)**

A WORD FROM THE AUTHOR

Sometimes I feel such a rapport with my fellow Christian teachers that our fellowship becomes almost tangible. We often labor in loneliness and isolation. It is very comforting to know others who share our experiences, our frustration, and our joys. No one else can truly understand the tremendous task our Lord has given us.

One day as I was teaching, I watched the faces of my students. Their expressions reflected an entire gamut of emotions from near catatonia to polite interest. It struck me what a difficult job we have. If the Word of God is spiritual food, then we teachers are chefs of a sort. Every day we set a table and prepare food in a palatable and attractive way. For a variety of reasons (some valid and some not), I don't always have enough time to prepare a gourmet feast every day. The truth is, I'm probably closer to a spiritual brown bagger than a gourmet chef. I pack the class a good lunch. It's well balanced. It contains all the daily requirements. But its packaging often leaves something to be desired.

Our culture teaches our students to crave novelty. My students are used to being stimulated and entertained. They have grown accustomed to consuming spiritual junk food done up in attractive packaging that sometimes makes my "brown bag lunch" seem uninteresting by contrast. Keeping students interested and motivated every day requires time and creativity that I don't have.

I need to remind my students and myself of the life-giving power of God's Word. Once ingested, this food nourishes God's people. While I continue to work on a more dynamic presentation and while I ask God for the time, creativity, and energy to design lessons that will touch the hearts of my students, I must remember the nourishment is not in the packaging.

Praise God that He forgives my sins of poor preparations. And praise Him that He has promised us that His Word always does its life-giving, life-sustaining work in the hearts of His people.

GETTING INTO THE LESSON (Objective 1)

Begin with prayer.

Then ask a student to read the opening illustration about the marriage of the perfect husband to his not-so-perfect wife. Compare it with **Rom. 6:13.**

God knows us so well. He knows our sin and weakness. He knows we can do nothing about our miserable condition. More often than not, though, the problem seems to be that we do not know this. Or at least we live as though we didn't. We continue to delude ourselves with the idea that as long as we *try* to keep the Law, we are not such miserable sinners as others we could name.

Paul's allegory and personal testimony in **Rom. 7** can help us recognize that God's law drives us away from our dependency upon ourselves and our righteousness.

The Law does curb the gross outbreaks of sin in the world. And, once we become believers, the Law shows us how to live in a God-pleasing way. But the one main function of the Law is to show us how powerless we really are to obey God in and of ourselves.

God gave His law to drive us in despair to the cross. The Law shows us our sin and our need for the Savior. A marriage to the Law can lead only to frustration and defeat.

Share briefly the three uses of the Law. Ask students for examples of each from Scripture and from their own lives. Move quickly into the next section.

IN THE WORD

Verses 1–3: Married to the Law (Objectives 1 and 2)

1. If you use the passages given in the student book for class discussion, it may take up more time than you wish to use. Students can get very interested when the subject of marriage comes up. **Eph. 5,** especially, may provoke much discussion. Spend just enough time on the topic to get your class thinking through the basics of marriage and the commitment husbands and wives make to each other, for instance:

Marriage is a literal union that becomes a permanent oneness through the sexual act **(1 Cor. 6:15–17).**

Marriage is lifelong **(1 Cor. 7:10).**

The institution of marriage is the best example we have to explain what our oneness with Jesus is like **(1 Cor. 6:15; 2 Cor. 11:12; Eph. 5:22–32).**

2. If we choose to live under the Law and to trust in pacifying God by our own obedience, two things are inevitable. First and foremost, we will fail. Second, if we break even one commandment, God counts us guilty—it's just as if we had broken every one of God's commandments **(Gal. 3:10; James 2:10).**

Verses 4–6: Married to Christ (Objectives 2 and 3)

1. Let volunteers share their paraphrases. Challenge them to think through these paraphrases. Be sure everyone understands Paul's allegory.

2. Paul's answer to "How do we die to the Law?" is found in **verse 4: "You also died to the law through the body of Christ, that you might belong to another."** Paul says here and in 1 Cor. 1:30 that on the hill of Calvary Christ did it all for us. God has taken us and made us one with Jesus by faith. His experience became our experience. He died; we died. He rose; we rose—to a new life as His bride.

3. Traditionally a woman takes the name of her husband when she marries. She changes her name to his. The wife becomes co-owner of all her husband possesses.

In a similar way God remarkably enriches us when He gives us the name of Christ. Everything God has is at our disposal; all of His vast resources are ours to draw upon. We no longer have to worry about working to please God. Now we bear fruit to God, a natural by-product of our intimacy with Him. Paul describes this as "serving in the new way of the Spirit, not in the old way of the written code."

You could also use **1 Cor. 1:30** to illustrate the blessings of our union with the Lord. Paul says that because we are in Christ Jesus we have access to wisdom, righteousness, holiness, and redemption.

4. See the outline at the beginning of this lesson for the things from which Jesus has freed us.

5. Have students share insights with one another in clusters of three or four students. Then discuss it with the whole group.

Session 18: Our Struggle with Sin

BIBLE BASIS
 Rom. 7:7–25

CENTRAL TRUTH

In our baptism, God has made us His new creation. All God's children will struggle with sin as long as they remain in the flesh. But God uses His Word and the Sacraments to strengthen our new self and to weaken our old self as we grow to become more and more like our Lord Jesus.

OBJECTIVES

By the grace of God students will
1. identify the effects of God's law in their lives;
2. tell what it means to be God's new creation;
3. relate Paul's personal struggle with sin to their own;
4. use the power of the Word and Sacraments to strengthen the new self and weaken the old self.

OUTLINE OF ROM. 7:7–25

A. The effects of the Law (vv. 7–13)
   1. The Law defines sin (v. 7a)
   2. The Law provokes sin (vv. 8–11)
   3. The Law reveals sin (vv. 12–13)
B. The struggle with sin (vv. 14–24)
   1. Our carnal nature (v. 14)
   2. "I can will what is right, but cannot do it" (vv. 15–17)
   3. The Law produces despair (vv. 18–24)
C. God's answer in Jesus (v. 25)

A WORD FROM THE AUTHOR

"Let those who love the Lord hate evil" (Ps. 97:10).

I often find myself hating my students' sins more than they do (at least more than they appear to). When I see sin in a student's life, I often confront that student. I want my student to feel the same way about their sin that God does. As a result of my sometimes misguided interference, the student resents me and clings to the sin even more tightly.

It seems to me that whoever advised us to "hate the sin and love the sinner" probably never worked with teenagers day after day. When I begin to react to the sin in my students' lives, I need to make sure my motives are godly ones. I need to make sure I have the student's welfare at heart—not just my own comfort or convenience. Otherwise, the line of distinction between sin and sinner begins to blur. I suddenly can find myself disliking the sinner as well as the sin. My students, of course, can sense this attitude in me, and then they react by disliking me in turn. I have built a wall between myself and my students, a wall through which very little of Jesus' love penetrates.

It's the Holy Spirit's job to convict people of sin. He is the One who must teach us to hate our sin. He is the One who must teach us how to discipline and correct our students in a way that brings blessings to both them and us. He is the One who must teach us how to help our students develop a spiritually mature attitude toward sin and sure confidence in Jesus as the Savior from that sin.

The apostle Paul vividly describes his own struggle with sin in today's text. Before you teach, pray for yourselves and for your students. Ask that the Holy Spirit will teach each of you gathered around His Word today. Ask for a clearer picture of who you are in Christ and a clearer understanding of the cleansing power of forgiveness as you continue to struggle with sin.

IN THE WORD

Verses 7–13: The Effects of the Law
(Objective 1)

As you begin, ask students to read the opening narrative to themselves. When everyone has had a chance to do so, discuss the questions at the end of the selection. You will return to these later, so you need not complete your discussion now.

1. The Law may seem like an unpleasant taskmaster. Some may even think of it as bad, like a clumsy student who hates gym class. Paul wants to go on record as saying that the Law itself is good and just. Without it, we would never know the extent to which sin permeates our lives. Without it, we might live all our life thinking it is possible to please God by what we ourselves do.

The convicting power of the Law brought Paul to the uncomfortable point of seeing his utter helplessness and his total dependence on God to provide a way out. "What a wretched man I am!" he cries out. "Who will rescue me from this body of death?" Not *what*, but *who*—no longer does he look to his own futile efforts, but all his expectation now rests upon another.

Verse 7—The Law defines sin. It clearly distinguishes right from wrong. Many areas of human experience are not covered in human law. There is no law against hatred, selfishness, or lust.

Verses 8–13—The Law exposes sin by provoking it. The Law cannot be blamed for our disobedience, but it does stir up our hidden desires and points out how utterly sinful sin is. Like a "wet paint" sign on a park bench or a mother's "don't touch" warning to her toddler, the Law surfaces the rebellious disobedience that lurks in the dark shadows of every human heart, however self-righteously we try to deny its existence.

2. God gave us His law for our own protection. Without His law, society would soon slip into anarchy and chaos. He also gave us the Law to reveal to us our inability to keep it and thus to lead us to see our need for the Savior.

Verses 14–24: The Struggle with Sin
(Objectives 2, 3, and 4)

1. Not even a great evangelist and preacher like Paul experienced a life free from struggle with sin. What he has to say in these verses has great relevance for us in our daily battle with the sin in our own lives.

Take time for students to share their thoughts with one another. They will likely discuss the questions more freely if you put them into groups of three or four.

2. As your students write their own paraphrases, encourage them to write a specific sin with which they struggle into the paraphrase. (E.g., "I want to honor my father and my mother, and I don't want to be disrespectful, but I find myself talking back and disobeying, and I end up hating myself for it.")

After the students have finished, ask them to read their own paraphrase to themselves. Then ask volunteers to share their thoughts with the people in their small group.

3. Paul vividly describes the civil war that rages within him. You might point out that only Christians struggle with this kind of problem. Unbelievers have only a sinful nature and therefore do not experience the tension we feel between what we want to do and what we often end up doing in spite of ourselves.

People frequently misunderstand the concepts Paul presents here. While it may appear on first reading that the sinful nature (in the original Greek, *flesh*) has as much or at times even more power than the "new man" that lives inside us, a closer reading and a comparison of parallel passages shows this interpretation to be dead wrong.

Lenski comments on **verses 15–16:**

> Paul's personality itself is not divided, there are no two opposing [egos] in him, which would be unthinkable. Even when in common parlance we speak of a better self in some person we do not mean that two actual selves exist in him. This duality in Paul is the presence of an extraneous power in him beside his own [ego]: "the sin dwelling in me," i.e., the sin power mentioned so often before. This dwells in Paul, it does not possess him and control him entirely, it is only lodged in him. It still maintains itself in him but is not really a part of him, it is a foreign element that has not yet been dislodged and expelled.

(Reprinted by permission from *Interpretation of Romans* by R.C.H. Lenski, copyright © Augsburg Publishing House.)

The passage from **2 Cor. 5** says believers are in Christ. They have been made a new creation. That have been reconciled to God. God declares them to be Christ's ambassadors, and He calls them **"the righteousness of God in Jesus Christ."**

Gal. 5:17 presents in condensed form Paul's teaching in **Rom. 7**. That last sentence of the passage is instructive: "[The flesh and the spirit] are in conflict with each other, so that you do not do what you want." Notice, "*You* do not do what *you* want."

4. Putting all three Scriptures together leads us to understand that the real "us" is the new creation Paul so wonderfully describes in **2 Corinthians**. We have become the righteousness of God in Jesus Christ. The real "us" is a child of God, a joint heir with Christ. The sinful nature (flesh) still clings to us, but as Lenski comments, it's a foreign element. It's not who we really are any more.

That's not to deny the power of the flesh. Sometimes the struggle with sin seems to overwhelm us. We feel powerless against its fury. But knowing who we are in Jesus can give us strength to keep on fighting against it. The flesh can be weakened, and the new creation strengthened as we use the Word and Sacraments to grow in God's grace and knowledge of our Lord Jesus.

Refer students back to the opening story and the question about how our image of ourselves influences our behavior. Talk briefly about how knowing who we are in Jesus might help us when we struggle with temptation.

(For more background information, you may want to read Francis Pieper, *Christian Dogmatics*, vol. 1, (St. Louis: Concordia, 1950), pp. 515–64 and Paul E. Kretzmann, *Popular Commentary on the Bible,* The New Testament, vol. 2, (St. Louis: Concordia, n.d.), pp. 35–39.

In **Rom. 7:24** Paul asks a critical question. His answer is as powerful as it is brief: **"Thanks be to God through Jesus Christ our Lord."** Paul does not elaborate on this dramatic statement; he will deal with it more fully in the next chapter. Paul tempers his cry of relief with a summary of the struggle he has described earlier. It serves as a reminder that the struggle will continue. But, praise God, we have the assurance of certain victory. Without the intervention of the living Lord Jesus, the battle would have been strictly "no contest."

5. This question will help you assess your students' understanding of today's admittedly difficult lesson. As time permits, you may want to ask students to answer it in writing.

Session 19: Victory through the Spirit

BIBLE BASIS
Rom. 8:1–13

CENTRAL TRUTH
God's Holy Spirit indwells God's children and enables them to live victoriously over sin and even death itself. The Holy Spirit helps and encourages believers in our battle with sin. Those who have received the gift of new life that God gives through His Spirit will someday defeat even the power of death.

OBJECTIVES
By the grace of God students will
1. describe the power and results of the sin and death from which Christ has redeemed them;
2. explain the work of the Holy Spirit in sanctification;
3. trust God's Spirit rather than their own power as they battle temptation.

OUTLINE OF ROM. 8:1–13
A. No condemnation (vv. 1–4)
　1. Declared "not guilty" in God's court (v. 1)
　2. Set free from the law of sin and death (v. 2)
　3. The Law's requirements fulfilled for us (vv. 3–4)
B. Delivered from the power of sin and death (vv. 5–13)
　1. Natural man (vv. 5–8)
　　a) Mind set on the flesh which brings death (v. 6)
　　b) Hostile to God (v. 7a)
　　c) Rebellious (v. 7b)
　　d) Unable to please God (v. 8)
　2. Spiritual man (vv. 9–11)
　　a) Mind set on the Spirit which brings life and peace (v. 6)
　　b) Spirit lives in us (vv. 9–10)
　　c) Spirit brings victory over death (v. 11)
　　d) Spirit brings victory over sin (v. 13)

A WORD FROM THE AUTHOR
Perhaps you have seen some (or even many) of your students struggling with the deep truths Paul presents in Romans. It's definitely heavy going. But don't give up on the Word!

Remember that God's Spirit has promised to work through His Word. Scripture speaks for itself. The Word of God never returns to Him void; it always accomplishes what He sends it out to do.

Pray each day as you and your students study the Word together that it will deepen and strengthen your students' relationship with their Savior. And trust the Holy Spirit to do what He has promised. In the final analysis, He is the Teacher of the church.

GETTING INTO THE LESSON
Begin with prayer.

Up to this point in Romans, Paul has mentioned the Holy Spirit only twice—probably because the apostle has shown the hopelessness of trying to please or appease God by our own efforts. Now, in chapter 8, Paul begins to stress the solution to our dilemma of sin. He describes the role of the Holy Spirit in the hearts and lives of believers. In **vv. 1–13,** Paul refers to the Third Person of the Trinity no less than 10 times, using four different titles.

As you begin today's discussion, have someone read the Student Book introduction aloud. Explain the section summarizing **Rom. 7** and introduce the ideas Paul will explain in the rest of **Rom. 8.**

IN THE WORD

Verses 1–4: No Condemnation
(Objectives 1 and 2)

1. The word *Law* here means *a spiritual principle*. Paul contrasts the "Law of sin and death" with the "Law of the Spirit of life." We believers have been freed from our bondage to the principle of sin and death. Ask students to explain this deliverance, but if their answers are not complete at this point, go on. You can return to this idea later, if necessary.

2. After students have written their paraphrase, ask for volunteers to share their versions.

3. Jesus was like us in that He had a truly human, physical body with the same physical limitations and weaknesses as ours. It differed from ours in that Christ was born from the "seed of the woman." Because of His conception by the Holy Spirit and birth of the virgin Mary, Jesus did not inherit original sin. He did not have the sinful nature other human beings inherit from Adam.

4. **Verse 4** describes our deliverance worked by God through Christ for us. We no longer walk after the flesh, but after the Spirit by God's grace. If Paul were stating a requirement rather than giving a promise, no one could find comfort in salvation. We would have to do something to earn righteousness.

Verses 5–13: Delivered from the Power of Sin and Death (Objectives 2–3)

1. See the outline earlier in this session for the main contrasts between the natural man and the spiritual man.

2. Paul uses the following four titles for the Holy Spirit:

　a. "The Spirit of life" (**v. 2**) takes up residence inside believers and sets us free from the spiritual deadness that has kept us from serving God. Through His presence, deadness gives way to life, and slavery to freedom.

b. "The Spirit of God" (v. 9). Compare Gen. 1:2. Paul here reminds us that the Spirit present at the creation indwells and empowers the believer.

c. "The Spirit of Christ" (v. 9). The same Spirit that directed and filled the Lord Jesus in His triumphant victory over Satan and sin also indwells and empowers us.

d. "The Spirit of Him who raised Jesus from the dead" (v. 11). What greater demonstration of power could any skeptic demand than the resurrection of Christ? This same power will raise to life all who call on the Savior's name.

3. Paul has begun a section dealing with sanctification in the life of believers. Only as we are empowered by the Holy Spirit can we obey God—or even *want* to do so.

4. Use the questions and Scripture references given in the student book to stimulate discussion about God's promise to give life to "our mortal bodies." Stress the concept that our bodies are not evil. But we do use our bodies to commit all kinds of sins.

As time permits, discuss Jesus' promises from John and Paul's discourse from **1 Cor. 15.** Both deal with the doctrine of the resurrection of the body.

Students who have experienced the death of a friend or loved one will undoubtedly find these Scriptures most meaningful. Many teens feel they are "immortal." Ask students if they know people who feel this way. Why do they think this is? How does the hope of the resurrection help us face life here and now?

5. According to Paul, those who *live* according to the flesh will surely *die* eternally. But those who use the Holy Spirit's power to put to *death* the sin in their lives will *live*.

Use the student's paraphrases and their paragraphs to evaluate their understanding of sanctification by grace through the power of God the Holy Spirit rather than through our own human effort.

Session 20: Children of God

BIBLE BASIS
Rom. 8:14–25

CENTRAL TRUTH
The Holy Spirit leads us into a family relationship with God our Father. We have become fellow heirs with the Lord Jesus. This relationship gives us certain and tremendous hope, even in the face of problems and suffering.

OBJECTIVES
By the grace of God students will
1. list implications of their adoption into God's family;
2. explain the profound impact sin has made on the creation as well as on the human race;
3. thank God for the hope we have as God's sons and daughters.

OUTLINE OF ROM. 8:14–27
A. Members of the family (vv. 14–17)
   1. Led by the Spirit (v. 14)
   2. Intimate with God (Abba) (v. 15)
   3. Taught by the Spirit (v. 16)
   4. Coheirs with Christ (v. 17)
B. Present suffering (vv. 18–22)
   1. Personal (v. 18)
   2. Universal (vv. 19–22)
C. Future glory (vv. 23–25)
   1. First fruits, glory begins now (v. 23)
   2. Confidence (vv. 24–25)

A WORD FROM THE AUTHOR
One passage from Mark never fails to impress me with its importance. The disciples had just failed another test. For the second time they had been caught in a storm on the Sea of Galilee. For the second time Jesus had calmed both the storm and their panic. Then the Lord asks an important question, **"You of little faith, why did you doubt?" (Matt. 14:31).** Mark doesn't record the question, but he does provide the answer. I consider **Mark 6:52** one of the most significant verses in Scripture: **"For they had not understood about the loaves; their hearts were hardened."**

Certainly the disciples believed in the Lord Jesus. Certainly they had faith. But like too many Christians they did not bother to think very deeply about what the Lord Jesus had done. He had fed a massive number of people with five loaves of bread and two fish! There had been enough left over for each of the disciples to have his own basket of food! The disciples saw all this. They may even have felt great pride at what a remarkable Teacher they had, but they seemed unchanged. They had found no way to relate the truth about the Lord Jesus to their own lives.

Many of our students are like that. They believe. They agree that the teachings of Jesus Christ are good. They may even have a certain pride in being a Christian. But they remain dangerously unaffected: They do not "consider the miracle of the loaves." Yet, no one can walk away from the Word unchanged. If the Word of God does not nourish and sustain faith, there is a very real risk that it hardens the hearts of the hearers.

Jesus Himself echoes a similar warning as He explains the parable of the sower, **"When anyone hears the message about the kingdom and does not understand it, the evil one comes and snatches away what was sown in his heart. This is the seed sown along the path" (Matt. 13:19).**

We need to teach our students how to dig into

the Word of God, personalizing the truths buried there. We need to help them experience the excitement of discovering the significance God's truth has for their lives. We need to challenge them to allow the Holy Spirit to do His work in them through the Word.

I have found no more effective method of doing this than by example. The Word of God has great significance for my life. My students need to see this. Discovering the truths of God and their relevance for my life is tremendously exciting. My students can "catch" that excitement from me as the Spirit works a hunger and thirst for His Word in their hearts. Ask that He do that for you and for your students today.

GETTING INTO THE LESSON

Begin with prayer.

We saw in the last session that the apostle used a rich and varied vocabulary when he introduced the Holy Spirit and His work. In the rest of the chapter he emphasizes different aspects of the Spirit's role as he switches the Spirit's title from the "Spirit of God" to the "Spirit of sonship or adoption." Paul writes about the same Spirit, but introduces another aspect of His ministry.

We can't understand how the adoption process works and just exactly what the Spirit does to bring it about. But, there is no hiding the joy that comes out of this relationship. The joy, gratitude, and relief of a believer who knows the reality of being an heir of God and coheir with Christ can best be expressed in one word—"Abba."

IN THE WORD

Verses 14–17: Members of the Family
(Objectives 1 and 3)

1. Romans would have picked up on the extreme contrasts between living as a slave or as a child and heir of a wealthy father. Remind students that Paul presents the choice in lifestyle to people who had already been brought into a saving relationship with God through the blood of Jesus Christ. We do not decide to be saved. But once we have come to faith, we have the power of God's Spirit to choose to grow up in our faith. The alternative to growing up is growing cold—choosing to live to please our sinful flesh. One is slavery; the other is true family life.

2. Your students may find different ways of phrasing the four concepts listed in the outline. Don't dwell on uniformity of thought, but rather encourage comments that show an understanding of the Spirit's work in our lives.

Verse 14—The Spirit leads us. The Greek word for *led* means *to show the way or to guide*. As we make ourselves available to the Spirit through study of His Word, He acts as our Guide through life. Ask why this idea can comfort us.

Verse 15—The Spirit brings us into an intimate relationship with God our Father. God has not only saved us from sin, but He has brought us into His family. Our relationship with Him is such that we may approach Him in the same way Jesus does: "Abba, Father."

Verse 16—The Spirit teaches us. Being children of the Father is more than a simple academic fact. The Spirit impresses the reality of this relationship into the deepest recesses of our being.

Verse 17—The Spirit helps us see ourselves as coheirs with Christ. **"It does not yet appear what we shall be" (1 John 3:2 RSV).** But we shall be like Jesus, and we shall receive from the Father all that He has given the Son! What a fantastic promise!

3. This exercise might best be used by having the students read their prayers for the class. Each one will be different; yet every student will be able to relate because they have all worked through the process of finding personal value from the truths taught in **verses 14–17.**

Verses 18–22: Present Suffering
(Objectives 1 and 3)

1. Very often high school students feel that nobody has ever had the kinds of problems they have, and they can't understand why God doesn't do something about it. They, like all believers, must realize all that God the Father suffered for us by giving His very own Son into death to save us. When we begin to understand the deep love that moved Him to do this, we can trust Him to do His very best for using every one of our lives.

The list of sufferings Paul endured will help 20th-century students see their problems in the proper perspective. Point out that under Roman law, 40 lashes was a death penalty. Since the Jews did not have the right to impose the death penalty (*jus gladii*), they gave Paul 39 lashes—on five different occasions!

2. When Adam sinned, all of the created universe was also affected in some awful manner. Have your students read Peter's description of God's final resolution to the sin that has infected even the created universe **(2 Peter 3:7–13).**

Verses 23–25: Future Glory
(Objectives 1, 2 and 3)

1. Our status as children of God and coheirs with Christ is a tantalizing foretaste of the wonderful inheritance God has in store for us.

The final phase of this glory will be the redemption of our bodies. We have a Spirit-induced confidence that God will, in His own time, give us a glorified body free from pain, sickness, weakness, and death. We will be completely free from our sinful nature and will serve Christ wholeheartedly forever.

2. Provide Bible dictionaries for your students. As time permits, ask volunteers to share their paragraphs.

Session 21: The Power and the Promise

BIBLE BASIS
Rom. 8:26–30

CENTRAL TRUTH

In our struggle against sin and Satan, God does not leave us alone and helpless. The Holy Spirit intercedes on our behalf, asking for gifts we in our weakness and ignorance cannot ask. Because He intercedes according to God's will, we can be sure of God's help, whatever problems we face. God turns all the circumstances in our lives to our good.

OBJECTIVES

By the grace of God students will
1. describe the comfort they receive because the Holy Spirit builds them up and intercedes for them;
2. explain ways God has worked difficulties and joys for good in their lives;
3. define five of the abstract theological terms Paul is using.

OUTLINE OF ROM. 8:26–30

A. The intercession of the Spirit (vv. 26–27)
    1. In our weakness (v. 26)
    2. In our ignorance (vv. 26–27)
B. The love of the Father (vv. 28–30)
    1. All things work together for good (v. 28)
    2. God's plan for our lives (vv. 29–30)
        a) He foreknew us (v. 29)
        b) He predestined us (v. 29)
        c) He called us (v. 30)
        d) He justified us (v. 30)
        e) He will glorify us (v. 30)

A WORD FROM THE AUTHOR

A strange idea crops up whenever I begin talking about the power of God and His guidance and control in our lives. Invariably someone will object to the idea of total and complete dependence upon God. I'm surprised how often students will quote the same old adage, presenting it as Scripture: "God helps those who help themselves."

First, I have to convince them that this is not a verse from Scripture. That is sometimes very hard to do! One student insisted that it was her confirmation verse! Next I have to convince them that this "truism" is simply not true. In fact, one can scarcely think of a more unscriptural idea. Not only does God *not* help those who help themselves; He finds the whole idea repugnant.

In a world, or at least a nation, that prizes rugged individualism, it can be very difficult for students to unlearn one of the ideals they have been taught. As long as most of them can remember, they have been struggling to become independent, to be their own person, to be responsible to no one. At age 16 or 17 they seem to be on the brink of achieving this longed for state of freedom. Then we Christian teachers confront them with what the Bible has to say. God cannot use independent, self-reliant individualists. He demands complete trust and dependence upon Him. Many adult Christians find this the most difficult of all life's lessons.

At the other extreme we find fatalism. Some students resolve every issue for themselves with the idea that whatever happens was supposed to happen—all because God is in control. They see God as some kind of divine "fixer-upper," committed to sorting out the mess we make of our lives and relieving us of any negative consequences for our actions.

Students also have difficulty with the idea that God is far more interested in our eternal good than our temporal good. If present problems will produce future security, then God will use problems for our good. Paul goes so far as to suggest that we rejoice in trouble for that very reason.

God's goal involves making redeemed sinners—that's us—into children who will finally share the character and the glory of Jesus Christ, their older brother.

GETTING INTO THE LESSON

Begin with prayer.

Ask students to read the brief story about Mr. Meyer's religion class. Discuss the questions at the conclusion of the story. Encourage honest answers. Jeffery may not find much comfort in these words. On the other hand, if he has come to a deep, mature relationship with the Savior, he may be willing to rest in God's love, trusting Him to bring good out of the situation.

Move from this discussion into the text by asking someone to read **Rom. 8:26–30** aloud.

IN THE WORD

Verses 26–27: The Intercession of the Spirit
(Objective 1)

1. No matter how intense the spiritual battle becomes, the Lord never leaves us to our own resources. He has provided His Holy Spirit, who will help us in our weaknesses and intercede for us when we don't even know how to pray or what to ask. Some scholars feel that both promises are parts of the same thing. They believe the Holy Spirit helps us with our weakness by interceding for us. This may be true. But the meaning of "helps us in our weakness" may be broader than that. In any case, the Holy Spirit is there for us in our weakness and in our ignorance of what and how to pray.

Note: You may want to make sure all students

understand the terms *intercession* and *intercede*.

2. Because God's Spirit Himself intercedes for us and because He always prays according to God's will, we can *know for sure* that God will work every event and circumstance in life for our ultimate good.

This does *not* mean God causes everything that happens. It does *not* mean every circumstance in and of itself is good. Very evil things sometimes happen to God's children. Often we bring our troubles down upon ourselves, or they come as a result of the sin of others or the work of Satan directly. Yet God promises to weave even these darker threads into the fabric of our lives in such a way that they help to produce good for us and to stimulate Christ–like character within us.

Verses 28–30: The Love of the Father
(Objectives 2 and 3)

1. Your students may know the Joseph story well enough to answer correctly without referring to **Genesis** at all.

During a 12- to 15-year period God equipped Joseph to handle a position of power as the prime minister of Egypt. He did this through a process that was painful, humiliating, and dangerous. Joseph's brothers hated him and sold him into slavery. He tried to obey God in the matter of Potiphar's wife and found himself in prison. He was abused, slandered, misunderstood, and imprisoned. Yet God eventually worked all this for Joseph's good.

2. Joseph's brothers did not believe he could have forgiven them so completely, so they conceived a lie to protect themselves from his anger **(Gen. 50:15–18)**. The passage your students should find easily is **50:19–20: "Don't be afraid. Am I in the place of God? You intended to harm me, but God intended it for good to accomplish what is now being done, the saving of many lives."**

3. This activity grows easier as a Christian grows older and can view life from a bigger perspective. Therefore, the youth of your students may work against them. But there should be enough personal examples to generate a good discussion. The experiences of those who share will encourage other students to look more closely for the good God intends in their own life. For this reason class discussion is more desirable than writing.

4. **Rom. 8:29–30** has been called the "golden chain that ties together the acts of God." Both time and space preclude an in-depth study of any one of these terms, much less all of them. Give the students time to look up the references and think about how they relate to one another. Or assign this question as homework. Class discussion will have limited value without proper preparation. Encourage students to find the words in a Bible dictionary or to use a commentary to assist them in defining these doctrinal terms.

a. As you discuss *foreknowledge*, one or more students may ask, "If God knows everything ahead of time, doesn't that mean that nothing can be changed?" This question betrays the questioner as a fatalist at heart. Fatalists seem to like the idea that everything is predetermined, because it relieves them of any responsibility for their actions. You may have to help them by reviewing "free will." God chose to limit His power in our lives. He did not make us puppets or robots, but gave us the option of independent action and, of course, the responsibility that comes with free will. Because God knows what is going to happen does not mean that He makes it happen or even wants it to happen.

b. To *predestine* means literally *to define in advance the limits*. God has chosen His children from eternity to share His glory. He chose us and orders events in our lives so that eventually we will be "like Jesus." This doctrine is intended as a comfort to believers, not as an explanation of why some people are saved and some are lost.

c., d., and e. These verses should be fairly self-explanatory. Allow your students to share their research and expect the Holy Spirit to produce some exciting insights into God's plan of salvation. In the final analysis, it is a beautiful and wonderful mystery. We will never fully understand it here on earth.

Session 22: What Shall We Say about All This?

BIBLE BASIS
Rom. 8:31a

CENTRAL TRUTH
By our sins we have earned for ourselves God's wrath and eternal damnation. But in His great mercy and grace, God sent Jesus to bear our punishment. By faith in Him, we receive forgiveness of sins, the gift of eternal life, and the hope of even greater future glory.

OBJECTIVES
By the grace of God students will

1. summarize **Rom. 1–8** so they can more fully appreciate Paul's dramatic finale in the rest of **Rom. 8**;
2. evaluate their own understanding of the four basic topics Paul stresses in **Rom. 1–8**;
3. identify the implications these topics have for their everyday living.

OUTLINE OF ROM. 8:31a
What shall we say about all this?
A. The guilt of humanity (Rom. 1–3:20)
B. The grace of God (Rom. 3:20–5:11)
C. The greatness of salvation (Rom. 5:12–8:17)
D. The guarantee of glory (Rom. 8:18–30)

A WORD FROM THE AUTHOR

Teaching requires constant review. Students *must* realize how one lesson relates to another. In a systematic study of a book of the Bible, particularly an epistle, a teacher can easily lose the class. No matter how eloquently and insightfully we interpret the book on a verse by verse basis, our students will not see the full picture without review. They will miss out on the author's intended meaning.

Is. 28:9–10 talks about this need for continuing review. It refers to God's methods in teaching the people of Israel. They (like we at times) learned very reluctantly. The King James version brings home the tediousness of God's teaching task: "**Whom shall He teach knowledge? and whom shall He make to understand doctrine? them that are weaned from milk, and drawn from the breasts. For precept must be upon precept, precept upon precept; line upon line, line upon line; here a little, and there a little.**"

Without the power of God's Spirit working through His Word, our teaching task would certainly be futile! Before you continue your preparation, stop for a few minutes and acknowledge your helplessness to God. Ask for His direction and power as you prepare and as you teach. Then thank Him for His promise to use His Word mightily in your life and in the lives of your students.

GETTING INTO THE LESSON

Explain the purpose of today's review to the class. Your students may be reluctant to do what looks like a major undertaking of things they have already learned. Actually the activity can be done in one class period. Most of your students should be able to develop a good overview of **Rom. 1–8.** Once finished, they will also find it valuable. If you don't wish to use class time, you could assign it as homework, but then you will not be able to help and guide your students as they review.

Before the students start, pray with them for specific guidance from the Holy Spirit. Ask Him to direct their review of God's plan of salvation and to produce in all of you a greater understanding and appreciation of God's great work.

IN THE WORD
Verse 31a: What Shall We Say about This?
(Objectives 1, 2 and 3)

If you do this activity in class, spend some time "reading over your students' shoulders." Give them encouragement and assistance as necessary. If you use the outlines provided below, you can quickly locate the key passages for each topic. Note, though, that your students' outlines may vary. Help them express as thorough an understanding as possible, but allow for individual differences in style, ability, and experience.

1. The guilt of humanity
    a. Produces the wrath of God, **Rom. 1:18–32**
    b. Earns the judgment of God, **Rom. 2:1–16**
    c. Even the people of God are guilty under God's law, **Rom. 2:17–3:8**
    d. All people, Jews and Gentiles alike are guilty, **Rom. 3:9–20**
2. The grace of God
    a. Available to guilty humanity through faith, **Rom. 3:21–4:5**
    b. Shown through the forgiveness of God who is both just and the justifier of all believers, **Rom. 4:6**
    c. Produces great joy in His people, **Rom. 5:1–11**
3. The greatness of salvation is demonstrated in
    a. How God dealt with the problems of sin and death, **Rom. 5:12–6:12**
    b. God's use of the Law to produce repentance
    c. The Spirit-empowered, fruitful lives of God's children, **Rom. 6:13–8:17**
4. God's glory is shared with us through the intercession of the Spirit and continuing love of the Father, **Rom. 8:18–30.**

Session 23: Super Conquerors

BIBLE BASIS
Rom. 8:31b–39

CENTRAL TRUTH

No matter what happens to us, God's people overwhelmingly conquer through faith in Christ Jesus who loves us. Nothing in all creation can separate us from His love.

OBJECTIVES
By the grace of God students will
1. describe Jesus' love for them personally;
2. share incidents when God's love gave them courage and strength;
3. articulate assurance in God's love despite formidable foes which might attempt to separate them from that love.

OUTLINE OF ROM. 8:31b–39
A. More than conquerors (vv. 31b–37)
    1. Who can be against us? **(v. 31)**
    2. Who can accuse us? **(v. 31)**
    3. Who can condemn us? **(v. 34)**

4. Who can separate us? **(vv. 35—37)**
B. More than confident **(vv. 38—39)**

A WORD FROM THE AUTHOR

In **Ps. 119:11** David writes, **"I have hidden Your Word in my heart."** David understood the importance of God's Word—not just as casual reading material, but as a real and comforting power in his life. His 119th Psalm is the longest chapter in the Bible, and all but 5 of the 178 verses mention God's Word **(vv. 84, 90, 121, 132)**. Sometimes when I'm tempted to feel that I overstress God's Word, I go back and read **Ps. 119**. God shares *Himself* with us in His Word—not just facts *about Himself.*

I have hidden Your Word in my heart. I try to convey this value to my students. How does one go about explaining how to hide God's Word in our hearts?

First of all, students need a first-person acquaintance with the Word. I can't hide God's Word in anyone else's heart. That's something believers must do for themselves. We must read the Word as something more than just this morning's newspaper. Many of my students' experience with God's Word has involved primarily someone else doing their thinking for them. We teachers and pastors are often too ready to tell students what to think. Students need help in applying the Word to their own lives and in sharing God's work in their hearts through the Word.

It helps students personalize God's teachings if they must do something creative with the Word they have read. David went beyond studying the Word to hide it in his heart; He wrote and sang songs about it. There are many ways to provide for creative expression by your students. The simplest is to let them talk. When my class is working through a particular section of Scripture, I ask my students to select a verse(s) from the same chapter to share in class. They share both their thoughts and any pertinent application they see to their own lives.

If a student simply reads a verse (e.g., "If God is for us who can be against us?"), it will probably not have the impact that it could. However, if that same student stands in front of the class and spells out how this truth has impacted his or her life, the student is far more likely to remember and act upon this verse. They have seen a truth; they have thought about that truth; they have spoken out about the truth. All of this is involved in "hiding the Word of God in your heart."

GETTING INTO THE LESSON

The spiritual impact of the passage can hardly be overestimated. Also you will want to note the almost defiant tone Paul uses. He writes as though he is challenging his readers to question the validity of his grand view of God's plan for human salvation—the plan he has so beautifully described in the first half of Romans. As people of God, we are not victims, or survivors, or poor souls who suffer through a dreary existence in vague hope of a better life to come; we are super conquerors!

As you begin your class time today, pray together. Then have someone read **Rom. 8:31-39** and the opening story from the Student Book. Ask students why Paul could express such confidence in God's faithfulness. Why is that kind of confidence important in our everyday lives?

IN THE WORD

Verses 31b–37: More Than Conquerors
(Objectives 1 and 2)

As students work on their paragraphs, chat with individuals and offer help and leading questions as necessary. Students should share their paragraphs with one another. Arrange for this to happen, perhaps in small groups rather than having each student share with the entire class.

Some pertinent remarks:

1. **"Who can be against us" (vv. 31–32)?** What further proof do we need that God is on our side? He offered His own Son up for us on the altar of the cross. Since the Father freely made this ultimate sacrifice, will He not also freely give whatever else is needed to see us through the final victory? This is our first and most important piece of evidence that God is on our side.

2. **"Who can bring any charge against [us]" (v. 33)?** The chosen to whom Paul refers in **v. 33** are those whom God has foreknown, predestined, called, and justified. Those of us who believe in Christ have been declared righteous by the Lord God Himself by faith alone. No one can resurrect any sin from our past. We stand before God "not guilty" and, further, justified—"just as if I'd never sinned."

3. **"Who is he that condemns [us] (v. 34)?** Here we learn that not only is our Judge on our side, but Jesus Himself is our Lawyer. The Father has placed all judgment into the hands of the Son; He alone may condemn us. We realize that this will never, ever happen when we realize that Jesus is our Advocate at court. He intercedes for us at the right hand of God!

4. **"Who shall separate us" (vv. 35–37)?** The word *separate* is the same word Jesus used in His sweeping statement about the lifelong union of marriage. (**"Therefore what God has joined together, let man not separate" [Mark 10:9].**) We are truly one with Jesus, and it is permanent bonding. The oneness couples experience in human marriage pales when compared with the eternal intimacy we enjoy with our Lord Jesus. To speak of anything separating us from Him, the One who loved us, is unthinkable!

Verses 38–39: More Than Confident
(Objectives 1, 2, and 3)

This exercise is better suited to discussion than to writing. You, however, may want to have the class work in small groups to write down their conclusions and questions.

Having challenged the harsh realities of deprivation, danger, and disaster to do their worst **(vv. 35–36)**, Paul now directs our attention to more abstract dangers. His message remains the same—nothing can possibly change Christ's sacrificial love for us.

Life and death. Paul has ministered for years with the knowledge that **"to live is Christ and to die is gain"(Phil. 1:21).** He and his first-century Christian contemporaries had often faced the startling realities of both life and death, and found nothing to fear.

Angels or demons. Spiritual forces, whether angelic or demonic, have no power to do anything that would come between the Savior and the saved.

The present, the future, or any powers. Paul's imagination expands to include time itself as a possible enemy of the redeemed. He finds nothing in either the present age or in the age to come that could threaten our security in the Lord. Broadening his horizons, he rules out any earthly power as a danger to our relationship with Christ.

Height and depth. These are more than just spatial measurements. In Greek thought they were used to represent other-worldly concepts. Height was linked with astrology in theorizing about human fate or destiny in the stars. Similarly, depth referred to mystery and unknown powers to be feared. In any event, Paul concludes that no *power,* real or imagined, can touch our relationship with the Lord.

Anything else in creation. This sums it up! *Nothing* can take us away from Christ's love.

So we arrive at the breathtaking end of Paul's systematic treatment of God's plan of salvation. Note that he concludes with the words "our Lord." The Lordship of Jesus Christ remains the fundamental principle of salvation; but even beyond this, He is *our* Lord! This brings salvation down from the lofty heights of theological idiom and into the everyday lives of human beings. That transition brings with it all of Jesus' life-transforming power!

Session 24: Concluding Activities for Unit 2

Open your class session with prayer. Thank God for His Word. Thank Him especially for the deep truths He has shared with you in Romans. Ask the Holy Spirit to create in you and your students a fervent love of God's Word and the spiritual maturity to grasp the deeper truths of Scripture. Ask specifically that God would guide and direct each of you in applying today's review of Romans to your own lives.

Use this review to encourage your students to organize their knowledge and recognize the potential for personal application. The work your students did in session 22 should have laid the groundwork for the activities in this review.

The activities are similar to the review of unit 1 in session 13. Refer back to the comments made in this guide for that session.

UNIT 3
THE RIGHTEOUSNESS OF GOD REJECTED

BIBLE BASIS
Rom. 9–11

Paul has concluded his tremendous account of the righteousness we have received from God. He ended on a high note: **"[Nothing] will be able to separate us from the love of God that is in Christ Jesus our Lord" (8:39)**. Now he turns to a matter that causes him sorrow and anguish **(9:2)**: the relationship of the Jewish people with God. These people from Paul's race and nation had been adopted into God's family, but had now, by and large, turned away from Him.

Paul reaffirms the love of God to these brothers and sisters of his. He also shows how God had used their apostasy to bring Gentiles into His fold, warns these new Christians against the same catastrophe (disobeying God and being cut off from His kingdom), and assures us that God brings all kinds of people, Jew and Gentile alike, into His kingdom. We too often are faithless, but God is *always faithful*.

Session 25: The Tragedy of the Jews

BIBLE BASIS
Rom. 9:1–5

CENTRAL TRUTH
God graciously gave many blessings and privileges to the nation of Israel. When the nation rejected God's covenant, God anguished over their sin. Even today, God desires to bless His people. Our sin and rebellion brings Him great grief and deep anguish.

OBJECTIVES
By the grace of God students will
1. express the depth of Paul's feeling for his nation and relate it to their own attitude toward people who are unsaved;
2. identify the source of Paul's concern and relate it to their own attitude toward ministry;
3. demonstrate an understanding of both the privileges and the responsibilities of God's people in Paul's time and in ours today;
4. express a desire to use their privileges and blessings to honor God and to be a blessing to others.

OUTLINE OF ROM. 9:1–5
A. Paul's attitude toward Israel Jews (vv. 1–3)
 1. Paul's sincerity (v. 1)
 2. Paul's love (vv. 2–3)
  a) Human ties—brothers (v. 3)
  b) National ties (v. 3)
B. Paul's pride in his heritage (vv. 4–5)
 1. Adopted by God (v. 4)
 2. Shared God's glory (v. 4)
 3. Received the covenants (v. 4)
 4. Received the Law (v. 4)
 5. Worshiped at the temple (v. 4)
 6. Received God's promises (v. 4)
 7. Claimed a godly ancestry (v. 5)
 8. Received the Messiah (v. 5)

A WORD FROM THE AUTHOR
"Commit your way to the Lord" (Ps. 37:5).

With rare exceptions the students in my classroom are Christians. I spend very little classroom time on personal evangelism. I do, however, make a conscious effort to teach commitment in every lesson. I view my ministry as a ministry toward commitment. I pray and counsel and teach all with an eye toward helping students develop a consciousness of commitment. That is of great importance, for without personal commitment to Christ, they can never attain spiritual maturity.

The people in the Macedonian churches first gave themselves to the Lord. Then the giving of money became a simple matter **(2 Cor. 8:5)**. In fact, even though the saints in this place were poor themselves, they gave freely, joyfully, even extravagantly! When Christians commit their ways to the Lord, all other sanctification goals can take place.

My students (like so many adults) have many things in life that clamor for attention and loyalty. Every waking hour we find ourselves bombarded by the philosophy of materialistic humanism. The advertising industry devotes itself to selling a life-style diametrically opposed to God's value system.

The ads try to convince us that we cannot be happy without the right clothes, the right soft drink, the right deodorant, and a big boom box with quadraphonic sound—"because you only go around once in life." All of us desperately need more epistles and less commercials! I teach for commitment every day.

GETTING INTO THE LESSON
Begin with prayer.
Then remind students of the great joy Paul felt

as he realized the magnificent plan of salvation he has shared with us in the first eight chapters of Romans. Next, ask if the students saw his mind abruptly shifting gears when they read **Rom. 9:1–5.** Ask what change they noticed in Paul's mood. Why does Paul's joy suddenly change to near gloom? (He has begun to think about Israel's rejection of God's plan of salvation and of His covenant with them.)

With few exceptions, his people, those in the Jewish nation, would never experience the same joy Paul felt in His salvation, and this intensified his sorrow for them. In **Rom. 9:1–5** Paul eloquently expresses his love and compassion for the unsaved. Talk about how tough it would have been for Paul to continue this love in light of the persecution he experienced **(Acts 17:10–15).**

IN THE WORD

Verse 1–3: Paul's Attitude toward the Jews
(Objectives 1 and 2)

After you have discussed how hard it must have been for Paul to feel such deep love and concern for his enemies, share with one another experiences you have had in showing love and concern for those who hurt you. Try to draw out the feelings all Christians experience as they try to put our Lord's command into practice—frustration, anger, guilt. Once these feelings have surfaced, assure students that in this lesson you will explore ways to get beyond this into power for love and obedience to the "law of love"—even for enemies. Then move into the next paragraph in the student book.

1. The intensity of the apostle's words impress upon the reader how genuinely he feels about the spiritual darkness of his own people. So fiercely does he want them to believe and be saved that he takes an oath. His opening statement, **"I speak the truth in Christ,"** calls Jesus to be his witness. Paul then states that his own conscience, which has been enlightened by the Holy Spirit, also bears witness. However anyone else might feel, there is no doubt in Paul's own mind that his feelings are genuine.

2. The reason for Paul's sorrow may be inferred from **verse 3** to be Israel's rejection of Christ, which will result in eternal separation from God.

3. Paul appears to be saying in **verse 3** that, if it were possible, he would be willing to give up his own salvation if that would result in salvation for Israel.

Some believe that Paul can't really mean what he's written. He must mean he would give up his life if it would do any good. The language he uses, however, certainly seems to imply the former interpretation. There is precedent for such a feeling. Moses prayed much the same thing in **Ex. 32:32.** It's difficult for most Christians to even guess at a circumstance that might induce us to give up our salvation for someone else. That kind of feeling truly is self-sacrificial, Christ-like love!

4. This activity should produce good discussion and often will result in some remarkably candid revelations. The Holy Spirit may even lead some students to confess sins against classmates and publicly ask for their forgiveness. If this happens, praise God for it, and be sure all parties concerned hear God's absolution as well as words of forgiveness from the classmate(s) to whom they have confessed.

Verses 4–5: Paul's Pride in His Heritage
(Objective 3)

Have students review **Rom. 8:15** as you begin this section.

a. To be Jewish was to be a part of the "adoption," literally the "placing as sons," or the special invitation of Yahweh to be His family. Hosea says, **"When Israel was a child, I loved him, and out of Egypt I called my son" (Hosea 11:1).** God has called and adopted each one of us into His family at Baptism. Do we ever take that fact for granted? ignore it?

b. Israel alone had seen the glory or, as the rabbis called it, the Shekinah. "The glory" described God's presence with His people in the pillar of cloud and pillar of fire during their wilderness wanderings **(Ex. 13:21).**

Compare **John 1:14.** Ask, **How does God's glory guide and protect us today?** (Jesus shows us the Father's glory. He is the One full of grace and truth. He has promised never to leave us or forsake us.) What difference does that make in our daily lives?

c. Only with the Israelites had the Lord entered into covenants such as those that promised lands to Abraham and special blessings to Isaac, Jacob, and David. Ask, **Do we have a covenant with God today as the "New Israel?" What are its terms, benefits, and promises?** Refer students to **Heb. 9:11–15; 10:14–17;** and **1 Cor. 11:23–26.** In what way can Christians abuse this covenant just as ancient Israel abused the first covenant?

d. God communicated His will in written from only to the people of Israel! They had the special privilege of knowing His law. What corresponding privilege do Christians enjoy today? (Having access to the written Scriptures.) **How could we abuse this privilege? For what reasons did God give us Holy Scripture in the first place—for His benefit or for ours?** Ask students to tell about a time when a Scripture passage was especially meaningful for them. Use this series of questions to bring out the idea that in Scripture God reveals *Himself* to us. He wants us to know Him better, because the better we know Him, the more we will want to love and obey Him. The better we know Him, the more we will trust Him. That's why He wants us to use the Scriptures.

e. It was to the Israelites alone that the order of worship in both tabernacle and temple had been revealed. The temple service at the time of Christ was regarded by the Jews as the pride of their nation. Ask, **Under what circumstances can our public worship honor God? dishonor Him?** (See **Matt. 15:8.**)

f. Only to Israel had promises for the whole human race been made. To them God promised the Messiah and the spread of true faith. **Give an example of how this special knowledge made the nation of Israel proud. Give an example of how "knowing the truth" might make a Lutheran high school proud today. How did (does) spiritual pride keep God's people from effective witness to unbelievers?** Talk about the specific examples students suggest.

g. The Jewish nation quite justly prided themselves on the long line of "fathers" that stretched back through the remarkable history of Paul's people. To call Abraham, Isaac, and Jacob their ancestors was a unique privilege. **We call Luther, Walther, and others our ancestors. When can such identification be a blessing? When might it be harmful or wrong?**

As you discuss this, refer to Israel's experience. Jesus commented that if the religious leaders of His day had truly been Abraham's children, they would have obeyed God as Abraham did. So with us. We can praise God for His care and love for our spiritual ancestors. We can learn many things about the grace of God as we study the lives and writings of godly people in the past. But we must remember that they, too, were forgiven sinners, adopted into God's family by grace through the shed blood of Jesus.

h. Of all the distinctions that went with being an Israelite, none was more illustrious than being part of the race that gave birth to the long-expected Messiah, the Hope of the world.

Ask, **How have we come into that same ancestry?** (By faith in Jesus.) Use this final item in Paul's list to stress the Gospel. Much of the discussion to this point has centered on ways we, too, abuse God's grace by taking it lightly, ignoring it, or by letting ourselves become spiritually proud—just as did the Jews of Paul's time. Still today God's compassion reaches out to repentant sinners. We can't make ourselves "unproud." We can't reverse the indifference toward God in our hearts. *He* must begin the process. *He* must give us the gift of repentance. *He* must assure our hearts of His forgiving love, and *He* must empower us to use rather than abuse our privileges as His children. Be sure no one leaves class today burdened by guilt, but rather rejoicing in God's love.

LOOKING AHEAD

As your students read ahead in **Rom. 9,** tell them they will discover that being a descendant of Abraham is not a matter of the flesh, but of the promise. Christians are the "true Israel" today—with all the same privileges and responsibilities that attend the family name.

Session 26: God's Chosen People

BIBLE BASIS
Rom. 9:6–21

CENTRAL TRUTH

God has not locked Himself into a system of election on the basis of bloodlines. The doctrine of election draws its dynamic from **"Him who calls" (v. 12).** It is not a process that relies on human worthiness or effort, but upon God's mercy.

OBJECTIVES

By the grace of God students will
1. demonstrate their understanding of God's grace in election;
2. explain the difference between a personal faith relationship with God and mere outward membership in a church or denomination;
3. praise God for His gift of faith in Jesus, the Savior.

OUTLINE OF ROM. 9:6–18

A. The true Israel **(v. 6)**
B. Children of flesh and children of the promise **(vv. 7–13)**
 1. Isaac and Ishmael **(vv. 7–9)**
 2. Jacob and Esau **(vv. 10–13)**
C. God's mercy in election **(vv. 14–16)**
 1. Salvation is not a response to anything we do **(v. 16)**
 2. God's glory **(Ex. 33:12–23)**
D. God's sovereignty **(vv. 17–21; Ex. 9:13–16)**

A WORD FROM THE AUTHOR

"This, then, is how you should pray: 'Our Father in heaven' " (Matt. 6:9).

For many students, God appears as a stern, intimidating judge, a father figure, but one whom it is impossible to please. Many students learn the factual truths about grace from Romans. They can repeat all the right words about justification by faith, not works. But buried somewhere deep in their subconscious sits a white-bearded, disapproving Old Testament deity who is never satisfied no matter how hard they try to please Him.

As we teach the truths of **Rom. 9,** we need to take care not to deepen this incongruous perception of God. As our students read lines like **"Jacob I loved, and Esau I hated,"** or **"He hardens whom He wants to harden,"** students can begin to sympathize with the rebellion of Israel. They develop lingering doubts about God's system of justice.

For this reason I find it necessary to remind them very frequently that God is our Father in every sense of that word. When Jesus introduced the idea of praying to God as "Father," He introduced a radical change in perception that would have made the orthodox Jew of His day cringe. These people regularly referred to "father Abraham," but calling God "Father" would have been an unthinkable presumption. Yet, what a world of comfort the term *Father* contains! Jesus obviously wants us to know that His Father is ours, also.

Every chance I get, I encourage my students to think of God as their Father. They can relate to this metaphor when they stop to analyze how a good, kind human father acts in everyday situations. Of course, a good earthly father wants only the best for his children. Of course, a good earthly father will hate the very thought of anyone abusing or molesting his children. Of course, a good earthly father will discipline his children when it becomes necessary. Even during those times when we don't understand our parents, there can be no doubt that we are loved and that good parents do what they consider best for us. As Jesus reminds us, if even sinful human parents deal lovingly with their children, how much more God, the perfect Father, will do so **(Matt. 7:9–11)**.

GETTING INTO THE LESSON
Begin with prayer.

Israel's rejection of their Messiah did more than provoke deep emotions of both grief and love in Paul. It stirs in him a fervent desire to counter their questions and misconceptions with undeniable examples of God's "standard operating procedures" from their own Scriptures. So Paul takes his readers on a tour through Biblical history, beginning with God's call to Abraham. God decided to bring from Abraham's descendants that One by whom all nations on earth would be blessed. Abraham had more than one son, and as his family branched out through the succeeding generations, God consistently chose the branch of the family from which His Messiah would come. God chose Isaac over Ishmael, Jacob over Esau, Judah over his brothers, and so on down Abraham's line until Christ's birth. God chose, and God had the perfect right to do this choosing.

IN THE WORD
Verse 6: The True Israel (Objectives 1 and 2)
1. As your students consider Christ's dialog with the teachers of the law and Pharisees **(John 8:31–41)**, challenge them to condense the point of Jesus' argument into one phrase. Jesus points out that if they were Abraham's children they would do what Abraham did. Ask the class what Abraham did. Someone should come up with **Gen. 15:6: "Abram believed the Lord, and He credited it to him as righteousness."** Jesus states point blank that they are not Abraham's children—**"You have no room for My Word"** (v. 37). Abraham believed the Word of God, the Father. The teachers of the law and Pharisees had no room for the Word of God, the Son.

2. Humans commonly derive a false sense of security from mere church membership or association with a denomination. Some people even believe that anyone born in the U. S. is a Christian—after all, isn't this a "Christian country"? Help students remember that saving faith involves a relationship between the Savior and the saved; anything less is hypocrisy and leads only to eternal death.

Verses 7–13: Children of the Flesh; Children of the Promise (Objective 1)
1. In all of the rhetoric about election, predestination, and the sovereignty of God, we can lose sight of the one elemental truth of Paul's teaching. **Gal. 3:26–29** sums up this truth with a simple eloquence. The "children of God" and the "seed of Abraham" include all those, and only those, who have faith in Christ Jesus.

2. As your students read the first five verses of Malachi, they should discover that the verses refer to the people of Esau, the Edomites. The descendants of Esau earned God's wrath when they refused to come to the aid of Israel in a time of great need **(Deut. 20:14–21)**, thereby demonstrating their rejection of God and His covenant. Point out the figure of speech presented by the word *hate*. We might paraphrase the verse, "My love for My people Israel is so great that my feelings toward Edom look like hate by comparison." Scripture uses this kind of comparison elsewhere. Be careful students do not come away with the impression that God plays favorites. Edom rejected God's love and His covenant. God will not zap anyone into a robotlike faith—not even to save us!

Verses 14–16: God's Mercy (Objective 1)
Paul offers clear evidence of God's insistence that He is free to deal with human beings as He sees fit. At the time, Moses needed some divine reassurance. He asked God for some visible evidence of the Lord's presence—"Show me your glory." God replied, in effect, "though you have been a faithful servant, you must realize that I do not grant such a request on the basis of merit, but on what I consider best." Moses had to content himself with a view of God "from the rear," a less than full view of God's glory.

Verses 17–21: God's Sovereignty (Objectives 1 and 3)
1. The dramatic story of God's dealing with Pharaoh is filled with references to a kind of spiritual hardening of the arteries. Again and again, God tries to move Pharaoh to yield to His will. Again and again, Pharaoh reverts from shallow and temporary repentance to arrogant resistance. Pharaoh, acting as a free agent, repeatedly hardened his own heart against God's demands until finally God finishes the job for him.

God tells us that He raised Pharaoh up to a place of international visibility so that he could become an international example of the futility of arrogantly opposing God's will **(Rom. 9:17)**. If Pharaoh had been a slave rather than a monarch, his sin would have been neither lesser or greater. Pharaoh freely chose to be arrogant and stubborn. God was free to place this arrogant man in a position where his pride would not only lead to his downfall but would also produce a vivid demonstration of divine power. The freedom to do this is incontrovertibly God's. Help individual students with their paragraphs as necessary.

2. One distinction between Calvinism and Lutheranism revolves around the emphasis given to either God's sovereignty or God's mercy. Lutheran Christians see the correct accent as resting on mercy. Only then can we be assured of eternal life. God *is* merciful. He *did* send Jesus to die for us. We can cling to that objective truth rather than struggling with doubt about whether or not God has sovereignly chosen us.

Session 27: "In Wrath, Remember Mercy"

BIBLE BASIS
Rom. 9:22–33

CENTRAL TRUTH
God has called His children to be "objects of mercy." He surely will punish those who reject His grace and try to achieve a righteousness based on human works. Yet, God's heart yearns that all—Jews and Gentiles alike—would be saved and come to the knowledge of the truth in His Son, Jesus.

OBJECTIVES
By the grace of God students will
1. acknowledge that God's wrath and mercy are necessarily inseparable parts of His divine character;
2. define the term *remnant* and apply it correctly in both its Old and New Testament meanings;
3. explain how Jesus is on the one hand the "Rock of offense" and on the other, the "Rock of salvation."

OUTLINE OF ROM. 22–33
A. A two-sided coin (vv. 22–29)
   1. Objects of wrath (v. 22)
   2. Objects of mercy (v. 23)
   3. The remnant (vv. 24–29)
B. Pursuing righteousness (vv. 30–33)
   1. Righteousness by faith (v. 30)
   2. Righteousness by works (vv. 31–32)
   3. Jesus—the Rock of offense/salvation (v. 33)

A WORD FROM THE AUTHOR
Paul told the Philippian Christians, **"Do not be anxious about anything, but in everything, by prayer and petition, with thanksgiving, present your requests to God" (Phil. 4:6).**

I must confess that I am anxious at times. I do worry about my students. I worry about their spiritual well-being. I especially worry about those who don't seem to worry about themselves. In short, I often find myself more concerned about my students than they are themselves.

This may, at first, sound like the attitude of a devoted teacher, but it can be very unhealthy. When I see the strength and power of the spiritual forces Satan mobilizes against the fragile faith of my students, worry leads easily to despair. At times like that, I find myself longing for the days when I taught other subjects; having students fail a vocabulary test didn't keep me awake at night.

Certainly concern for students characterizes good teachers, but we must be careful to channel our concern into positive actions. That's why I have found **Phil. 4:6** to be such a helpful verse. Paul encourages us to get rid of our cares by committing them to the Lord in prayer.

This seems so simple that I am embarrassed when I discover I'm not doing it! Perhaps I have an ego problem. I see a cause for concern and begin to feel that if I'm not a part of the solution, the situation will not be resolved. I usurp to myself responsibility that belongs only to God. I forget that my job consists of keeping the Lord Jesus front and center in my classroom. I am given the responsibility to share His grace with my students with clarity and enthusiasm. Then I am to trust the Holy Spirit to use His Word to complete the good work He has begun in their hearts.

When I fail to entrust my concerns to the Lord, all sorts of unhealthy things begin to happen. I begin to nag my students. I find my supposed realism slipping into cynicism. I find my excitement turning into apathy.

One of the best things I can do when this happens is to go back to basics—to pray for my students. When I find myself getting depressed because I am worrying about them, I ask my class to spend some time in silent prayer while I pray myself. I don't tell them I am praying for them, but I spend the time praying for every individual in the classroom. It takes a little while, and this procedure may not work for every teacher, but I find great comfort in it.

It's not by accident God promises that when we commit our worries to Him, **"the peace of God, which transcends all understanding, will guard your hearts and your minds in Christ Jesus" (Phil. 4:6).**

GETTING INTO THE LESSON
Ask the students to read the first paragraph in their books. Then ask them to jot down their picture of God in 30 words or less. Have them do this without referring to their Bibles or to other reference materials. As they work, walk around the classroom noting the kinds of responses they are giving. When everyone has finished, ask volunteers to share their descriptions. On the chalkboard or large piece of chart paper, ask the class to mention similarities and differences in the de-

scriptions as they are read. What common attributes recur in the student descriptions? What attributes appear only once or twice?

IN THE WORD
Verses 22–29: A Two-Sided Coin
(Objectives 1 and 2)

1. Have someone in the class read the passage from **Ex. 34** aloud. Compare God's description of Himself with the attributes you noted on the chalkboard earlier in the session. Tell the students that the description of God given in **Ex. 34:6–7** is repeated frequently throughout the Old Testament. In these words, God gives us a succinct description of Himself. As He does, He stresses two main attributes—His justice and His mercy. These, like two sides of the same coin, cannot be separated.

2. The attributes called for here are, of course, justice and mercy. Accept reasonable variations of these terms. Then lead students in a brief discussion of how inseparable these two attributes are. For example, in His just anger God destroyed the people of the world in Noah's time. That same act was, however, an act of grace toward Noah and his family. They were living as the only righteous, God-fearing people in a world of perhaps millions of unbelievers. Unless God had intervened, what might have happened to their relationship with Him? Also remind the students that God in mercy waited 120 years for the wicked people of earth to repent before He sent the Flood. They refused to turn to Him and thus earned for themselves God's judgment.

Lot's case parallels that of Noah. God judged Sodom and Gomorrah for their gross wickedness. This act of judgment toward the ungodly was, on the other hand, an act of mercy toward Lot and his family. (See **2 Peter 2:6–8**.) Ask students to cite other Biblical examples. Then ask if they can think of cases in which God's judgment on wickedness today serves as a blessing or vindication for His children.

3. This question will probably not prove too difficult for your students. Help them see that God's heart yearns to be merciful. His grace calls and calls and keeps on calling sinners to repent. If we refuse His invitation of grace, we will receive His just judgment.

As time permits, refer students to the title of this lesson, telling them that it comes from the last part of **Hab. 3:2**. Calvary is, of course, the place where in His justice, God remembered mercy. There, God's judgment fell on Christ so that we might receive God's mercy.

4. Provide reference books for students to use as they do their research. Any good Bible dictionary, concordance, or topical Bible should provide the information students will need.

You may wish to assign the paper as homework. Or, you might ask groups of three or four students to work together as they study the word *remnant*.

When all have finished, ask each group to report its findings. If students worked individually on this project, ask volunteers to share what they have found.

Verses 30–33: Pursuing Righteousness

1. Let students share experiences as directed in their books. You may want to share a personal incident yourself first to "prime the pump" for them.

2. The people of Israel had an excellent goal—righteousness. Rather than reaching that goal through the grace that God provides, however, many of the people chose to pursue a righteousness by works. Such a righteousness is not possible for sinful human beings. In reality, it constitutes the ultimate blasphemy. By relying on a righteousness produced under our own power, we call God a liar and reject the unimaginable sacrifice our heavenly Father made for us as He gave His only Son into death for our justification.

The Gentiles, on the other hand, received the righteousness God offered by His grace through faith. That righteousness clings to Christ alone. That kind of righteousness honors God. That kind of righteousness is the only kind of righteousness acceptable in the courtroom of heaven.

3. This question should lead into a discussion of human pride and our tendency to want to do things ourselves rather than having to admit our need for God's help. Luther once said, "The Law is a constant companion in human hearts; the Gospel, a rare guest." What evidence of this do the students see in their own lives?

The last two questions in this section lend themselves well to private meditation by individual students. If you intend to use them in this way, set aside some class time for quiet reflection. You might also ask your students to write out their answers—it will probably help them think through their responses more deeply.

4. In one sense, the Cross is the ultimate insult to our human pride. The Cross shouts at us, "You can't save yourselves. You must trust *Me* for salvation! *I* took the punishment you deserve! Receive the free gift I offer!"

Still today, people stumble at the idea that they can be justified only by faith in Jesus. Jesus Christ is the Rock of offense to unbelievers and the Rock of salvation for those of us who have put our faith in Him. For every human being, Jesus is one or the other!

Session 28: Zeal, Truth, and Knowledge

BIBLE BASIS
  Rom. 10:1–13

CENTRAL TRUTH
  Many people who are zealous for God base their zeal on something other than a knowledge of the Gospel. No person, no matter how sincere, can save himself or herself. The mistaken notion that we can save ourselves leads to damnation. But God gives us Good News: no one who trusts in Jesus for salvation will be disappointed.

OBJECTIVES
By the grace of God students will
1. identify ways to recognize and confront error in a truly loving, evangelical way;
2. identify religious systems today that stress works as a means of pleasing God;
3. explain the important link between faith and confession of faith, and see the implications of that link for their lives.

OUTLINE OF ROM. 10:1–13
A. Israel's error (vv. 1–3)
   1. Paul's deep concern for his unsaved people (v. 1)
   2. Zeal without knowledge (v. 2)
   3. Ignorance (v. 3)
   4. Arrogance and independence (v. 3)
B. The Gospel truth (vv. 4–13)
   1. Jesus fulfilled the Law for us (vv. 4–5)
      a) Gospel is done (v. 4)
      b) Law is doing (v. 5; Lev. 18:5)
   2. The convenience of the Gospel (vv. 6–8)
   3. The confession of the Gospel (vv. 9–10)
   4. The availability of the Gospel (vv. 11–13)

A WORD FROM THE AUTHOR
  "Nazareth! Can anything good come from there?" Nathanael asked.
  "Come and see," invited Philip in **John 1:46**.
  Most of my students are truly Christians. But as I teach, I remember that invariably some students do not believe. More and more students who come to my class say they used to believe but no longer do so. Then I occasionally get a Buddhist or Hindu in class. While these students are only a small minority, they nevertheless must not be ignored.
  I have never yet argued a student into the kingdom of heaven, but I have found Philip's witnessing method very effective. Nathanael didn't know Jesus, but he knew Nazareth as a town with a bad reputation. Little good could be said about it so far as he was concerned. Philip refused to get pulled into an argument about the town; he simply invited Nathanael to come and meet Jesus.
  In most cases of unbelief that I confront, the individual doesn't really know Jesus, but has developed an opinion about Him based on experiences with people who claim to know Him. Unfortunately, these experiences are often negative. It is pointless to try to change these individuals' perceptions of Christians, but pointing them to Christ is effective. If they will meet Him face to face in His Word, Jesus will reveal Himself to them in much the same way as He did for Nathanael. There is no greater thrill for a Christian teacher than to hear a former skeptic echo Nathanael's conclusion about the Savior, "You are the Son of God!"

GETTING INTO THE LESSON
  Begin the session with prayer.
  Have the students read the introductory comments about zeal from their books and discuss the questions there.
  Then tell the class that the section from Romans they will study today has a lot to say about right and wrong kinds of zeal.
  The introduction to **Rom. 10** can be found in the last few verses of **Rom. 9**. Here Paul concludes that those in Israel who tried to earn righteousness by keeping the Mosaic Law failed to achieve it. By the same token, the Gentiles who received God's righteousness by faith had the assurance of their salvation. Israel's rejection of God's plan of salvation did not stop Paul from praying for his fellow Jews. His greatest desire was for his people's salvation, even though he knew they were **"seeking to establish their own [righteousness]"** (v. 3 RSV) rather than accepting God's plan by faith. Just as the majority of people today, many Jews of Paul's time refused to submit to God, thereby becoming victims of their own arrogance.

IN THE WORD
Verses 1–3: Israel's Error
(Objectives 1 and 2)
  1. Discuss the questions together. Probe as necessary to help students express reasons for reluctance to confront others who are headed for trouble. Point out the sin involved in many of our excuses: fear of rejection or ridicule, unconcern about the other person's spiritual needs, etc.
  Move from the students' experiences to Paul's model approach. He identifies himself with the people he is confronting. He expresses his motivation—love and deep concern for the spiritual welfare of his people. He compliments them for their zeal. Then he gently eases into the error he wishes to help them see.
  Our Lord Jesus taught His disciples again and

again about the importance of love in effective ministry. Paul clearly and deeply expresses his concern about the people themselves. He does not see them as mere statistics or as evangelistic scalps that will prove to the world his prowess as a missionary. We see no trace of arrogance in his approach, only a humble reliance upon God, to whom he prays.

2. Paul has been where his Jewish readers are. With the energy and misdirected zeal of a fanatic, Paul actually persecuted the people of God. He truly believed that by doing so he was pleasing God. He had been a living fulfillment of Jesus' prophecy in **John 16:2.**

3. Paul confronts his Jewish readers with the fact they are in error even though they are zealous for God. Contrary to popular belief (both then and now), it doesn't matter how sincere we are, or how fervently we believe, or even how deeply we are committed. If what we believe is fundamentally wrong, only tragedy can result. Israel in Paul's day, as many movements today, ignored the availability of God's righteousness through faith in Jesus Christ. Anyone who endeavors to communicate the Gospel today can profit by noting Israel's errors because they are common to most people in one form or another.

Your students should have little trouble developing a list of both "religious" and "nonreligious" groups that fit into the same mold (e.g., Jehovah's Witnesses, Moonies, Mormons, Ku Klux Klan, the Way, pragmatism, and any number of cultlike trends that frequently pop up in the media).

4. Two characteristics the groups mentioned above share are (a) a basic ignorance of how God has chosen to impart His righteousness by grace; and (b) an attempt to establish their own alternative to justification by faith.

Even though these characteristics may vary dramatically from one group to another, each group reflects an arrogant human declaration of independence from God.

Verses 4–13: The Gospel Truth (Objective 3)
1. Without cramming it down his readers' throats, Paul clearly states that Christ is the fulfillment of the Law. The "doing" part of salvation is over, and righteousness is now available to all who believe. Work righteousness, by contrast, says "The one who *does* these things [obeys the Law] will live by them." The Gospel is done; the Law is doing. There may be more eloquent ways of expressing the difference between Law and Gospel, and your students may have a variety of fine definitions, but it all boils down to the difference between *done* and *doing*. Thus **verse 4** is the key verse that summarizes the section. Ask students which verse they chose as they read the section in preparation for today's class session. (See session 27 in the Student Book, **"Looking Ahead."**)

2. Paul has thoroughly established the principle of justification by faith alone. He is not here adding another element to the process. In the apostle's mind, however, it is impossible to separate salvation from confession. Theoretically, it is possible to live an entire lifetime and never once mention the name of the Lord Jesus. But, practically speaking, if you believe in your heart that Jesus is Lord and that God has raised Him from the dead, you are no more able to keep quiet about it than you are to stop breathing!

The word *Gospel* means *Good News*. Good News must be shared! Ask your students how they would feel if something truly wonderful happened to them but they were forbidden to tell anyone about it. Most will probably agree that such a restriction would spoil much of their pleasure. Then have them share some of their feelings about witnessing and about why they find it hard or awkward to witness.

You might suggest practicing in class a way to share the Good News of Jesus Christ so it will be easier in other settings. Whatever else you do, this is a good subject to pray about. Have a volunteer offer a prayer of confession for times all of you have neglected or ignored opportunities to witness. Ask for the Spirit's power in becoming more effective witnesses to the love of Jesus Christ. Be sure to thank God for His full and free forgiveness, even for sins of neglect in this area. Or, pronounce an absolution before students leave.

Session 29: Evangelism

BIBLE BASIS
Rom. 10:14–21

CENTRAL TRUTH
The Good News of salvation is exciting. Sharing this Gospel with others is equally so. God gives us the privilege of both knowing and sharing His love and forgiveness in Jesus.

OBJECTIVES
By the grace of God students will
1. express gratefulness to those who have had a part in bringing them to saving faith and nurturing them in that faith;
2. discuss the concept that every person is either a missionary or a mission field;
3. explain the process the Holy Spirit uses in evangelism and the paradoxical way the Spirit works to bring people to Himself.

OUTLINE OF ROM. 10:14–21
A. The process (vv. 14–15)
   1. Calling upon God (v. 14)

2. Believing **(v. 14)**
   3. Hearing **(v. 14)**
   4. Preaching **(v. 15)**
   5. Sending **(v. 15)**
B. The response **(vv. 16–19)**
   1. Receiving **(v. 16)**
      a) Foolish **(1 Cor. 1:20–25)**
      b) Unattractive **(Is. 53)**
   2. Hearing **(vv. 17–18)**
   3. Understanding **(v. 19)**
C. The paradox **(vv. 20–21)**
   1. **Is. 65:1**
   2. **Is. 65:2**

A WORD FROM THE AUTHOR

"Whoever turns a sinner from the error of his way will save him from death and cover over a multitude of sins" (James 5:20).

Sometimes I wonder whether I'm doing any good at all. Is the kingdom of God any richer because I am working in it? Maybe you've wondered that yourself. I know it is both sinful and counterproductive to doubt the power of God's Word, but I still do doubt on occasion. And when I do, I try to remember **James 5:20.**

The privilege of saving a soul from death is simply breathtaking. In the student book material for this session, I have shared my conversion experience. This experience is always with me. No words of mine could ever express how I feel toward the man who allowed God to use him in such a way. And nothing would mean more to me than to have God use my witness in someone's life the way God used his in mine. He died never knowing what sort of fruit his witness would produce. Possibly he wouldn't even remember how he shared. But every person God touches through my ministry owes a debt of gratitude to that man! All the men and women I have taught, and who are now themselves in ministry around the world teaching others, are in some way, large or small, a product of this man's ministry. What a chain of blessings a single act of witness can set in motion!

I guess all Christian teachers sometimes grow weary. I guess we all wonder sometimes if we are doing any good at all. But I believe that those doubts grow out of Satan's attempts to blind us to the magnificent possibilities God gives us every time we share God's Word. I was a mission field; now I am a missionary. Isn't God's grace amazing?

GETTING INTO THE LESSON (Objective 1)

Begin the session with prayer.

Read and discuss the introductory material in the student book. What opinions do your students have about the writer? about the person who witnessed to him?

Too often the people charged with the responsibility of teaching God's Word are regarded as pests, especially by the people being taught. Talk to your class about the people (including yourself) who have brought them to know their Savior and to become members of His holy Christian church. Encourage them to thank God for these people in their prayers.

Then have your class read **Gal. 6:6.** Discuss what Paul means by **"sharing all good things with his instructor."** Suggest that these good things are not necessarily material things but, rather, respect, love, and gratitude. Encourage the students to write notes of thanks to the people most responsible for their spiritual training.

IN THE WORD

Verses 14–15: The Process (Objective 2)

Having established the universal relevance of the Christian Gospel in **verse 13,** Paul, with relentless logic, establishes the process by which that Gospel spreads. This message is relevant and necessary for those of us who sit comfortably in Christian pews, untouched by the condition of over half the world's population who live and die knowing nothing of Jesus Christ, the Son of the only true Savior. How will these people call on the Lord if they don't believe? Isn't their faith dependent upon hearing? And how will anyone hear unless someone tells—unless someone feels the burden of the commission Jesus gave to His people to take His message to the uttermost parts of the earth?

1. As your students ponder the process of evangelism, have them share their thoughts with the class. An Old Testament example of a loving, concerned witness would be Naaman's servant girl. The apostles' fear at the crucifixion became Easter joy which, in turn, became fervor and fearless witness after Pentecost.

Have students share names and situations of people for whom they feel concern. This might best be accomplished in small groups of two or three students. Encourage students to pray regularly for a set time period (a week or two) for each other's "special people."

2. If the students have trouble with any of the four steps, it probably will be with the first one. Many Christians don't seem to grasp the link between "believing in the heart" and "confessing with the mouth." We need to understand more clearly that witness is not just the work of a few dedicated souls who feel the call to serve God in the jungles of Africa or in the rain forests of Brazil. God wants to send *everyone*—*all* who believe that Jesus is the Christ. We witness, and those who believe as a result of our witness are then called to share with others, as they set the whole process of witness in motion for yet another cycle. This constantly renewed cycle, experienced and expressed, would produce a church in which everyone is filled with a sense of privilege and joy in being sent by our great God and Savior to tell His message to others.

Verses 16–19: The Response (Objective 3)

1. Some will reject the Good News of our witness. Some will not understand. Some will refuse to believe.

Refer students to **verses 12–13**. In doing so, remind them of the positive response you discussed earlier: some will receive the Gospel, believe it, and be saved.

    2. Students often fear that no one will listen, even if they do share their faith. Paul explains one reason people reject the Gospel in **1 Cor. 1:20–25**. The whole business seems foolish from the world's point of view. **Is. 53** explains that the suffering Servant-Savior does attract us to Him. The portrait Isaiah paints is not a pretty one. We humans prefer strength to weakness, ruling to serving. We prefer a crown rather than a cross.

    3. This is a key question. We do not want to build a self-fulfilling prophecy of rejection into our students' attitudes about witnessing. Christian witnesses need to be realistic, but not pessimistic! We have been chosen and called by God to be His witnesses. What a privilege! We are not responsible for the response of those to whom we witness. Sometimes the most unlikely people hear and believe, while those we expect will come to faith do not **(Rom. 10:20–21)**. Sometimes the seed of the Word lies in the ground of a person's heart for months or years before the Holy Spirit causes it to produce faith. We go on sowing seed, assured of the harvest. If you have personal experiences that will make this point personal for your students, by all means share them.

Verses 20–21: The Paradox (Objective 3)

    1. A paradox is a statement that seems contradictory, but is, in fact, true. Paul quotes **Is. 65:1–2**, which explain that the people (Gentiles) who are not looking for God find Him, while the people (Israel) to whom God holds out His hands day and night lose Him.

    2. Spend whatever time you have left in the period assisting your students in seriously considering what they can do to further equip themselves to share the Gospel and to actually do some sharing. Depending on your situation, you may want to require that they join their congregation's evangelism callers for one, two, three, or four weeks to observe firsthand.

    As you close today, pray with the students that the Lord will equip them to do and be what He has asked them to do and be. Before you offer this prayer, draw their attention to **Rom. 10:15**. Tell them this is a quote from **Is. 52:7**. Ask them to consider their feet. You might even have them take off their shoes and socks. Ask them if they think their feet are beautiful. (Almost no one does.) Then remind them of what God thinks of anyone who shares the Gospel.

Session 30: Cast Away or Set Aside

BIBLE BASIS
    Rom. 11:1–15

CENTRAL TRUTH
    Even in times of great national or global apostasy, God always preserves for Himself a faithful remnant who receive God's gift of salvation on the basis of grace, not of works. God used Israel's apostasy in Paul's day to spread His plan of salvation to the Gentiles.

OBJECTIVES
By the grace of God students will
1. tell how God always preserved a remnant of people faithful to Him throughout history;
2. relate the cause and cure for depression in their lives, especially as it relates to perceived, personal spiritual failure;
3. identify God's grace as the only source of forgiveness for spiritual failure and strength to continue as faithful witnesses for our Savior.

OUTLINE OF ROM. 11:1–15
  A. God always preserves a remnant **(vv. 1–10)**
    1. Paul, an example **(v. 1)**
    2. God will *not* reject His people **(v. 2)**
    3. Elijah and the 7,000 **(vv. 2b–4)**
    4. Remnant preserved by grace **(vv. 5–6)**
    5. The hardening of those who reject the Gospel **(vv. 7–10)**
       a) Is. 29:10 (v. 8)
       b) Ps. 69:22–23 (vv. 9–10)
  B. Failure of the Jews resulted in salvation for the Gentiles **(vv. 11-15)**

A WORD FROM THE AUTHOR
    In the student book for this session, we will ask the class to think about Elijah's ministry and his depression as he thought about the apostles he saw in his nation. This account may prove easier for you than for your students.

    As a teacher, I can identify with Elijah's depression. I have had my own pity parties, usually variations on Elijah's theme:

    "Lord, I'm tired. Lord, I'm all alone. Lord, nobody understands. Lord, I have had enough."

    Sometimes I feel like a spiritual manic-depressive. At times, like Elijah in **1 Kings 18,** I stand on my own Mount Carmel. Confident in my God, I challenge the very forces of hell. Then, when God produces the spectacular victory I have come to expect from Him, the enemy begins to take notice, and I begin to fear. In my fear, I grow depressed and downright peevish—even with my God.

    At times like this, fire doesn't come down from heaven as it did for Elijah. A violent storm or an earthquake doesn't reassure me of God's love and protection. Instead, I get the same answer Elijah did— a still, small voice that asks, "What are you doing?" After pouring out my complaints, both real and imagined, I hear the gentle whisper again asking, "What are you doing here?" As I really listen to God's question and begin to answer it, I can feel my fear and depression slipping away.

I am in the service of God, my king. But sometimes I become so busy serving God that I forget to let Him serve me. Then I begin to feel afraid and depressed. The still, small voice reminds me to stop, to listen, and to draw strength from my God. Then He sends me back to work for Him.

GETTING INTO THE LESSON

Begin the session with prayer.

Paul begins this chapter with a question: **"Did God reject His people?"** Two more questions arise from this one: Who is meant by "His people"? Does "rejected" mean permanently cast away? Paul seems to be saying in **Rom. 11** that "His people" means Israel as a nation and that "rejection" means temporarily set aside. He totally rejects the idea that God has turned His back on Israel. In fact, he begins to argue that Israel has a magnificent future in store for her. In the meantime, however, she is experiencing the discipline of her God.

IN THE WORD

Verses 1–10: God Preserves a Remnant
(Objectives 1 and 2)

1. The three arguments Paul uses might be summarized in the following way:

Verse 1: If God had cast off the entire nation of Israel, then no Jew could be saved. Paul, however, was a Jew, and he had been converted **(Acts 9)**. So long as there are people like Paul, there can be no such thing as a rejection of the whole nation of Israel.

Verse 2: Furthermore, the principle of **"those God foreknew He also predestined" (Rom. 8:29)** applies here. God has selected Israel to fulfill a special role in His plan of salvation. God will not reject His chosen believers.

Verses 3–6: As in Elijah's time, when God preserved 7,000 faithful to the Lord, so God always preserves a remnant for Himself. Sometimes individual members of this remnant are highly visible (e.g., Moses and Elijah). At other times, they are practically lost from sight in the apostasy of a nation (e.g., Anna and Simeon, **Luke 2:21–40**).

2. Spend some time talking with your students about why Elijah felt as he did. Was it lack of faith? Did he have good reason to be afraid? Did he handle it the right way? You might find this a good time to discuss serious topics like teenage suicide and drug abuse. The subjects usually come up when teenagers discuss depression. Take advantage of the situation by letting students talk as much as they will.

A number of factors probably led to Elijah's problems:

fear of Jezebel instead of faith in God **(1 Kings 19:3)**;

physical fatigue and hunger **(19:5–9)**; and

social isolation **(19:3b, 9)**.

You might also help your students see that Elijah may have been isolating himself spiritually. Over 7,000 believers in Israel had not bowed to Baal, and Elijah apparently did not know even one of them. We all need Christian friends with whom to laugh, cry, and pray.

Elijah's sin was partially responsible for his problem, but not exclusively so. Help students see that to be useful in God's ministry, we need to take care of ourselves physically, socially, and emotionally as well as just spiritually.

3. In **verses 7–10** we discover that those Jews who have not exercised faith in Jesus Christ have been "hardened" by God. The more they resisted God's grace, the more hardened they became.

4. The situation in Paul's day differs only in detail from the society in which we live. Many people today practice what can be called "safe religion." Without getting too "religious" themselves, they identify with a church group or a denomination, adopt the name of this group, and assume they are saved. Refer your students to **Matt. 7:14** and ask their opinion. The road to heaven can be very lonely—ask any who belong to the remnant.

Verses 11–15: Salvation for the Gentiles
(Objectives 1 and 3)

1. Paul claims that God was trying to make Israel jealous by offering to the Gentiles what Israel had refused. It would seem that God sometimes has to deal with His children literally as children. Many of your students will have had experiences babysitting. Perhaps they have given the child a toy. The child rejects the toy by throwing it back at the baby sitter. But, if the same unwanted toy is given to a second child, the toy suddenly can become enormously desirable to the first child.

2. Paul seems to be telling us that Israel is down—but not out. He seems to say Israel will, in actual fact, rise again. Her failure will give way to fullness. Her rejection will be replaced by reception. There will, indeed, be a day when Israel will again be the people of God, through faith. See session 31 for a fuller discussion.

Session 31: Baking and Botany

BIBLE BASIS
   Rom. 11:16–25

CENTRAL TRUTH

   Gentile Christians now enjoy that which was originally reserved for the Jews. But the privilege of being God's children offers no basis for smugness or pride among the Gentiles, for they receive this privilege as a gift of God's grace. Furthermore, God brings Gentiles and Jews alike into His church.

OBJECTIVES

By the grace of God students will
1. demonstrate their understanding of Christianity as the fulfillment of God's promises to His Old Testament people;
2. relate the metaphors of Paul concerning Jews and Gentiles into meaningful experience in their own lives;
3. point out that, even though the Jewish nation was cut off from God's church, God still calls Jewish people into His family.

OUTLINE OF ROM. 11:16–25

A. The metaphors (vv. 16–17)
   1. Baking (v. 16a)
   2. Botany (vv. 16b–17)
B. The warning (vv. 18–25)
   1. Don't be arrogant (vv. 18–20)
   2. Kindness and sternness of God (vv. 22–25)

A WORD FROM THE AUTHOR

   "Come to Me, all you who are weary and burdened, and I will give you rest" (Matt. 11:28).

   Until I started teaching, I thought I had a pretty good understanding of this verse. But then my perception of *rest* changed from the spiritual concept of "I will give you rest" to the secular concept of "no rest for the weary." Like so many first-year teachers, I found myself getting assignments from lunch-room supervision and coaching to teaching at least one subject where I knew little more than the students.

   Much about that first year of teaching seemed impossible. Fortunately, I had to turn to the Lord for support, because there was nowhere else to turn. That, of course, is exactly what God wants! At that time I rethought what I understood about **Matt. 11:28** and found I didn't really understand Jesus' message. Until then, I pictured myself digging a hole and getting tired and sweaty. Jesus would stand on the edge of the hole, lead a prayer, and tell me to keep up the good work. During those first years of teaching it dawned on me that I needed to let Jesus get into the hole with me. His hands would join mine on the shovel, and He would provide the power for me to complete the task.

GETTING INTO THE LESSON

   Begin with prayer.

   The preceding verses have informed us that the Jewish people are not irretrievably lost. As a nation they have been set aside so that the Gentiles might gain what the Jewish people have lost. But even in this, we find the underlying thought of the recovery of the Jews. Paul fully shares the longing of God for the Jewish people. He yearns for them to repent of their unbelief and become recipients of the blessings originally given to their nation. To clarify his point, Paul now uses two metaphors.

IN THE WORD

Verses 16–17: The Metaphors (Objectives 1 and 2)

   1. Apparently Paul is saying that the patriarchs (Abraham, Isaac, and Jacob) were the first part of the dough. Through faith they were recipients of God's righteousness. The "whole batch" represents the nation of Israel. If the first generations of Israel were set apart to God, then so is the entire nation.

   2. This can be a very interesting activity. It can also degenerate into a gripe session about all that is wrong with the church, so be careful with it. The discussion or writing activity should promote unity in the church.

   Often many older, regular church-goers are somewhat chagrined and put off by the rather startling styles in hair and clothing that the younger members have adopted. By the same token, many young people think of their elder co-worshipers as a bunch of old fuddy-duddies. Through the power and influence of the Holy Spirit these two divergent groups can come together for the good of both. The centuries of thought and wisdom behind the traditions of the church can provide a steady flow of life from the experienced believers into the lives of the young believers, while the "wild life" of the young people can bring the energy and vitality that so often leaves when people mature. When this happens without compromising God's Word, both groups profit, and God is honored. This is a tricky grafting operation, one that can succeed only through God's power.

Verses 18–25: The Warning (Objectives 2 and 3)

   1. Use class discussion for this activity, and move through it rather quickly. Too many students still support a prejudicial attitude toward Jews, thinking of them as a people in rebellion against God. Since this may be the only time in their lives that many in your class will be exposed to this portion of Scripture, you have an obligation (as well as an opportunity) to provide instruc-

tion about God-pleasing attitudes of Gentiles toward Jews.

2. Very likely the imagination of your students will be a powerful ally for you in this exercise. They may come up with examples that completely baffle you until they explain the thought process behind them. Whenever students ponder over Scripture, they are giving the Holy Spirit quality time in their lives, so the activity will probably be more important than the results.

As examples to get the class started, you can suggest organ transplants as a modern metaphor to explain the intimate relationship between Judaism and Christianity, or Jew and Gentile. A body without a liver or kidney cannot survive. Organs without bodies are no good at all. The idea of corneal transplants illustrates the point. You might use the healing of the blind man in **Mark 8:22–26**. Jesus came into his life and gave him sight. Today God enables us to use corneal transplants to provide the gift of sight. Compare this to a Jewish person living in spiritual darkness and a Gentile who has received God's wonderful light.

Session 32: Mercy and Majesty

BIBLE BASIS
Rom. 11:26–36

CENTRAL TRUTH
God used the apostasy of the Jewish nation to bring salvation to the Gentiles. Still today, sometimes in a similar way, God offers mercy to all, Jew and Gentile alike—mercy that appears more majestic each time we recall the disobedience from which God rescued us. True Israel includes those from every nation who in faith acknowledge Jesus as their Lord and Savior. Knowing this, we can shout our appreciation for the infinite love of God and acknowledge the centrality of the Lord in all things.

OBJECTIVES
By the grace of God students will
1. acknowledge the bittersweet reality (joy of salvation offered to all; sorrow over those who are lost) that permeates the life of every believer;
2. describe the interaction between Jew and Gentile as God worked out His salvation for all people;
3. demonstrate their appreciation of God's unfathomable love and ineffable majesty.

OUTLINE OF ROM. 11:26–36
A. All Israel will be saved (vv. 26–32)
   1. Salvation for all, Jew and Gentile alike (vv. 26–27)
   2. The status of Israel (vv. 28–29)
   3. A reminder to the Gentiles (vv. 30–32)
B. Wisdom and majesty of God (vv. 33–36)
   1. Exclamation that needs no proof (v. 33)
   2. Questions that need no answer (vv. 34–35)
   3. The universality of God (v. 36)
      a) From Him
      b) Through Him
      c) To Him

A WORD FROM THE AUTHOR
"When an evil spirit comes out of a man, it goes through arid places seeking rest and does not find it. Then it says, 'I will return to the house I left' " (Luke 11:24).

By nature each of us is filled with all sorts of evil. By grace God enters us and cleans that evil out of us. Then it is necessary to get filled up again—by Him. Only when that happens can we be of real use to God.

The **Book of Acts** refers over 20 times to this refilling process: **"Peter, filled with the Holy Spirit, said . . ."** (4:8). **"They were all filled with the Holy Spirit and spoke . . ."** (4:31). **"Brothers, choose seven men from among you who are known to be full of the Spirit and wisdom"** (6:3).

When an evil spirit is driven out, the vacuum must be filled by God or the demon returns with friends **(Luke 11:24–26)**.

Being filled—being controlled by a force from *within;* that's what religion is all about. For some people, however, religion is more of an obsession—a fixation upon something *without.* We teach and believe in the indwelling Lord Jesus. Such a filling produces evangelism. Obsession produces fanaticism.

GETTING INTO THE LESSON
Begin with prayer.

Paul has made it quite clear that, while there is a partial hardening among Israel, God is using it to bring His blessing and mercy to the Gentiles. When He has done that, **"all Israel will be saved"** (11:26). Paul does not stipulate the exact timing of this prediction, nor do theologians agree on the exact meaning of *all Israel.* One interpretation, that it refers to the great majority of Jews of the final generation, is inconsistent with **"some of them"** in **verse 14**. A second interpretation, that it refers to the Jews of every generation who have faith in Christ, is plausible. More likely, however, Paul is referring to all those who are saved, both Jew and Gentile. The student book uses this definition.

IN THE WORD
Verses 26–32: All Israel Will Be Saved
(Objectives 1 and 2)

1. See the notes above. Paul continues the theme he expressed in **verses 23–24**: Jewish people

who come to faith in Jesus as their Savior will be saved. Paul continues to make it abundantly clear that race or nationality are not criteria for salvation. Gentile and Jew alike receive God's mercy.

Is Paul predicting a major revival among Jewish people, a revival that will occur after **"the full number of Gentiles has come in"?** Probably not, but that question misses the major point, that salvation comes to all, both Jew and Gentile.

2. As he does so often when speaking of the Jews, Paul quotes the Old Testament to prove his point. See the message recorded in **Is. 59:20–21; 27:9;** and **Jer. 31:33–34.**

3. Paul is speaking to the Gentiles and saying that God used the rejection of Christ by His people as a means of reaching the Gentiles. Paul is *not* saying that God *wanted* the Jewish nation to reject God so that the Gentiles could be saved. Rather, Paul is just telling what happened. Furthermore, this in no way affects God's love for the Jewish people, which began with their first ancestors and continues to this day. He chose Abraham and his descendants, and He continues to regard them with interest and love, fully desiring to restore them to His mercy. God's gifts and call remain in effect even though most Jewish people reject the salvation He offers. God, unlike humans, is truthful, reliable, and does not change His mind.

4. Paul sums up the Gentile background in one short phrase, **"you who were at one time disobedient to God" (v. 30).** In **Eph. 2:1–2** and **11–12** Paul gives a fuller account of the Gentiles' spiritual condition. The apostle proceeds to explain that, despite their background, they now receive mercy as a result of Jewish disobedience. Because Israel rejected Jesus and attempted to gain salvation through works, they had been hardened against the truth and temporarily set aside. As a consequence, many Gentiles have now believed God's plan of salvation **(v. 30).**

But God has not abandoned His people. He has shown His mercy to the Gentiles so that through them the Jews **"may now receive mercy" (v. 31).** Have your students look back to **verses 13–14,** where Paul is expressing the same idea. This text is teaching that all people are caught in the trap of sin. God's mercy is the only release from this trap, and He has mercifully provided His only Son to free all people, Jew and Gentile alike, and to bring them into His wonderful presence.

Verses 33–36: The Wisdom and Majesty of God
(Objective 3)

Perhaps Paul was prompted in part to utter this profound doxology because he realized how difficult these three chapters would be for his readers. We may misunderstand Paul's message, but that makes no difference at all in God's resolution of the Jewish problem. God has not altered His plans, violated His principles, besmirched His character, forsaken His people, or ignored the Gentiles. God is God, and that is more than enough to generate the praise of mortals.

1. **"Who has known the mind of the Lord?"** Since He is infinite, no creature could ever begin to comprehend the mind (or the love!) of the Creator. Many human beings disbelieve God because they cannot understand Him or His ways. What a tragedy!

"Who has been His counselor?" God knows all things even before they happen, and God has boundless wisdom to apply His knowledge. Surely none of His creatures could give advice to Him!

"Who has ever given to God, that God should repay him?" God is the Sustainer and Provider of all. No creature could ever make God a debtor to him or her. Unfortunately, we too often feel we are doing God a favor by our deeds or contrition or church attendance. This is yet another form of work righteousness.

2. **From Him**—a reminder that He is the Source of all things. **James 1:16–18** says the same thing very nicely.

Through Him—a reminder that He is the Sustainer of all things and is able to cause all things to work for the good of those who love Him **(Rom. 8:28).**

To Him—a reminder that He is significant in all things. We recognize Him as the Source of all life, the Force that sustains life, and because of Him we are constantly being drawn back to Him. To Him all glory rightly belongs!

Session 33: Concluding Activities for Unit 3

Open your class session with prayer. Thank God for His Word, and especially for the truths He has provided in Romans. Ask the Holy Spirit to transform these truths of God's Word into living applications for yourself and your students.

Use this review to encourage your students to organize their knowledge and recognize the potential for personal application.

Plan to use at least part of the class session for students to share their knowledge and applications. As you have probably discovered, some of their applications are remarkably creative and valuable. When students share with one another, God multiplies the blessings of His Word.

The activities are similar to the review of units 1 and 2 in sessions 13 and 24. Refer back to the comments made in this guide for those sessions.

UNIT 4: THE RIGHTEOUSNESS OF GOD APPLIED

BIBLE BASIS: ROM. 12–16

Justification and sanctification—many of our Christian beliefs fall under the umbrella of these two doctrines. Elsewhere Paul summarizes the relationship of these doctrines as follows: **"He died for all, that those who live should no longer live for themselves but for Him who died for them and was raised again" (2 Cor. 5:15).**

In a general way, we can use these two doctrines to summarize the content of Romans. The material we studied in the first three units **(chapters 1–11)** opens up to us some of the most beautiful teachings God has given us about justification. A key word at the beginning of **chapter 12 ("therefore"—v. 1)** signals a new emphasis. In the last chapters of this epistle, the content for this unit, Paul speaks about our response to justification. In unit 4 you will have the opportunity to help students understand what God teaches about sanctification.

As you teach about sanctification, remember to always place it into the cradle of justification. We do not earn any special favor from God by trying to live a sanctified life. As emphasized often during the first three units, everything God gives us comes to us as a gift of His grace. Sanctification, too, is a gift from God. As the Holy Spirit enables us, we respond to His goodness, a response prompted by what God has done for us in the saving work of Jesus, through which we have been justified.

Session 34: Therefore . . .

BIBLE BASIS
   Rom. 12:1–2

CENTRAL TRUTH
God has shown limitless mercy and compassion toward us, His children. Realizing this, we respond by presenting our whole selves to Him in sacrificial service.

OBJECTIVES
By the grace of God students will
1. review the mercies of God described in the first 11 chapters of Romans;
2. offer themselves to God as living sacrifices in response to God's amazing grace;
3. daily renew their minds as they study God's Word so they may be transformed more and more into the image of Christ, resisting the pressures to conform to the value system of the world around them.

OUTLINE OF ROM. 10:14–21
A. Offer your bodies **(v. 1)**
   1. Therefore . . .
   2. Living sacrifices
B. Have your mind transformed **(v. 2)**
   1. Don't conform to the pattern of this world
   2. Test and approve God's will

A WORD FROM THE AUTHOR
Young people today experience heavier pressure to conform to the world's way of thinking than at any other time in history. You may argue this issue and claim that people have always felt intense pressure from the world system around them. But I disagree, and I offer this quote as evidence:

David Crosby (of Crosby, Stills, and Nash, a soft rock group) recently said, "I figured the only thing to do was swipe their kids. I still think it is the only thing to do. By saying that, I'm not talking about kidnapping. I'm just talking about changing their value systems which removes them from their parents' world very effectively" (*Rolling Stone Interviews,* 1:401).

The media, particularly the music industry, have to a great extent concentrated their efforts on stealing the minds and hearts of 8- to 18-year-olds. Only God's Word can effectively combat this malevolent influence. Paul writes, **"For though we live in the world, we do not wage war as the world does. The weapons we fight with are not the weapons of the world. On the contrary, they have divine power to demolish strongholds. We demolish arguments and every pretension that sets itself up against the knowledge of God, and we take captive every thought to make it obedient to Christ" (2 Cor. 10:3–5).**

God's Spirit Himself renews our minds through His Word as we fight the unhealthy influences our students face every day of their young lives. And we thank Him that He provides weapons that work effectively! Next to the home, the Christian school can be the best place to help young people wage their battle with worldly influences—and win!

GETTING INTO THE LESSON (Objective 1)
Begin the session with prayer.
Have someone read aloud the two paragraphs that introduce unit 4 **(Rom. 12–16).** Then explain that the word *therefore* that begins **Rom.12** is a very important key to understanding the following verses (and even chapters)! Give students time to work indepen-

dently as they scan the first 11 chapters of the epistle. Ask them to look for the most significant truths from these chapters. They should also note the chapter and verse in which they find each. Ask that they limit their list to about 8 to 10 important concepts. Plan to spend about 10 to 15 minutes on this review and the following discussion.

When most have finished, compile a class list on the chalkboard or on a large piece of poster paper. The majority of the texts should highlight God's grace toward sinful human beings in general and toward each of us personally in particular.

Explain that the writers of the New Testament epistles often use the word *therefore,* and that it is much more than an insignificant conjunction. Often it connects doctrinal principles with practical applications to daily living. Ask why the students think this connection is so critical. (Without sound doctrine, our lives soon degenerate into amoral living—see, for example, **Jude 3–4** and **2 Tim. 3:16–17**; but when we fail to apply to our lives the sound doctrine we believe, we live hypocritcal, even pharisaical lives.)

IN THE WORD
Verse 1: Offer Your Bodies

1. Just in case we missed the significance of his *therefore,* Paul reminds his readers once again of God's mercy. Lives of sacrifice and unselfish service come as a *response* to God's great grace poured out upon us. Paul wants to make sure his readers understand this concept. Or, as the apostle John puts it, "We love because He first loved us."

2. God's Holy Spirit **works in [us] to will and to act according to His good purpose (Phil. 2:13)**. The New Testament makes it abundantly clear that we cannot "clean up our own act"—either before or after our conversion. The Spirit works sanctification in us. Knowing this eliminates any sinful pride that tends to sprout up in our hearts when we feel we've done what God expects from us. It also eliminates despair when we fail to obey God. As believers, we have the Spirit's power to "present our bodies" to Him for His use. We trust Him to do in us what we cannot do ourselves. And we rely on His forgiveness when we do stumble.

3. The verb translated *offer* is the technical term used when a worshiper presented a victim for sacrifice. These two words *offer* and *sacrifice* clearly indicate that God here calls for His people to totally dedicate themselves to Him.

While the Old Testament believers offered some meal sacrifices, most offerings consisted of dead animals. Here in Romans, God asks us to offer the living sacrifice of ourselves. As time permits, ask students to use Bible dictionaries and encyclopedias to research some of the Old Testament sacrifices and the customary ways they were offered.

4. The words *holy and pleasing to God* must point us back once again to God's grace in forgiving us for Jesus' sake. Because of what our Savior has done for us on the cross, God not only forgives our sins; He also declares us to be righteous, holy (set apart for His service), and pleasing to Him. So complete is His grace that even though our motives are very seldom pure, even though our attitudes seldom conform precisely to what the Law demands, and even though our best efforts are marred by sin, God accepts our sacrifice of service. He declares it to be holy and pleasing to Him. And He works continually to conform us more and more into the image of Jesus.

Verse 2: Have Your Minds Transformed
(Objectives 2 and 3)

1. Your students should have little difficulty developing an extensive list of things that pressure them to conform. Peer pressure can be the single greatest influence in their lives, both for good and evil; so, when they find themselves doing what everyone else is doing, they might look carefully at their actions. Other items on the list could include music, fashion, entertainment, friends, fads, ambitions, and even attitudes about what behaviors are acceptable.

Some worldly influences are more subtle. The world around us operates according to certain principles, principles that for the most part are diametrically opposed to Scriptural principles. For example, the world tries to tell us that a person's worth can be determined by what that person does for a living or by how the person looks or dresses. The world system tells us that world-class athletes are worth more than preschool teachers. The world system declares nuclear physicists to be worth more than persons who are mentally retarded. The world system says that rich people have more value than the beggars on the streets of third world countries. Our Lord tells us, on the other hand, that all human life is of infinite value—Jesus gave up His very life that *all* might be forgiven and live with God eternally.

The world system tells us that truth is relative and that all people are entitled to their personal opinions. The world system says that we can't be certain about anything we can't prove in a laboratory. Scripture teaches that God has given us absolute truth. Jesus claimed to be "the Way, the Truth, and the Life." He went on to warn that no one comes to God except through faith in Jesus as the Savior. Individuals may sincerely hold differing opinions, and those opinions are protected by law in our democracy. But God's Word declares those opinions false, and if persisted in, damning.

Ask your students to be on the lookout for other principles by which the world lives. Ask them to listen closely to newscasts and television documentaries. Ask that they examine ads and commercials they see and hear. What assumptions lie beneath the surface? Are these assumptions and principles in line with God's Word or not? Why not? If you make this assignment today, allow a few days for students to gather their information. Then follow up in class. Ask students to bring samples illustrating the principles they find.

2. Assign the paragraph as homework or allow some time at the end of the class period for students to write. As you read the papers, check to see how thoroughly students understand the idea that God remolds our minds as we hear and study His Word. Also look for the idea that this change takes place by God's grace and not as we "try hard" to conform to our Father's expectations.

3. You might point out that this Greek word is translated *transfigured* in the account of our Lord's transfiguration. As the Holy Spirit remolds the attitudes in our minds and hearts, God's glory begins to show in our lives. People begin to see Jesus in us. This change takes place from the inside out. As our thoughts and attitudes become more Christ-like, our words and actions will become that way, too.

4. This question refers to the last phrase of **verse 2**. For many believers the will of God seems to be some mystical ideal that we have little hope of ever understanding. Paul disagrees. He insists that, as we present our bodies and allow the Holy Spirit to transform our minds, a life-style of fruitful activity will result, and we will provide evidence of God's good and perfect will in our lives.

Session 35: Evaluate and Activate

BIBLE BASIS
Rom. 12:3–8

CENTRAL TRUTH
Christ has called us to be His body, the church. As such, He has given each of us functions and different gifts. Rather than to use these gifts to promote ourselves, by our faith we rely upon God to use us for the common good of His church.

OBJECTIVES
By the grace of God the students will
1. view the church through Christ's eyes—that it is His body on earth and that the student is one member of that body;
2. distinguish the difference between being free agents working for their own purposes and being Christ's members working for Christ's purposes for the general good of the entire church;
3. employ a sober judgment when realizing the important calling they have in Christ's church on earth.

OUTLINE OF ROM. 12:3–8
A. Use sober judgment (**v. 3**)
B. Act for the good of the church (**vv. 4–5**)
   1. One body (**v. 4**)
   2. Many members (**v. 5**)
C. By grace, we have different gifts
   1. Prophesying ("proclaiming")
   2. Serving
   3. Teaching
   4. Encouraging
   5. Contributing
   6. Leadership
   7. Mercy

A WORD FROM THE AUTHOR
"**Come, follow Me,**" Jesus said, "**and I will make you fishers of men**" (Mark 1:17).

Every time I stand in front of a new group of students, this promise of the Lord comes to mind. I find a great comfort when I realize that Jesus takes responsibility for equipping me to do the work He has given me to do. I feel a kinship with Peter, Andrew, James, and John, who didn't really know what they were getting into, but trusted Jesus to provide the leadership.

These four fishermen were raw recruits where ministry was concerned, but they knew how to catch fish. And I think they probably understood the three steps involved in Jesus' command. The first step is "Come, follow Me," which they did instantly. Second, allow Jesus to do the equipping, a lesson that took Peter three years and a bitter failure to learn. And, finally, be "fishers of men." Jesus used a frame of reference they could understand. They knew the fishing business, and they realized the skill needed to make a living at it.

To achieve success in the fishing business, one has to be willing to fish at inconvenient times. Fish are often hungriest and nearest the surface in the predawn hours. To catch fish we need to know where to fish and what kind of bait will attract them.

All these rules apply directly to our job. A 3 a.m. phone call from a deeply depressed student may present the best opportunity for ministry you will ever have with that person. Effective ministry also occurs in the lunchroom, on the athletic field, or at a sock hop. Finally, you must know your students and their interests. You must capture their attention before you can focus it upon their Lord and Savior.

LOOKING AHEAD
In session 53, during the study of **1 Corinthians**, you will again examine the topic of spiritual gifts. Read both the Student Book and Teachers Guide for that session now. Decide how you will teach the two sessions so that session 53 will reinforce and complement today's study.

GETTING INTO THE LESSON

Begin with prayer.

Ask the students to briefly read through the opening section of the Student Book and to list some differences between talents and gifts. Draw two columns on the chalkboard, under the headings "Talents" and "Gifts." As the students offer opinions, write them down under the column headings. Ask others whether they agree or disagree and why. Keep in mind that gifts may not be quite so obvious, simply because they are used by God for the benefit of the church. Of course, a high-scoring basketball player is talented; but that does not necessarily help in the work of the church (even if he or she plays on a church league). Ask your students why not.

IN THE WORD

Verse 3: Use Sober Judgment

By saying, **"Use sober judgment,"** Paul was telling the Christians to put all things in perspective, to see themselves from God's point of view. Obviously, many had an ego problem that split the church down the middle. Apparently they developed a superiority complex when they evaluated their gifts from God. Instead of thanking God for the gifts they had, they lorded their gifts over others. Cliques formed within the church; it was the (vainly imagined!) "haves" against the "have nots." Showy gifts were elevated; the humble gifts of genuine service were disregarded. The "haves" believed they were special to God. Understandably, that made the "have nots" feel quite left out.

Point out to your students that the crisis was caused by the vanity that comes from worldly thinking, not by God's gifts. Paul's comparison of the body of Christ to the human body showed masterfully that no part of the body, the church, can function well without all the other parts. You may wish to refer your students to **1 Cor. 12**, especially **verse 7**.

Encourage your students to talk freely of their own experiences with feelings of superiority and inferiority. Remember, though, that high-school-age people may not easily expose their opinions of themselves before a class of their peers.

Look for a way to show that Paul's admonition to use sober judgment does not mean discrediting the gifts He has given us. False humility is as dangerous as pride and, in fact, may have the same root. In a strange way, those with inferiority complexes commit the same sin as those with superiority complexes: both are too wrapped up in the self; the self (for both) has consumed them.

Point out that we can escape the trap of superiority or inferiority complexes only by accepting (by the Spirit's power) Jesus' invitation: "Lose yourself for Me and My Gospel, and then you will find it."

Verses 4–5: One Body, Many Members

The church is frequently called the body of Christ, based primarily on this passage of **Romans** as well as **1 Cor. 12:12–31**. Encourage your students to use these Scriptures to reexamine the reasons for superiority or inferiority complexes that may hurt the church. The church in Corinth suffered greatly when this problem hit. The questions in the Student Book may prompt your students to illustrate how this problem can cause suffering in the church today. Your students do not have to think of remote examples; some may be as close to them as themselves.

This section may offer you a golden opportunity to help your students see the great value of each member of Christ's body. Each of us belongs to the others **(v. 5)**. We obscure this value when we permit worldly standards to intrude into our thinking. That is why it is no coincidence that this segment is placed so closely to Paul's encouragement to **"be transformed by the renewing of your mind" (v. 2)**. By the Spirit's power, we surrender (daily!) the worldly viewpoint and its Hollywood-style standards of judging both others and ourselves.

Verses 6–8: Different Gifts

Paul does not mention any specific gifts until he first gives his readers a proper understanding of their place. With that accomplished, Paul now lists seven gifts as examples.

1. Help your students through the exercise of writing briefly on each gift. Some of your students may need help relating these gifts to specific functions of the church. Explain that the gift of prophesy, for instance, probably refers to the proclamation of the Word. If it helps, refer back to some of the Old Testament prophets. Not all prophets foretold future events (e.g., Nathan, who pointed out David's sin with Bathsheba). The gift of teaching also refers to the teaching of the Word. You might ask your students how proclaiming differs from teaching the Word of God. Point out that those with both teaching and prophesy gifts may make dynamic preachers for the church.

With a little help from you, your students may (with more ease) relate the rest of the gifts to functions within the church. Be sure to mention that each Christian has one or more gifts.

2. Encourage your students to select a gift (or gifts) that interests them. It may be far too soon in their lives to determine which gifts they may have. (How many adult Christians know?) Urging them to do a little envisioning and dreaming (and praying!) may be planting seeds for service to Christ and His church.

When your students have completed this work, return to the list of "Talents/Gifts" that you drew on the chalkboard or newsprint. Ask your students whether they would allow their original list to stand, or whether they would make some changes. Provide help as needed. List those changes (if any) and ask them to support those suggested changes with reasons from Scripture.

Session 36: Love, the Real Thing

BIBLE BASIS
   Rom. 12:9–13

CENTRAL TRUTH
Love, to be genuine or sincere, is a self-giving-up, a self-sacrificing for others. Remarkably unlike our society's notions of love, this unconditional *agape-love* is not just the love we are to give others, but the love God gives us in Christ Jesus.

OBJECTIVES
By the grace of God the students will
1. point out that those things that propose themselves as love in our society fall miserably short of God's standards;
2. demonstrate a clear understanding that genuine agape-love is self-giving, self-sacrificing love and is the love that God invites us to give others;
3. explain that this unconditional agape-love is precisely that which God has already given them in Christ Jesus.

OUTLINE OF ROM. 12:9–13
A. Agape-love is self-giving, self-sacrificing **(vv. 9–13)**
   1. It hates evil and clings to good **(v. 9)**
   2. It devotes itself to others **(v. 10)**
   3. It honors others over self **(v. 10)**
B. Agape-love serves our Lord zealously **(vv. 11–13)**
   1. It hopes joyfully **(v. 12)**
   2. It takes affliction patiently **(v. 12)**
   3. It prays faithfully **(v. 12)**
   4. It shares, even hospitality, with those in need **(v. 13)**

A WORD FROM THE AUTHOR
In another Pauline letter, the superiority of love is proclaimed in this familiar verse: **"And now these three remain: faith, hope and love. But the greatest of these is love" (1 Cor. 13:13).** As teachers we have no trouble believing in the truth of this verse, mainly because we have so many opportunities to practice it. God calls these clusters of adolescents we teach "communion of saints." My flesh objects and comes up with all sorts of other names to describe them, but God insists on calling them saints. Furthermore, He demands that I treat them as saints, love them, and as Peter says, not lord it over them, but lead by example.

The most profound example I can set for my students is to genuinely love them. Of course, this does not mean complete permissiveness in the classroom; but when I need to discipline, I know that this too is a characteristic of love. **("Those whom I love I rebuke and discipline"—Rev. 3:19.)** If my students are able to see all the different aspects of the love Paul describes consistently working in my life, then my job is half done. If they don't see love, no amount of effort will make me an effective teacher. Meticulously prepared lesson plans and brilliant lecturing can never compensate for indifference and noninvolvement.

My flesh rebels at this. If this is my job description, it sounds impossible. Who can consistently, genuinely love all his or her students? None of us, if we rely upon ourselves. But God promises to give us His power. With Paul, we can then say, **"I can do everything through Him who gives me strength" (Phil. 4:13).** By the grace of God, we can put our students' best interest above our own. We can teach with loving enthusiasm, effort, patience, humility, joy, and prayer.

GETTING INTO THE LESSON
Begin with prayer.

God certainly calls for our love to be genuine and sincere. Yet, called as we are to be not *of* this world, we are still *in* this world and highly influenced by it. Your students are no exceptions. They, as all Christians, witness the cheapening of love by the worldly attitudes and behaviors of people manipulating people. They see it highlighted and romanticized in video, movies, T. V., and other media. We need to have Christ Jesus define what He means by love. And He not only defines it but gives it to us from His cross. That agape-love, self-giving-up and self-sacrificing-for, is His gift to us. Only His Holy Spirit can enable us to offer that agape-love to others.

IN THE WORD
Verses 9–13: Be Sincere (Objectives 1, 2, and 3)

A. The Dilemma

You might open a class discussion by asking the students to review this segment of Romans and then to read this section in the Student Book. Ask your students to help determine when love is sincere and when it's not. Write out their responses on the chalkboard.

Ask students to show how even our sincere love for a loved one is tested. **What does it take, sometimes, for us to blow up at a loved one? When we become angry, moody, or hurt at a loved one's response, does that show some lack of sincerity in our love? Why or why not?**

If this is the difficulty we encounter even with those we love, what about those we don't? What if these "not so loved" ones are fellow Christians? Since we are called to love them, too, in what ways do we often disguise our lack of love?

Share Jesus' words in **Matt. 5:44, 46–48.** Ask, **How do Jesus' words make you feel?** Students' responses will probably show not only their own dilemma, but also the dilemma of most Christians.

B. The Definition

Familiarize yourself with the activity, "Imagine!" before this session begins. Use it to help students look more objectively at their own particular world and society, and critically look at their world's views on love.

Under the segment, "Your Research," the students may give a wide variety of answers. Encourage them to select a stanza, scene, phrase, and point of view from a few of their favorite tunes, videos, and movies. Offer no opinion of your own on the students' choices; the activity will be far more effective if students are allowed to come to their own conclusions on the basis of the Romans text.

Under the segment, "Your Observations," the students are asked to jot down statements that reflect the view of love of their selected song, movie, etc. This may reflect a 20th-century view. Encourage the students to think for themselves. As you have probably seen yourself, the students' completed answers are meant to help them see that the world's view of love is conditional, rooted in the self, and (perhaps) temporal. Human love looks for lovable qualities in the beloved; it often changes as human mood and character changes.

"Now, Some First-Century Conclusions" brings in God's Word as an objective norm by which to measure the authenticity of the world's loves. **Rom. 12:9–13** may sound to some students as a harsh standard, as though God is expecting too much from us. If this challenge comes up, be prepared to return with a loving counterchallenge: **Would you wish to be loved less than this?** Woven into the text is God's protecting love for all of us. It is not His will that any of us are loved by anything less than genuine love.

"My Conclusions about Agape-Love" encourages the students to contrast the world's view of love with God's view. Obviously, God's love has no conditions. His commitment is total: **"He . . . did not spare His own Son, but gave Him up for us all" (Rom. 8:32)**. Needless to say at this point, while human loves may last a lifetime (at best), God's love reaches out to eternity.

Allow your students to share (only if they wish) some of their overall conclusions with the class. Call for discussion by asking if others wish to express agreement or (friendly!) disagreement, additions, or other comments.

C. The Delivery

By now the students may have reached the conclusion that not only does society fail to reach God's totally committed, completely self-giving-up kind of agape-love, but so do we, His called people.

Yet, even if we have failed to be doers of this agape-love, we are still receivers of it! This would be an opportune time to express how infinitely we are loved by God; how hard it is to miss seeing that love as we see Jesus on the cross. To wind down your class, ask students how they think and feel about being so loved by God. Ask, further, how this enables us (by the Holy Spirit's power) to fulfill the invitation to agape-love others.

Session 37: Good Swallows Evil

BIBLE BASIS
Rom. 12:14–21

CENTRAL TRUTH

Failing to love our persecutors, we hate them. In revenging ourselves on them, we become exactly like them, and we have let ourselves be overcome by evil. Our only salvation is Christ Jesus, who calls us to follow Him and love our enemies and who gives us the power to love. Loving them means losing ourselves in Christ and praying and working for our enemies' best and eternal interest. In a way echoing the way that Christ Jesus saves us, we save our enemies. Then Christ's goodness swallows evil.

OBJECTIVES
By the grace of God the students will
1. demonstrate an understanding that by giving in to revenge we allow evil to overcome us;
2. identify the only way to overcome evil as agape-loving the evildoer;
3. explain that only by Christ Jesus' power can we bless our persecutors, thus overcoming evil with good, as Jesus did for us.

OUTLINE OF ROM. 12:14–21
A. The only way to resist evil and not let evil overcome you is to agape-love the evildoer.
   1. Bless, not curse, the persecutor **(v. 14)**
   2. Do not repay evil for evil **(v. 17)**
   3. Leave all vengeance to God. It corrupts us; it cannot corrupt Him **(v. 19)**.
B. Christ's goodness is the only power that can swallow up, or overcome, evil **(v. 21)**.
   1. Rejoice with rejoicers, for it doubles joy; weep with weepers, for it halves the suffering **(v. 15)**.
   2. Giving up one's pride promotes harmony, even among Christians of lower position **(vv. 16, 18)**.
   3. Christ rescues your enemy by putting His agape-love to work through you.
      a) If he is hungry, feed him; if thirsty, give drink **(v. 20)**.
      b) Christ's agape-love, not vengeance, acts as burning coals that may save the enemy **(v. 20)**.

SPECIAL NOTE

As a change of pace, seriously consider extending this session into two parts. As part two, we recommend the video *Truce in the Forest*, a powerful, true drama about Christians overcoming evil with good. Set during Christmas Eve, 1944, during the Battle of the Bulge, the story will give your students a vision of Christ's power of love. You may purchase or rent this 30-minute video cassette from Concordia Publishing House (VHS 87-0191).

GETTING INTO THE LESSON

Begin with prayer.

Revenge is so seductively delicious, especially when we have been innocently attacked, that we can taste it! Its powerful lure comes from the appearance that revenge is so right, so fair, so just; and a little twisting of the Old Testament ("Eye for eye, tooth for tooth!") can make it appear that even God would not dare hold us back from seeking sweet revenge!

Very likely this segment of Romans will prove most challenging to you, and you may expect your students to challenge you as you teach them, **"Do not repay anyone evil for evil"** (v. 17), and **"Do not be overcome by evil, but overcome evil with good" (v. 21).**

Begin the session by asking your students to tell you of cases of helpless human victims to some cruelty, big or small (e.g., the millions Jews and others who died at Hitler's hands). Agree with every reasonable case your students offer that, chances are, the victims were, indeed, powerless to stop the evil from hurting them. In this sense, the victims are helpless.

Then begin to question whether or not the victim is still helpless *after* the attack. Ask, **Doesn't the victim now have enormous power over the attacker? Doesn't the attacker owe the victim?** In a just society, the attacker may be answerable to a school official or to civil authorities. But even in an unjust society, the attacker will not always get by with evil. As silent as He may appear for now, God remains in control.

Now the victim has power—even at the present time! What will the victims do with their power over their attacker? Will they use that debt, that power to make their attacker pay? Or will they use that enormous power to forgive?

Let the students discuss their options for a few minutes. Then direct them to read the case of Brett, written in the Student Book.

IN THE WORD

Verses 14–21: Overcoming Evil with Good
(Objectives 1, 2, and 3)

A. The Danger: Evil Overcoming Us (Objective 1)

Allow your students to read through the initial paragraphs of this part of the session and then to prepare some answers to the questions by jotting down some notes.

Because most of your students know the "right answers," you may have to push them into admitting that they may not believe the right answers!

Question 1 allows your students to offer justifications for revenge. Write these justifications on the chalkboard. For example:

How would Brett ever get his honor back if he did not take on Jack? (On chalkboard, write, "Honor!")

Isn't Brett's case exactly like the theme of *Karate Kid*? (On chalkboard, write, "Justice!")

Question 2 may help to draw answers out that challenge the initial conclusions of question 1. The point is: Julie saw through all of Brett's justifications and saw that he had changed, that he had been overcome by evil. Let the students discuss how the desire for revenge can change any of us.

Question 3 seeks to show that being overcome by evil does not mean suffering from evil attacks. It means that we have been tainted or changed by evil and have become evil ourselves.

Question 4: Despite protests to the contrary, in principle, little or nothing would separate Brett's actions against Jack from Hitler's revenge against the major European powers. Hitler felt he was merely getting back for the suffering caused by Germany's surrender after World War I. But the Allied nations felt they were only getting back at Germany for beginning World War I. Evil never stops evil; it only brings on more evil.

If necessary, remind the students that the question asks "If Brett were suddenly thrust into a position of power. . . ." Brett's actions multiplied by power would bring havoc.

Question 5: The quotation is not from Scripture, but it was placed here for the purpose of debate. Encourage some students to try to disprove it. Ask why the thought of becoming like our enemy is so repugnant.

B. The Dilemma: Unstoppable Evil? (Objective 1)

This section is meant to bring to the surface one more justification for revenge that sounds terribly convincing: "If we obey God's Word in **Rom. 12,** evil will go on a rampage, and nothing, not even God, will stop it!" Cunningly, it puts God on the defensive (or seems to!), making Him ultimately responsible for evil, since He does not permit us to take justice into our own hands.

Humorously, you may now play the strange role of being devil's advocate for God. Again, push your students to see the basic illogic of this fear: God, on the side of evil? Ask your students to consider the source of that notion. It is not the throne of grace!

It is a satanic ploy to present evil as so powerful that it is unstoppable unless we pay back evil for evil. God still sits on the throne; He's still in control, as **verse 19** strongly hints.

Evil is stoppable—but not by further evil. Evil can

be swallowed up, or overcome, but only by Someone who can take it on to Himself.

If the role of government comes into question, you may point out that there is a difference between justice and revenge and that governments were established by God to execute justice. Defer questions on this until the next session.

C. The Defense: Only Christ's Undefeatable Good (Objective 2)

Allow your students to read this section and to research the Bible texts. They show that only Jesus Christ can stop evil, because only He is good enough. This is not at all funny, when it comes to overcoming evil. This is a job for the only Super Man, i.e. the God-Man, Jesus Christ.

1. Each Biblical text shows an incident in Jesus' passion where He returned evil for good and thereby swallowed up evil.

Mark 15:3–5: Jesus is silent before His lying accusers in Pilate's court.

Luke 22:47–51: Two blows of evil were hurled against Jesus: betrayal and arrest. Jesus returns with two acts of agape-love: friendship and healing.

a. Notice Jesus' action to Judas's evil and compare this with His comments in **Matt. 26:50.** He still calls Judas, "Friend"!

b. When His disciples react against evil with evil violence, Jesus reprimands them and heals Malchus's ear.

Luke 23:33–34: The best for last! From the cross comes the ultimate defeat of hell and evil, Jesus' classic and powerful Word: "Father, forgive them!"

2. Help students see the incredible "why" behind Jesus' returning forgiveness and goodness for evil. He really means to save His enemies! Why? He loves them. Why? We can give no "reasonable" answer for that; God's love does not make sense to us. Thank God, it doesn't have to!

3. Challenge the thought that revenge is a powerful tool. Actually, revenge is the tool of the weak, and that is why it is so evident in our world today. Love and forgiveness take superhuman, supernatural power, which only God has. The unbelieving world might see this nowhere except in Christ's faithful people today.

D. Cross Purposes (Objective 3)

The referral back to **Rom. 6:1–7** shows that God makes the impossible possible. Not only did Christ Jesus die for His enemies, He invites us to do the same. Point out that those who feel like saying, "It'll kill me to love those who hate me," found a most accurate description of the process! The old nature that wants to get even is precisely what is killed-off daily in repentance and forgiveness! By the gift of Baptism, God has planted the new (Christ) nature in us. And this is His power working in us to share Jesus' work: loving enemies into the kingdom of God.

Students may need your guidance to reach the amazing thing God is up to here. Remember, once the attack is done on us, victims have tremendous power over their enemies. We can vengefully hate them and contribute to their condemnation. Or we can forgive them, and (so to speak) contribute as instruments of Christ to rescue them. In ways that no one else can, victims can best play the role of Jesus Christ and thus witness to the Gospel, acting it out in their own lives.

Question 3 refers to **verse 20,** which shows some practical ways in which to love our enemies and thus rescue them.

Point out that in the Jewish custom of that day eating and drinking with another person was the second-most-intimate thing one could do. No one ate and drank with enemies, until Jesus ate with sinners.

"You will heap burning coals on his head" cannot mean a subtle form of vengeance. The context of **Rom. 12:14–21** prevents us from falling to that conclusion. Taken from the Old Testament, the meaning must be closer to what we mean by the "burning desire" of love for someone. Perhaps it means "melting someone's hate."

Ask students to imagine agape-loving an enemy as fiercely as they love their steady girlfriend or boyfriend. If that surprises them, imagine how much more it would surprise their enemy!

Session 38: Citizenship

BIBLE BASIS
Rom. 13:1–7

CENTRAL TRUTH

God has established civil government to maintain social peace and justice. Therefore a government's authority comes from God, whether or not that government recognizes God's authority. As God's people, we are called to give honor, respect, and duty to government for the one in authority is God's servant.

When human authorities run into conflict with God's authority, however, we, like the apostles, are called to **"obey God rather than men"** (Acts 4:18–21; 5:29).

OBJECTIVES

By the grace of God the students will

1. demonstrate their understanding of obedience to the authority of the government as obedience to God;
2. explain how government officials are God's servants who work (knowingly or not) for God's purpose in promoting peace and justice on the earth;

3. identify points of conflict between human authority and God's authority when they occur and demonstrate the faith of a true Christian disciple to "obey God rather than men."

OUTLINE OF ROM. 13:1–7

A. God's people are called to honor and obey the civil government **(vv. 1–5)**
   1. Because all authority comes from God **(v. 1)**
   2. Those who rebel against civil authority rebel against God **(v. 2)**
   3. The government is God's servant to
      a) Implement God's will **(v. 2)**
      b) Reward and protect good conduct **(v. 3)**
      c) Punish evildoers **(v. 4)**
B. Therefore, in response to Christ, Christians are to pay their dues to civil government **(vv. 5–7)**
   1. We pay our taxes and revenues as opportunities to serve God **(vv. 6–7a)**
   2. We give our respect and honor as opportunities to serve God **(v. 7b)**.

GETTING INTO THE LESSON

Begin with prayer.

Things are not always what they seem. That corrupt politician in Washington, the bureaucratic official in your county courthouse, the hard-nosed cop patrolling your favorite highway may not look at all like a servant of God, but that is precisely what he or she is! And if that is a hard pill for us, the servants of God, to swallow, imagine how your students may choke on it.

Despite the way we may feel about it, the apostle still writes, **"Everyone must submit himself to the governing authorities, for there is no authority except that which God has established" (Rom. 13:1).**

Begin the session by asking your students to read through Case 1 (of William Kent) and Case 2 (of Sölveg Segezha), two scenarios presenting young people in conflict. Use this exercise to help students think through (on the basis of **Rom. 13:1–7**) a Christian's duty to government. Give the students time to draw their conclusions before opening the question for class discussion.

IN THE WORD
Rom. 13:1–7

A. Called to Honor and Obey
(Objectives 1, 2, and 3)

1. Do not allow the Case of William Kent to be oversimplified. Many of your students may believe Kent should join the American Revolution against the British government simply because we have been taught that it was justified. **Rom. 13:1–7**, however, calls our simplified justifications into question.

Suggest to the students that there be a mock (and fun!) debate on the issue facing William Kent. Ask for their answers as to what Kent should do. Ask the students to defend their answers. Ask upon what laws or principles they are resting their case.

Push the students here, especially if you sense they are too quickly concluding that the cause for American independence was "right." You may ask, **Right according to what or whom? Scripture? Wasn't the king of Great Britain the rightful ruler over the colonies? Then wouldn't rebellion against the king be rebellion against God, too?**

You may need to take the other side, too, especially if no students are volunteering to take up the American cause. Ask, **Which government, the Pennsylvania legislature or the British crown, had the authority from God? Does Scripture support the "divine right" of kings to rule? Did not Pennsylvania (and the other colonies) have a legal charter from the British government to govern that colony? Didn't King George III's new tax laws violate that original charter? Some of the colonies had been nearly self-governing for over 150 years; didn't that fact mean something to the British crown and parliament? And didn't the Magna Carta extend also to colonists?**

The debate should not lead to a clear conclusion for one side or the other. Simply illustrate, as colorfully as you can, that Christians cannot be swayed by popular notions (of either side of an issue) in choice making. William Kent, as well as your students, must use only God's Word to reach their conclusions.

In the case of the American Revolution, once it can be determined who was established by God (the colonial government or the British government) the following choices become much more clear. Kent would have to follow one or the other. Ask your students, **What if William Kent made a mistake in choice?** Be sure to point out that he would have the invitation from Christ to repent and receive forgiveness.

2. The Case of Sölveg Segezha is much different than Kent's. Remind your students that for a Soviet citizen, the U.S.S.R. is the legitimate government established by God, notwithstanding that the Marxists came to power through a bloody and corrupt revolution. The Soviets justify their revolution as many Americans justify ours— without God's Word.

Nevertheless, that makes little difference. **"The authorities that exist have been established by God" (Rom. 13:1).** Just as one cannot Scripturally justify a rebellion against the United States government, neither can a Soviet citizen justify a rebellion against that government.

Agree, as much as possible, with students who may protest these points, and listen closely to what they say while examining it all by **Rom. 13**. Simply because a government may be atheistic does not justify a rebellion. Point out that Paul wrote this letter to the Roman Christians, and one day soon he would be in Rome himself—in prison. Eventually, Paul would be executed and martyred for the faith. But Paul never advocated rebellion against Rome.

Sölveg's case, however, is not so much open rebellion as it is possible disobedience. Ask, **What happens when a government, a Soviet government or our own, creates laws which counter God's Word? What would you do if you were in Solveg's situation?**

B. Caesar or God?

1. Jesus would not involve Himself in this debate because, first of all, it was a trap set for Him by His enemies. Either way He answered, His enemies would use His testimony to accuse Him. Had Jesus answered in favor of Caesar, the Pharisees would accuse Him of heresy. Had He answered in favor of God, they would have had no scruples against charging Jesus with conspiracy to overthrow Rome. As a matter of record, they did just this when they finally brought Jesus before Pilate.

But more importantly, Jesus was not going to be distracted or diverted from His real mission. He came to save us from the penalty of our sin and to bring us into the kingdom of heaven. Human politics was not Jesus' purpose; human souls were.

2. Jesus' statement is fairly clear. Encourage your students to explain it more fully and allow them to test their study of Scripture with others. God has allowed and sanctioned human governments to provide for good order in human society. He will judge human leaders as to whether or not they were faithful in their offices. As King of kings, Jesus delegated this responsibility to human governments. And He is not in competition with His own servants, whether or not governmental servants realize they are serving God.

3. This section calls for a Biblical example of God who is still in control, ussing even corrupt or pagan civil authorities for His divine purposes. A few examples to help stimulate the students' remembering may include:

- Belshazaar and the Babylonian Empire fall to Darius, king of the Medes **(Dan. 6)**. God's covenant people will soon be released from their captivity, and some will return to Jerusalem and Judah.
- The young Israelite, Joseph, interprets Pharaoh's dream and ascends to a position of authority in the empire. In that way God uses the Egyptian empire and its pharaoh to feed and protect the children of Israel during famine **(Gen. 42)**.
- God uses the mighty Roman Empire and its emperor, Augustus, to bring Mary down from Nazareth to Bethlehem. Augustus, by issuing the order for a tax-census, actually becomes God's agent to fulfill a prophecy: that the Messiah would be born in the royal city of King David **(Luke 2)**.

C. When Caesar Plays God (Objectives 1, 2, and 3)

Acts 4:18–21 and **5:25–29** are vital for an understanding of the limits of government's authority. Governments have authority from God, but if they use that authority to force us to disobey God, we "must obey God rather than men."

That still does not give us the right to rebel. It gives us only the right to disobey. Ask, **Will there be consequences for our disobedience to government?** Your students will probably agree that there will be consequences. These consequences, however, are part of the cross carrying that some Christians must carry; especially Christians in Marxist countries.

Sölveg had to face the very real situation of helping to smuggle the Bible into her country. That would have been discipleship to Jesus Christ, and it may have been a costly one for her. Point out, however, that she could rely on our faithful Lord to uphold her throughout the ordeal. Ask your students, if they were Sölveg, and were arrested, how would knowing that they had been faithful to Christ give them strength—and even joy?

Sometimes rulers do forget the limits of their authority. Write out on the chalkboard the principle: *Forbidding what God commands, and commanding what God forbids is an inexcusable abuse of authority.* Ask your students, **What possible conflicts between God's law and human law might one face in America today?**

Follow, but do not be tied down to, the questions in the Student Book for discussion.

Session 39: Wake Up

BIBLE BASIS
Rom. 13:8–14

CENTRAL TRUTH

Since Christians are in and surrounded by a sin-darkened society, we can easily fall into a sleepy insensibility towards immorality—even in ourselves. We are called, however, to wake up, arm ourselves with the Word, and remembering our baptism, clothe ourselves with Christ.

OBJECTIVES

By the grace of God the students will

1. identify paying our debts with loving our neighbor;
2. recognize that spiritual slumbering fogs our vision of ourselves as Christ's redeemed people;
3. use the power of the Word and Sacraments to wake up to the opportunities we have as people clothed in Christ.

OUTLINE OF ROM. 13:8–14

A. Love is the fulfilling of the Law **(vv. 8–10)**

1. Love is the only debt we should owe our fellow man **(v. 8)**
2. Love harms no one; it's the summing up of the Ten Commandments **(vv. 9–10)**

B. The day is near. Wake up! **(vv. 11–14)**
   1. Slumbering through the darkness of sin must end **(vv. 11–13)**
      a) Alerted to society's immorality
      b) Alerted to our own
   2. Putting on the armor of light empowers us to put aside the deeds of darkness **(v. 12)**
      a) "Darkness," from orgies to jealousies, gratifies only sinful nature **(vv. 13–15)**
      b) "Darkness" blinds us to the reality of the day Jesus returns.

C. Clothe yourself with the Lord Jesus Christ **(v. 14)**
   1. He already clothed us with His new life **(6:4)**
   2. In this way, we prepare for His return

A WORD FROM THE AUTHOR

Often a teacher, particularly a young teacher, has great confidence in his (or her) ability to coach an athletic team or teach an academic subject, and yet is very insecure about being able to effectively teach religion. Certainly teaching the precepts of God to His lambs can be an intimidating experience, but it is a labor that God asks us to undertake with absolute confidence, confidence in Him and in ourselves. We can have that confidence because God really does work in and through us.

Just before Jesus ascended into heaven, He told his disciples, **"You will receive power when the Holy Spirit comes on you" (Acts 1:8).** As you remember from session 2, the Greek word for power is *dunamis*, from which we derive the words *dynamic* and *dynamite*. We defeat ourselves when we attempt to obey Jesus' command to witness without trusting His promise to provide the dynamics. Our power source is the Holy Spirit working in and through the Word. Personally, I'm relieved when I realize that the responsibility for equipping the saints is not mine, but the Spirit's. As I dwell in the Word, the Spirit enables and empowers me to be His tool. God intends that we rest secure in His power. This is dynamite.

GETTING INTO THE LESSON

Begin with prayer.

This segment of Romans takes a definite line of direction. From our relationship to the government and paying our taxes **(13:1–7)**, to paying our personal debts **(13:8)**, to our duties to our fellow humans **(13:9–10)**. It may seem, then, like an incredible jump to speak of our Lord's promised return and the exhortation for Christians to wake up out of spiritual slumber, but it is not.

The apostle Paul is only pointing out that Christians, while in the world, are not of the world. Therefore we must not allow the false securities of the world to lure us into a spiritual fog. Our Lord Jesus will return, and we must act on that promise. How? Not by being slack in our obligations to our neighbors, but by faithfully fulfilling our responsibilities. Not by conforming to the immoralities of the worldlings, but by arming ourselves with the Word and clothing ourselves in Christ.

The danger always lurks for teachers to become moralistic and perfectionistic when these teachings about the Christian life appear in Scripture. The tendency is to teach, "If you are a Christian, then this is what you will do! You will pay your debts. You will not fall into sexual immorality!" And, of course, that is true. The law of God is always true.

But the law of God does not give us (pastor, teacher, or student) the power, desire, or motivation to fulfill the Law! The Law exposes and provokes sin. The Gospel alone provides the power for salvation **(1:16)**, and the Gospel alone provides the motivation to do God's will. As a help for understanding, you may wish to guide your students back to session 18 **(Rom. 7:7–25)** and the story of Carla. Ask the students to recall what motivated clumsy Carla to become a runner.

IN THE WORD

Verses 8–10: Love, the Fulfilling of the Law
(Objective 1)

Lead the students through this section of Scripture, guiding them to see that there is only one debt that is good to keep: to love. Paying our financial debts off is faithfulness to Christ, because it is one way of showing love and concern for others—Christian or non-Christian ("fellowman" in **v. 8** makes clear our obligation to both).

Likewise, by listing four of the commandments from the Mosaic law, Paul is showing that all the commandments of God can be boiled down to love.

Have your students define love in their own ways. Write some of their definitions on the chalkboard or on newsprint until you come up with a composite definition. Then target who should be loved—who is our neighbor? This may help students work through the exercises in this section.

Verses 11–14: The Day Is Near. Wake Up!
(Objective 2)

Many Christians are in spiritual slumber, or else Paul would not have sounded the alarm. As it usually goes, however, those most deeply in the slumber or fog may be the last ones to know it. Sometimes it takes a jolt, like Paul's, to arouse us out of our sense of comfort. Guide your students to realize that the best way to measure whether we ourselves have slipped into slumber is to measure ourselves by the Word spoken here. This is what the activity in the Student Book is designed to help your class do.

1. The cause for urgency is our Lord's imminent return on the world's last day. Every day brings us closer to that day when the world, and everything we know of it, will utterly vanish. If our desires center only

on this world, we will end up empty-handed, to say the least.

2. Paul zeroes in on evil desires, many having to do with immoral sexual gratification. Unfortunately, that may be the very problem for a number of your students, and you may be speaking to some who are in that spiritual fog. Don't dwell, however, only on sexual sins. Anything that lures, or attracts, our hearts away from Christ—whether it is good or bad—gets in God's way. A perfectly happy husband and wife, if so drawn into themselves and not into Christ, are also in a spiritual slumber. Why? Because they are self-content.

The student activity with the contrasting columns is designed to lead your students to open themselves to the Word and see God calling them out of their slumber. Encourage your students to use somebody other than themselves as the example. Ask for examples—both for the "deeds of darkness" and for the "armor of light." Encourage your students to see the contrasts as God's Word sees them.

3. **Why are the world's promises so attractive?** Ask your students to share their opinions. They may have some deep insights to share. To help the class move into the subject (if no one is volunteering to begin), ask someone to compare what Paul is talking about to someone on dope or crack. Isn't being on crack or other similar drugs a slumber of sorts? Why do some people get hooked on it? like it? find it hard to get off of it? Being on drugs brings out the worst in people. Why? Although it causes untold heartache, especially among loved ones, why doesn't the addicted person admit it?

4. God provides the power to pull us out of the spiritual fog. Christ says that He chose us out of the world (see **John 15:19**), and the Holy Spirit called us by the Gospel. We can be certain that God will use His redeeming, rescuing power. He already has—in our baptism.

Verse 14: Clothe Yourself with Christ
(Objective 3)

Leading the students through this section will help them to bring the Gospel into focus. If the words, "clothe yourself with Christ" was merely a command, we would have to despair. We don't have what it takes.

Paul refers to the same picture in **Gal. 3:27,** and the Student Book directs the class to study that text.

1. The Galatians text makes it clear that we were clothed (note passive) in our baptism. Ask your students to share their baptismal birthdays.

2. The question really calls students to answer the question, "What does being a child of God mean to me?" Listen to their answers and encourage students to take heart in the Gospel: despite who they are or what fogs they are in, through the Gospel the Holy Spirit has reached out with love for them. The atoning work of Jesus gives them the status as "sons of God." That provides the power that enables us to go on. Let your students express this in their own words.

3. The example of Carla might give hope to the students who have difficulty seeing themselves as God's people. Approached from this way, Paul's words to "clothe yourself with Christ" is an invitation to live in our baptismal covenant.

Session 40: The "Weaker Brother"

BIBLE BASIS
  Rom. 14:1–12

CENTRAL TRUTH
  Paul warns against dividing the church over non-Biblical issues. Often those who are weak in faith hold rigid views about nonessential or human matters. Others, those strong in the faith, may view the former group of Christians with contempt. Christ's death empowers us to love fellow Christians instead of judging them.

OBJECTIVES
By the grace of God the students will
1. describe Paul's solutions for dealing with a "weaker brother";
2. demonstrate their ability to discern essential truths from nonessential opinions;
3. identify examples of adiaphora they are likely to run up against;
4. display an attitude of love (instead of judgment) towards fellow Christians.

OUTLINE OF ROM. 14:1–12
A. Who is a "weaker brother"? **(vv. 1–6)**
   1. One who sets limits that God does not set
      a) Diet **(vv. 2–3)**
      b) Holy days **(v. 6)**
   2. One who is threatened with his Christian liberty
B. Live with the "weaker brother" for the Lord's sake **(vv. 7–12)**
   1. Because none of us lives to ourselves **(vv. 7–8)**
   2. Because Christ died for him **(v. 9)**
   3. Because God will judge us both **(vv. 10–12)**

A WORD FROM THE AUTHOR
  "When the Spirit of truth comes, He will guide you into all truth" (John 16:13).
  As teachers of the Word, our principal function is to lead the student into the Word so that the Holy Spirit can do the teaching. The religion teacher is a pedagogue in the purest sense of the word. For Greek and Romans boys, the *paidagogos* was not their teacher so much as he was their guide and protector. He would

take them to the teacher, sit with them, see that they paid attention, and, after escorting them home, would help them with their homework.

The role of the religion teacher is surprisingly similar to the *paidagogos*. We lead the students to the Spirit and the Word, allow the Spirit to do His work, and then help the students understand what they are learning. The Spirit is the Teacher; we are the *paidagogi*. He is the Tutor; we are the servants who escort the students through the streets to meet Him. He is the Motivator; we are more like the facilitators. And it's best not to get our role mixed up with His role. In other words, He will be the One doing the teaching, faith building, and the changing. In His own good time.

Trusting the Holy Spirit to do His work will make our work much easier.

GETTING INTO THE LESSON

Begin with prayer.

In the preceding chapters Paul taught us who and how to love. In **chapter 14** we face the reality that too often our capacity to love is most severely tested among our Christian brothers and sisters. The "weaker brother's" judgmental, holier-than-thou attitude and the stronger brother's contempt for legalism produce an atmosphere more conducive to division than devotion. The apostle realized that the issues about which he wrote were not as much theological as they were attitudinal. The crucial problem that needed to be addressed was the negative responses of the groups to one another.

IN THE WORD

Verses 1–6: Who Is the "Weaker Brother"?
(Objective 1)

Paul set forth several principles that we must consistently remember and apply as we deal with one another. The following guidelines show how two factions who disagree on the "nonessentials" of the Christian faith can live in harmony.

1. Because we are justified freely by grace alone, we can take the correct view on the nonessentials (adiaphora): the stronger Christians have the responsibility to accept the weaker, and the weaker can surrender their judgmental attitudes towards the stronger. The stronger Christian may even help others towards the day when they also may enjoy more fully the freedom of the Gospel.

2. All Christians are under the same Head **(v. 4)**, Jesus Christ. Because we are all servants of the one Master, we do not have the authority to condemn other believers. Only the Lord has the right to evaluate the practices of His people. We are accountable to Christ, not to other Christians.

3. Christians should be fully convinced of their position **(vv. 5– 6)**. We should be as certain as possible that whatever position we hold on nonessential issues is consistent with what we know about the Lord Jesus.

Verses 7–12: Harmony for the Lord's Sake
(Objectives 2, 3, and 4)

1. In the area of spiritual freedom and Scriptural silence, some believers are intimidated. They would much prefer to have everything spelled out in black and white so they know what the rules are.

Paul's only hint of criticism is in the use of the word *weaker*. He did not argue about the rules they developed for their own lives as long as what they did was compatible with the Lordship of Jesus. He was concerned, however, about the weaker believers exercising a kind of tyranny over the others by forcing their legalism upon the whole body.

Have your students read **Acts 15** to see how easily this can happen. Weaker believers tend to criticize those who exercise their freedom, and the stronger Christians too often react with utter contempt for those who are weaker.

Criticism and contempt were equally unacceptable to Paul, and he deals with both in **verse 10**. To the weaker he says, "Why do you judge your brother?" and to the stronger he says, "Why do you look down on your brother?"

2. This activity can be done as class discussion. If your students are slow in getting started, give them a few examples. Some Christians believe that drinking any alcoholic beverage is wrong. Point out that, from a purely Biblical view, it is not possible to argue against drinking in moderation. Paul even seems to endorse the use of wine for medicinal purposes in **1 Tim. 5:23**. On the other hand, though, the Bible does warn against abuse of alcohol, and alcoholism has become a serious problem in the United States. Therefore one may find good reason for total abstinence.

Other areas of adiaphora that trouble some Christians are smoking, movies, dancing, the wearing of makeup, and proper dress for church. Some Roman Catholics still cannot bring themselves to eat meat on Friday.

3. Unfortunately, on too many occasions in the history of the church, these matters have resulted in selfish feuds rather than in selfless acts of love.

Weave throughout your teaching that Jesus Christ provides the real basis for our unity. Under Him we all have the same status as the redeemed children of God. Encourage students to provide very concrete examples of ways people handle an issue. Point to the power we receive from the Gospel **(v. 9)** to respond in love instead of judgment **(vv. 8 and 10)**.

Session 41: The "Stronger Brother"

BIBLE BASIS
Rom. 14:13–23

CENTRAL TRUTH

Those who are strong in faith know they may enjoy Christian liberty and do not need to submit to human regulations for salvation. Strong Christians, however, are also called on to act in Christ's love so they do not hurt or offend the weak. We may rejoice because God gives us the power to show such love.

OBJECTIVES

By the grace of God the students will
1. demonstrate a distinction between God's law and human rules;
2. develop Scripture-based principles that support living in the freedom of the Gospel while at the same time loving those with a weaker faith;
3. explain the Gospel paradox that we are at the same time free lords and dutiful servants;
4. demonstrate an understanding of Biblical paradox.

OUTLINE OF ROM. 14:13–23

A. Strong Christians
  1. Should not let Christian liberty be a stumbling block for others
  2. Know that, of themselves, all foods are clean and all things are permitted **(vv. 14, 20, 23)**
      a) But for weaker Christians, some foods are unclean if they regard them as unclean **(v. 14)**
      b) If stronger Christians distress the weaker by flaunting their liberties, they are not acting in love **(v. 15)**
  3. Are called on to love the brother as one for whom Christ died
      a) Therefore do not destroy the brother by free eating **(v. 15)**
      b) Do not flaunt Christian liberty so that others will think ill of it **(v. 16)**
  4. Are blessed
      a) When they keep their Christian liberty as a private matter between them and God **(v. 22)**
      b) When they are led to express (or not express) their Christian liberty by faith in God and by their love for the brother **(vv. 22–23)**
B. The kingdom of God is a matter of righteousness, peace, and joy **(vv. 17–23)**
  1. Not of eating and drinking; these are minor matters **(v. 17)**
  2. Work then to build up the weak in Kingdom matters **(v. 19)**
      a) Avoid destroying God's work on account of minor matters **(v. 20)**
      b) Find that it would be better to refrain from liberties than to cause the brother to fall **(v. 21)**

A WORD FROM THE AUTHOR

"When I came to you, brothers, I did not come with eloquence or superior wisdom as I proclaimed to you the testimony about God" (1 Cor. 2:1).

The apostle Paul was one of the most highly educated men of his day, fully versed in rhetoric and debate in the fashion of the classical Greeks. Yet here, Paul claims not to rely on any of his rhetorical skills, but in a straightforward manner said, **"I resolved to know nothing while I was with you except Jesus Christ and Him crucified" (v. 2).** The persuasive logic or clever debate tactics of the Greeks would not bring Christ crucified to the Corinthians. That would happen by the power of God the Holy Spirit **(vv. 4–5)**. I find no small amount of comfort there for us who teach God's Word!

Yet another point from Paul which attracts teachers' attention waves to us from **verse 3**, where the apostle writes, **"I came to you in weakness and fear, and with much trembling."**

Fear? In the mighty Paul?

Perhaps Paul's anxieties stem from the same things that intimidate us. When we focus on the enormity of our calling, on our weaknesses and unworthiness, fear and trembling are the only possible responses.

Yet, in a sense, the feelings of personal inadequacies might even be healthy if they compel us to do just what Paul did: trust the Spirit to accomplish through us what no amount of human training can ever equip us to do.

GETTING INTO THE LESSON (Objective 4)

Begin with prayer.

Read through the introductory material in the Student Book. Point out that, while there may be other definitions of paradox, we will use the definition given in their book. Proceed, then, to ask the students to resolve the four paradoxes listed. To help get the class started, you might help them with the first paradox:

1. *Poor/Rich:* Hardly anybody in our American society thinks they are rich, but in fact, by the world's standards most of us are. Your students may feel they are nearly broke. Ask, however, how many of them drove to school in their own cars? How many of them live in homes owned by their parents or guardians? have several meals a day? have closets and dressers rather full of clothing? In addition, if your students are

mostly middle class or higher, they are among the 10 percent wealthiest people in the world.

2. *Kid/Adult:* What youth hasn't felt this paradox? Let your students express their feelings as to how they have felt both ways at the same time.

3. *Dumb/Smart:* This remark was overheard once in reference to a simple man who seemingly did not possess great intelligence. Yet he kept his life simple, uncluttered, and uncomplicated by the fast-paced living of our society. Eventually he was seen as one of the best managers of his time, finances, and stewardship to our Lord. Use your own example to illustrate this paradox to your students.

4. *Smart/Dumb:* We all know or have heard about people of such brilliance that they have no common sense and can barely function normally in a practical everyday world. Ask the students to share experiences (but no names) if they have witnessed this paradox.

Moving to Scriptural paradoxes, the Student Book explains that many of the key doctrines of the Bible are, in fact, paradoxes. Help your students through the activity:

1. *Weak/Strong:* Paul, **2 Cor. 12:10.** Paul recognizes his own weaknesses, but this moves him to depend on Christ's strength.

2. *Mourners/Comforted:* Jesus, **Matt. 5:4.** Those who cry over their condition will find, in Christ, tears wiped away.

3. *Save/Lose:* Jesus, **Matt. 16:25.** Holding out ourselves from Christ will result only in our eternal loss; but Christ invites us by His Gospel to give ourselves up to Him, and thus we will be rescued.

4. *Live/Die:* Jesus, **John 11:25.** Spoken to Martha at the death of her brother, Lazarus, Jesus assures that He will give victory over death to all believers. Lazarus's case was an immediate example.

5. *Sinner/Saint:* Paul, **Rom. 7:18–25.** Even Christians have the old nature still rebelling; but the new nature planted in us at Baptism makes each of us redeemed by Christ, therefore a saint.

6. *Foolishness/Wisdom:* Paul, **1 Cor. 1:25.** To the unbeliever, it does look foolish that God would rescue us in such a way as grace. But the world's wisdom will never understand God's "foolish" love.

Briefly review some of the other Biblical paradoxes that can be found in Scripture's teachings. Be sure to ask your students to mention other paradoxes.

Background

Have your students read through this section of the Student Book so that they may begin to grasp the controversy faced by the church in Rome. The strong believers now had to ask what to do with their Christian liberty. The paradox, of course, was that the strong Christian appeared weak, and the weak Christian appeared strong.

It's Not Sin Just Because Someone Calls It Sin
(Objectives 1 and 2)

1. Allow the students free discussion on this question. You might wish to move the discussion towards speaking about our Christian love for the "weaker brother." Would we give up some liberties for someone we loved? Are there times when we could enjoy our Christian liberties and not offend the weaker Christian?

2. Some activities today are considered as sin by some and not by others, and activities Scripture neither commands nor forbids might be either. Dancing, drinking alcoholic beverages (if one is of legal age!), wearing makeup, listening to rock music (ask, **What kind of rock?**) or smoking might start out the list. Be sure to ask students for their own suggestions.

Guide the students through (a), which asks who considers what to be sin. Be sure to keep urging students back to Scripture as the sole norm and guide on this point.

The following questions will probably provide a good, hearty debate in your class:

"Is gambling-as-recreation a liberty that a Christian can take?" This question can take on more interesting aspects if you reside where there is a state-operated lottery.

"How much liberty can a high school Christian take on a date? Where are the lines drawn for showing love and affection? What is a God-pleasing dating relationship?"

3. The pogo-stick jumping example is, admittedly, ridiculous, but it is meant to draw students away from heated and emotional issues in order to develop Scriptural principles objectively. Encourage the students to write out some principles to determine what is within the bounds of Christian liberty, and what is not. Ask students to volunteer their findings, and write some of them on the chalkboard or on newsprint.

When No One Says It's Sin, but It Is!
(Objectives 1 and 2)

The "sin against one's conscience" is difficult not only for high school students, but for more adult Christians, too. Paul knows from Jesus Himself that nothing is unclean or unholy by itself (and he is speaking of kosher and nonkosher food, specifically). It only becomes unclean when a person believes it to be so.

Paul aims his comments here at the strong Christians who have a weak Christian "brother" beside them and who may easily fall into a serious mistake. A weak "brother" may believe or feel something not forbidden by Scripture is still forbidden him. This belief could be due to something in his or her own mind, or it could be due to some fear, ignorance, faulty thinking, misinformed ideas about others, and so on. A weak Christian may believe that any Christian who drinks alcoholic beverages is an alcoholic. This person is not only misinformed but may be reacting emotionally. Why? Perhaps the weak Christian grew up under an alcoholic parent or was raised in a denomination in which drinking was seen as one of the worst sins a human could possibly commit.

Freed or Enslaved? The Paradoxical Answer
(Objective 3)

Pietistic church bodies have added so many DOs and DON'Ts to Christian life-styles that for some people Christianity is little more than "Rules to Live By." Rather than living under the Gospel, many are running back to the Law. If you have time, you may ask your students to offer opinions why such legalistic approaches to Christianity are so popular today.

Ask the students to read through this section in the Student Book. Help them become aware of the dangerous lure of legalism in our relationships with weaker Christians. Although, out of Christian love, we do not wish to do anything to offend the "weaker brother," at the same time we cannot allow ourselves to be manipulated into following human regulations. We find an answer to this tension in Luther's great paradoxical statement, which is part of his treatise of 1521, "The Freedom of the Christian."

Session 42: God-Given Unity

BIBLE BASIS
Rom. 15:1–13

CENTRAL TRUTH
True unity in the church comes to us as God's gift. He desires all believers to praise Him with one heart and mind. The Holy Spirit works this kind of unity in God's people as He encourages us through His Word.

OBJECTIVES
By the grace of God students will
1. repent for times they have selfishly failed to build others up, choosing instead to please themselves;
2. define true Christian unity and seek the Spirit's help as they work toward that unity within their own school and congregation;
3. accept other believers and bear with their weaknesses in a spirit of true Christian servanthood.

OUTLINE OF ROM. 15:1–13
A. The responsibility of the mature (vv. 1–7)
   1. Bear one another's burdens (**Gal. 6:1–2**)
   2. Please our neighbors; build others up
   3. Christ, our ultimate example
   4. God's equipping power
   5. The goal: God's glory
   6. Accepting one another
B. Unity produced by God (vv. 8–13)
   1. Unity based on God's truth
   2. Jews and Gentiles united to God's glory
   3. All believers receive joy, peace, and hope from God

A WORD FROM THE AUTHOR
We live in an age in which educators of foresight share some justifiable concerns about being replaced by computers. Indeed, some computer technologists steadfastly maintain that by the year A.D. 2000, teaching machines will be doing the job of the classroom teacher—more efficiently and more economically than humans now do it.

Whether this claim will prove to be true or pan out to be mostly science fiction, teachers of God's Word can stand secure in the knowledge that they have job security. The Christian teacher is irreplaceable for the simple reason that God Himself has chosen human beings as the means by which He shares His life-giving plan of salvation.

If I were ever tempted to question the wisdom of God, it would be on this point. How could God entrust a task of such eternal consequence to flawed and incompetent human beings? But the fact is that He did; and since He did, we must trust that He will also provide the grace and power we need to accomplish the task. As a Christian teacher, I feel a great sense of awe because God has equipped me and included me as a participant in His grand scheme!

GETTING INTO THE LESSON
(Objectives 1 and 2)

Begin the session with prayer.

Judging from Paul's comments in **Rom. 12–14**, we can deduce that at least two elements of schism had arisen in the Roman church. Apparently a strong group of Gentile believers and an equally influential group of Jewish believers, each holding opposing views, had begun to threaten the unity of the congregation. Some points of contention may have been:

- **Rom. 12:3–8:** Selfish and arrogant use of spiritual gifts
- **Rom. 14:1–23:** Questions about Christian freedom as it applied to eating meat offered to idols; and in a more general way, the larger question of "strong" Christians offending their "weaker brothers" as they used their freedom in the Gospel

In addressing each issue, Paul urges the believers to be considerate and caring about one another's spiritual welfare. As the first verses of **Rom. 15** show, there will always be differences in background, convictions, and spiritual maturity—all of which can threaten the unity of the local congregation. In the verses that follow, the apostle outlines Biblical priciples for producing harmony without destroying variety of expression in nonessential matters.

If students did the dictionary study of the word

unity before class, share the results of that study now. If not, have dictionaries available, or copy the definitions on an overhead acetate sheet and display it for use by the class. Depending on the dictionary you use, the definitions and synonyms may shed further light on your students' understanding of this word. Keep the definition handy and refer to it later on in the class period whenever you think it might prove helpful.

As time permits, you might compare the dictionary definition with that found in a Bible dictionary. If you still have time, ask students to read Jesus' high priestly prayer from **John 17.** Talk about issues like: For what kind of unity did our Lord pray on the night before His death? What importance did He place on the unity of His body, the church? What implications does that have for us as we think about relationships with other people in our school or congregation?

IN THE WORD
Verses 1–7: The Responsibility of the Mature
(Objectives 1 and 2)

1. We all frequently act to please ourselves rather than acting for the good of our neighbors. This kind of selfishness and sinful independence accounts for most of the problems we experience in society. The church has, likewise, suffered down through history when members of the body adopted this kind of attitude. In **verses 1–2** the Holy Spirit exhorts us to center our concern on the needs of others.

Ask your students to read **Gal. 6:1–2.** Then ask them to explain what bearing one another's burdens means to them.

2. To see the ultimate example of a life-style devoted to the good of others, we must look, of course, to our Lord Jesus Christ. His entire life demonstrated the kind of care-filled, sacrificial living that sets the standard of behavior for all mature believers.

The quote from **Ps. 69** refers to Jesus' vicarious atonement for us. Our Lord enjoyed limitless glory and unbroken fellowship with His Father. But He descended to earth, became flesh, and made Himself vulnerable to the heartaches, frustrations, and pain human beings experience. He went so far as to suffer death for us. He willingly threw Himself between sinners and His holy Father to intercept the consequences we by our sin had deserved. These He bore in His own body to the cross. The insults we had deserved fell instead on our Savior.

3. Paul has just presented a striking passage from the Psalms to demonstrate His point. The power of this verse illustrates the point the apostle goes on to make in **verse 4:** the Holy Spirit uses His Word to work in us the endurance and courage we need as we practice the loving unity to which He calls us.

Precisely because the Scriptures give us such courage and endurance, it follows that we cannot compromise God's Word in a misguided attempt to create artificial unity of faith where it does not exist. Rather, our unity with other believers must be based upon the truths of God's Word, the authority of that Word, and the agreement the Spirit works through that Word.

4. Refer back to your definitions of unity as you talk about **verses 5–7.** When Paul prays that we will praise God with one heart and one mouth, he is not asking us to become a group of spiritual clones. Rather, we are to form a body of believers who have the same focal point for our lives—namely, Jesus Christ. The ultimate purpose for this unity is that we can render genuine, heartfelt praise to God without being distracted by trivial quibbling.

Verses 8–13: Unity Produced by God
(Objectives 1, 2, and 3)

1. Paul quotes Old Testament Scriptures that talk about all people—Jews and Gentiles alike—bringing true praise to God.

We can hardly imagine two groups that could have been much more opposite than these. The Jewish leaders of Paul's day were superreligious separatists with an infuriating arrogance about them. They maintained a narrow and rigorous belief in one God and adhered to a strict, legalistic code of behavior. The Gentiles, on the other hand, were by Jewish standards morally bankrupt. They seemingly enjoyed the relaxed, almost nonchalant attitude toward idolatry that their culture encouraged.

The two groups had one thing in common—their mutual animosity. And yet the Son of God united these two groups under the common bond of their Christian faith. Paul writes to encourage his readers to emulate Christ's servant role when necessary to preserve the unity He won for us by His suffering, death, and resurrection.

2. Without harmony among believers, we can expect little abiding joy, corporate peace, or lasting hope. However, where Christian unity is a reality and where God's people are using the Spirit's power to live in humility as servants for one another, then our Lord's promise of joy, peace, and hope also becomes a reality. The full power of the Holy Spirit is constantly at work in our lives to this end.

When the Rubber Meets the Road
(Objectives 1, 2, and 3)

The case studies in the Student Book have been designed to help your students think through some of the implications of Paul's words for their everyday lives.

If possible, assign students to one of three small groups. Assign one case study to each group. Ask that the students discuss the situations. Tell them to draft a list of actions that would increase disharmony in a given situation and a list of actions that could bring more unity. Then they should decide what course of action they would recommend to the people involved.

As time and your situation permit, ask the students to roleplay the situations and their solutions. Then open up the solution for discussion by the whole group.

How satisfactorily was the conflict resolved? What might the apostle Paul have said to each person involved in the situation? What better solutions might there be?

Obviously, there is no easy answer to any of the three stories. All of them represent the kinds of "sticky wickets" God's people sometimes encounter. Perhaps you or someone in the class has a real dilemma like these that you might like to discuss instead.

The key to solving all unity-threatening dilemmas involves God's people assuming a servant's role. God cares more about our heart's attitude than about whether we win or lose in a given situation. He is well able to vindicate His people. Of course, left to our own resources, we will act to please ourselves. Only as the Spirit works a servant's heart in each of us through His Word, will we be able to express the true unity that our Lord so desires for His body, the church.

Session 43: Personal Notes

BIBLE BASIS
Rom. 15:14–33

CENTRAL TRUTH
As Paul nears the end of his letter, he assures the Roman Christians of his confidence in their mature faith, shows his deep concern for a ministry to the Gentiles, and shares his faith that whatever he accomplished occurred by the power of God. He also shares with them his itinerary for the coming months and years and requests their prayers on his behalf.

OBJECTIVES
By the grace of God students will
1. identify the elements of a mature faith and examine their own lives for evidence of it;
2. express their support of mission work and how they plan to participate in church expansion;
3. affirm their reliance upon God's grace and power;
4. articulate the importance of personal prayer and prayer support in their lives.

OUTLINE OF ROM. 15:14–33
A. Personal care and ministry **(vv. 14–22)**
   1. Encouragement for the believers **(v. 14)**
      a) Full of goodness
      b) Complete in knowledge
      c) Competent to instruct one another
   2. Concern for ministry **(vv. 15–22)**
      a) Ministry to the Gentiles **(vv. 15–16)**
      b) Rooted in Jesus **(vv. 17–18)**
      c) Proclaimed Jesus **(vv. 19–21)**
B. Personal planning **(vv. 23–29)**
   1. To Jerusalem
      a) Contribution from Macedonia and Achaia **(vv. 26–27)**
      b) Desire to complete his task **(v. 28)**
   2. To Rome
   3. To Spain
C. Personal prayer **(vv. 30–33)**

A WORD FROM THE AUTHOR
The religion classroom can be exciting, but it can also be one of the most frustrating places in the world! Almost every religion teacher I have known has been a deeply committed, highly concerned individual. Far too many of them, however, have also been discouraged and frustrated. Some of them quit, and some of them quit caring. How can this happen? Sadly, if I am boring my class to tears, if they are falling asleep or studying for a biology exam, I can save my sanity and some vestige of self-esteem if I stop caring. After all, if the students don't care, why should I? God, however, takes a dim view of this. He insists upon teachers who care.

We need to remember that Satan causes this form of oppression. But the power of God working in us gives us unlimited potential for doing damage to the kingdom of Satan. Of course, Satan will try to render us ineffective.

We also need to remember that what we teach is only one part of our task. How we teach is also very important! If we teach with the enthusiasm of a Paul, knowing that God will provide the blessing, our enthusiasm tends to rub off on the students. Perhaps most of all, we need to remember how God responded to Moses when he questioned God's wisdom in choosing him to speak. God said, **"Now go; I will help you speak and will teach you what to say"** (Ex. 4:12.)

GETTING INTO THE LESSON
Begin with prayer.

The last section of **Rom. 15** deals with three different topics. In **verse 14** Paul gives the Roman Christians his complimentary assessment of them. Then the apostle shares some things about himself **(vv. 15–29)**. In the last four verses Paul shares a prayer request.

IN THE WORD
Verses 14–22: Personal Care and Ministry
(Objectives 1 and 3)

1. Be sure the students recognize that Paul is not speaking about characteristics the people had developed in themselves. Rather, these were evidences that he expected to see in the people because God had placed them there. We are good, we have knowledge, and we can instruct one another because the Holy Spirit lives in us and causes such behavior.

a. **"Full of goodness."** Like a good teacher, Paul realized the importance of statements of encouragement for those whom he was instructing. This first phrase conveys a genuine desire to do what is right. This demonstrated the Spirit's sanctifying work in their lives. Christians who are "inwardly good" don't need rules imposed on them from the outside; they are motivated from within. Ask the class to think of school rules they could do without if the student body, as a whole, were "inwardly good" (e.g., dress codes, tardies, chapel behavior, fighting).

b. **"Complete in knowledge."** Your students are in this class and studying Scripture so they may grow in knowledge, but knowledge alone is but one facet of their lives. By God's grace that knowledge leads to a living faith. Also, we must know the truth before we can be faithful in doing the truth (living by it). That the Roman Christians were knowledgeable is evident from the difficulty of the subject matter Paul sends their way. Romans is not a book for spiritual infants.

c. **"Competent to instruct one another."** The believers in Rome loved their Savior and were deeply caring. They were ready and able to share the love of Jesus and to admonish those who were falling away as well as to instruct, remind, warn, encourage, and teach others. Mature believers are willing to take the time and risk to lovingly confront those in their midst who are erring or in need of training in God's Word. But more than that they are willing to take the time and risk to speak a word of forgiveness to repentant sinners who have wronged them.

2. Paul talks about his evangelistic ministry as though it were the work of a priest bringing his offerings before God. A priest is concerned with not only converting souls but also with their sanctification. When we serve others as priests, we must be as concerned with their continued spiritual growth as we were with their becoming baptized.

3. Paul was proud of his numerous achievements, but it was pride in God. The victories God had produced in his life brought him an inner sense of reward and joy that he was delighted to share with others. At the same time he is able to give all the credit to the Lord. Jesus told His disciples **"Apart from me you can do nothing"** (John 15:56). Paul understood this truth.

Invite students to suggest ways this truth can, by the power of God, affect their lives.

4. Paul had a true pioneer spirit. He had a burning desire to carry the Gospel to regions where no one had gone before. He was not interested in reevangelizing areas. That was for people with smaller goals. Paul's vision was as large as the world he lived in, and he lived in hope of the Gospel reaching it all in his lifetime. Emphasize the context; all this happened through the power of the Spirit (**v. 19**).

Verses 23–29: Personal Planning
(Objectives 2 and 3)

This activity does not need to be in writing, except for the prayer. The words of Paul in **verse 23** bear testimony to the thoroughness of his evangelical labors, and now he is ready to take on an even larger task.

1. As students read this, encourage them to pause to consider their own fervor for mission work. Talk about their potential and desire as well as their gifts in this area.

2. Have some of the class read their prayers. Paul's dream to evangelize the unevangelized was both realistic and optimistic. How can we be less on fire for the mission field when the end is so much nearer?

3. You might encourage students to discuss this question in pairs.

Verses 30–33: Personal Prayer
(Objective 4)

This activity could use up an entire period. Prayer contains so many important facets, and Scripture teaches so much about prayer. Point out the elements of Paul's request. We need to make people aware of our needs. Students seem to never tire of prayer requests, perhaps because it gives them a sense of worth in situations in which they are helpless to aid any other way.

In **verses 31–32a** Paul gives specific information as to what they were to pray about. Sometimes we are afraid of limiting God, but He certainly encourages us to tell people what we would like them to pray about. Prayer is as essential to our spiritual life as fresh air is to physical life.

Session 44: Warm Regards and a Strong Warning

BIBLE BASIS
Rom. 16

CENTRAL TRUTH

After the challenging theology of the preceding chapters, Paul now concludes with a personal and intimate series of greetings. In the middle of these he takes steps to warn the believers in Rome about the dangers of teachers with less than honorable motives.

He concludes with a stirring doxology giving glory to our eternal God.

OBJECTIVES
By the grace of God students will

1. express their concern and establish their plan for positive demonstrations of Christian love for one another;

2. demonstrate their understanding of how we are to

recognize and deal with false teachers;
3. show their insights into the nature of God as expressed in Paul's doxology.

OUTLINE OF ROM. 16:1–27

A. Greet one another (vv. 1–16)
B. Look out for troublemakers (vv. 17–19)
   1. They cause divisions and give offenses (v. 17)
   2. Avoid them (v. 17)
   3. Watch out for their smooth talk and flattery (v. 18)
   4. Be wise and innocent (v. 19)
C. To God be glory forever (vv. 21–27)
   1. A benediction (v. 20)
   2. Additional greetings (vv. 21–23)
   3. A final doxology (vv. 25–27)

A WORD FROM THE AUTHOR

Christian teachers have the same responsibility as parents—to provide the nutrition, the environment, and the training that will produce intelligent adults who can act independently of them.

In his first letter John warns his flock about the testing of their faith. He says in **1 John 2:26–27: "I am writing these things to you about those who are trying to lead you astray. As for you, the anointing you received from Him remains in you, and you do not need anyone to teach you. But as His anointing teaches you about all things and as that anointing is real, not counterfeit—just as it has taught you, remain in Him."**

The statement, **"you do not need anyone to teach you,"** is not written to spiritual babies. It shows the confidence a Christian teacher had in his students who had grown into a mature relationship with God and simply did not need him any more. John refers to the Holy Spirit as their teacher and does not mention his own role in their education.

This is as it should be. We, as teachers of the Word, are privileged to watch a miraculous process in action—the Holy Spirit sanctifying people for whom we have a deep affection. If we understand what is happening, we will also understand who should get the credit. Praise God and amen!

GETTING INTO THE LESSON

From the number of names he mentions, Paul obviously knew a lot of Christian people all over the world, and he had the ability and interest to keep track of them. We know about some; about others we know nothing but what is said here. Apparently Phoebe delivered the letter to the Roman church. This is the only place in Scripture where she is mentioned. Yet, Paul pays her great tribute in the way he introduces her to the believers at Rome. He calls her a servant and saint who is worthy and who has been a great help to many. We know how Paul met Priscilla and Aquila from Luke's account in **Acts 18,** but we have no idea how they risked their lives for him.

Some Bible scholars have suggested that Tryphena and Tryphosa were twins. Their names mean *dainty* and *delicate,* but the word Paul used for *work hard* suggests heavy labor or working to exhaustion. We are left to wonder what kind of work "Dainty" and "Delicate" performed for the Lord. Of such stuff was the church at Rome made, and our imaginations are fired by the untold stories they represent!

IN THE WORD

Verses 1–16: Greet One Another (Objective 1)

1. Encourage free sharing here. If you wish, place students in small groups, and ask each group to suggest a realistic display of affection in your classroom or in their congregation. Such responses ought to take into consideration the "accepted" norm, but should not be restricted to that. The discussion of the weak and the strong Christians in **chapter 14** ought to influence students to tread carefully when suggesting radical changes in practices.

2. For each directive invite two or three volunteers to read their responses. Then ask the entire class to evaluate them. Following are some comments about each directive.

   a. *Accept one another's differences.* All Christians are united by the common bond of faith in Jesus Christ. But this profound oneness does not dictate against individual differences. In **Rom. 16** we find Jews and Gentiles, men and women, couples and singles, slaves and people who came from the household of Herod. Paul remembers and appreciates all. He thus demonstrates that such diversity is to be channeled toward unity, not division.

   b. *Be willing to become a servant of others.* Many Christians labor in the service of the Lord without any special recognition or applause. They do this as a labor of love, love for the Lord and love for the brothers and sisters. Paul mentions some of these types of Christians in **Rom. 16.** In fact, we know nothing more about most of the people he mentions than what he wrote here.

   c. *Demonstrate your love to one another.* Paul expresses his deep affection for these people in the simplest of manners. He doesn't gush or try to produce deathless prose to show his love. He uses very unspectacular terms; yet, the sincerity of his words shines through. Christian love doesn't have to be expressed in a grandiose style; many show it in simple, yet sincere, ways. If a holy kiss doesn't do it for you, try a hug or a pat on the back or a gentle touch. Whatever you do, let your students know you care.

Verses 17–20: Look Out for Troublemakers (Objective 2)

1. Discussions about church fellowship frequently include discussion of these verses. While you

will probably want to prevent a debate that would lead students to challenge decisions that adults in their congregations have made, you will provide good groundwork for the future if you help them develop appropriate guidelines and philosophies for their relationships with others.

a. *What was happening?* Paul answers this in **verse 17.** Either some within the Roman church were causing trouble that would lead to divisions, or the potential existed for such trouble to occur. Besides this, others were setting up obstacles for the believers by giving offense, creating doubts, and promoting doctrines contrary to true Christian teachings.

b. *Why was it happening?* **Verse 18** tells us that these false teachers were doing it for selfish personal reasons. Apparently their interest and concern ignored the needs of the people and focused on what the believers could do for them. Throughout her history, the church has been exploited by these enemies of the cross. Every Christian has a responsibility to be informed enough to combat the deceivers.

c. *How was it to be handled?* Paul mentions two steps in our battle against these divisive individuals. First he calls for careful scrutiny **(v. 17a)**; he told the believers to keep a close eye on what others taught and how they behaved. Secondly, he told them to separate themselves from the false teachers **(v. 17b).**

d. *How could it be overcome?* Paul was not a pessimist. He states very clearly that believers should not be afraid of these people. We should watch and avoid them, but they cannot prevail. The apostle encourages the Roman Christians to continue their obedience and to **"be wise about what is good and innocent about what is evil" (v. 19).** Talk about that phrase. Help your students recognize how easy it is to get into trouble when we reverse that advice. Encourage your class to share ways in which people do the opposite of what Paul said. They learn all they can about evil (e.g., pornography, drugs, music that is overtly anti-Christian) but fail to learn about what is good (God's Word).

2. You might use this opportunity to emphasize the false teachings of various denominations, false doctrines that prevent The Lutheran Church—Missouri Synod from engaging in church fellowship with them. You could also look at problems within the closer fellowship of their class or congregations. Ask, **Has someone ever tried to smooth-talk you into believing that it's okay to drink alcohol at a party? curse or swear? engage is sexual intercourse or other such sexual activities outside of marriage?**

3. In connection with church denominations that teach false doctrine, consider such practices as not worshiping with them, not communing with them, and not listening to their services on radio or TV. In connection with peer pressures, discuss ways to say no—including ways to avoid situations where they're forced to say yes or no.

Verses 21–27: To God Be Glory Forever
(Objective 3)

1. As you discuss the doxology, emphasize the saving work of Jesus. Paul wrote everything in the context of 1:17—**"In the Gospel a righteousness from God is revealed, a righteousness that is by faith from first to last, just as it is written: 'The righteous will live by faith.' "**

a. *He establishes us by the Gospel.* Establish means *to prop up, make firm, or stable.* It conveys the idea of support. Because of Jesus' work on our behalf and through the Holy Spirit working in us, God supports us and stabilizes our lives.

b. *He proclaims the mystery of Jesus.* Only through Jesus can anyone come to God. Be sure your students read **Col. 1:26–27,** where Paul explains what the mystery is. Jesus is more than a conduit to the Father. He rescues us from damnation, and binds us together, and makes us one with the Father.

c. *He makes His will known to the nations.* Our gracious God has initiated His plan of salvation for the entire world **(John 3:16).** Therefore, He has made it known to all the nations **(Rom. 16:26b).** The Gospel is available to all! Since the Father's focus is on the world, ours should be also.

d. *He produces faith and obedience.* God does not tell us to convert anyone. Only God causes people to he born again **(1 Peter 1:3).** On the other hand He has chosen human beings to be the means by which He communicates the Gospel of salvation. He has given us the responsibility of getting the message out. Our Redeemer lives, our Redeemer loves, our Redeemer saves; believe on Him and receive eternal life!

e. *He receives glory through Jesus.* Because Jesus has saved us, and because the Holy Spirit has created and sustained faith in our hearts, our lives have changed. We now demonstrate (though imperfectly) our love for God through thoughts, words, and actions that bring glory to Him.

2. Encourage students to talk with one another about their faith in Jesus. God can use such sharing to cause their faith to grow!

Session 45: Concluding Activities for Unit 4

Open with prayer. Thank God for His Word, for Paul who was His dedicated servant, and especially for this letter to the Romans. Acknowledge the sanctifying work of the Holy Spirit who has produced the understandings and insights for this difficult and wonderful document.

Use this review to encourage your students to organize their knowledge and recognize the potential for personal application.

Plan to use at least part ot the class session for students to share their knowledge and applications. As you have probably discovered, some of their applications are remarkably creative and valuable. When students share with one another, God multiplies the blessings of His Word.

The activities are similar to the review of units 1, 2, and 3 in sessions 13, 24, and 33. Refer back to comments made in this guide for those sessions.

UNIT 5: FAITH BATTLES PRIDE

BIBLE BASIS: 1 COR. 1–11

Pride. Our lives as children of God face a struggle that never ends until we enter heaven. Because of the sin that still lives in us, we want to lift up ourselves instead of God and other people; we battle the sin of pride.

We quarrel.

We try to use our own wisdom to earn heaven.

We seek earthly pleasures more than heavenly treasures.

We let selfish desires affect our lives as singled or married individuals.

We try to use our own resources to battle temptation.

We even attempt to use worship to show our superiority over other Christians.

The statements above summarize the content of this unit. Read the central truths and objectives of all the sessions to identify more completely the direction taken with these issues.

Ask students to read in advance the portion of **1 Cor.** suggested for each session. To get them into the text, assign selected questions from the sessions as homework. Select questions that deal primarily with facts from the text. Do not ask students to work in advance with the questions that require discussion. If students become familiar with the facts in advance, you can use the class time for in-depth discussion of the issues.

Note: You will probably inhibit discussion of issues if you use class time to correct and grade student answers. If you must give grades for homework, we recommend that you make special assignments. Perhaps after each day's discussion you could assign one of the questions listed under "Essay Test" in session 52 of this guide.

Session 46: When Christians Quarrel

BIBLE BASIS
1 Cor. 1:10–17

CENTRAL TRUTH

Christ has molded us into a fellowship of believers through the power of the Gospel. We frustrate the unity to which Christ has called us when we quarrel with fellow Christians and divide His church into factions. Through Christ's healing love we can be restored to unity.

OBJECTIVES

By the grace of God students will
1. explain that Christ has created a fellowship of believers in His name through the power of the Gospel;
2. explain how sinful pride leads to quarrels and dissension in Christ's church;
3. identify the pride-filled behavior in their own lives and demonstrate a willingness to come to terms with it;
4. tell how Christ's healing love mends broken relationships and restores unity in the church.

BACKGROUND

The congregation at Corinth, to whom Paul addresses this letter, was established by Paul on his second missionary journey (see **Acts 18**). The city became renowned in Greece as a prosperous center of commerce due to its strategic location near major sea routes and its two magnificent harbors. In addition to being the capital of the province (Achaia), Corinth was the seat of the Roman proconsul. Because of its availability to travelers, Corinth emerged as a cosmopolitan metropolis made up of a mixed population of Greeks, Romans, Jews, and people of Eastern origin. When Paul preached to the Corinthians, he was literally preaching to the "world."

Paul appears to have worked in Corinth for about a year and a half, leaving behind a flourishing congregation of Jewish and gentile converts. His fellow workers were Aquila and Priscilla. After Paul's departure from Corinth the congregation was served by Apollos. There is no evidence that Peter ever visited this area.

When Paul was at Ephesus on his third missionary journey, members of Chloe's household reported to him that scandalous divisions were breaking asunder the unity of the Corinthian congregation **(1 Cor. 1:11)**. Other spiritual problems were rampant as well, all of which stemmed from a deep-seated sinful pride that characterized the Corinthian Christians.

In this pastoral letter to the church at Corinth, the apostle wastes no time in addressing himself to the root problem behind their spiritual immaturity. In the very first chapter he exposes the problem of their pride and calls them back to the power of the Gospel of Jesus Christ.

This lesson demonstrates how modern Christians suffer the same scandalous problems of bickering and quarreling with one another. How important it is that we acknowledge the real reasons behind such dissension and are drawn by the love of Christ to fellowship and unity.

GETTING INTO THE LESSON (Objective 2)

Use the opening section of the Student Book. Encourage students to give their opinions about quarreling and divisions in the church. Focus especially on what such quarrels do to a Christian's spiritual life and the unity of God's church. Point out that, although quarrels do happen in our congregations, God gives us His power to mend and heal all broken relationships.

Dissension in the Church at Corinth
(Objectives 1, 2, and 4)

To make more time available to discuss the issues during class, consider asking students to complete this section as homework. Have them write their answers on a separate sheet of paper or in a notebook to be used regularly in this class. This guide will generally suggest answers to the Student Book questions. Remember, though, that at times answers will vary.

1) a. The behavior of the members had actually broken the congregation into opposing cliques.

b. Each clique had a favorite leader—Paul, Apollos, Peter, and Christ Himself. Paul and Apollos were former pastors of the congregation. We are not sure about the connection with Peter. The "Christ" group may have been the most divisive and arrogant group of them all. Some scholars believe that this group had turned Christ into a moral philosopher and were introducing Gnosticism into the congregation (see the next session).

c. The Corinthians were making Baptism a human initiation ceremony. They were attributing the power of Baptism to the person who baptized them, not to the God of grace who through Baptism draws all believers into a unified fellowship with Jesus Christ. Paul is thankful he did not baptize many of the Corinthians because he wanted to take the attention off himself and direct it to his Lord.

d. These verses are the key in interpreting the proud and divisive behavior of the Corinthians. Spiritual pride and spiritual immaturity go hand in hand. This situation exists because quarreling and bickering result from human pride, and human pride is a strong sign of spiritual immaturity.

2) a. Christian unity is based on faith in Jesus Christ, our common Lord and Savior. Members of Christian congregations should behave toward one another as people united in Christ.

b. Perfect unity in Christ means that our hearts and minds are in exact agreement on the doctrine of Jesus Christ and in His love, which we have for one another. It does not refer to our opinions on church polity and practices that are not essential to the Gospel (see AC XV).

c. These verses point to God's promise to supply all our spiritual needs, especially His power and grace, to keep us spiritually strong.

d. No human power can build the spiritual unity that characterizes the fellowship of God's church. This is the work of the Gospel. In the Gospel, God's power is released and the Holy Spirit brings us into unity.

Am I a Part of the Church's Problem? (Objective 3)

The Self-Discovery Exercise has been designed to draw the students into a personal confrontation of the text. Spend some time allowing the students to work through the exercise. Then discuss it. At your discretion make this either a personal or class project.

If your schedule permits, mention to the students that you are available to discuss their discoveries with them personally. They may desire your support in this important decision-making matter.

His Love Makes Us Whole and Complete
(Objectives 1 and 4)

1. **Eph. 4:29–32** describes the "old" behavior of the nonbeliever and the "new" behavior of the believer, whose life is ruled by Christ's love and forgiveness. Point out how Christ's love calls us to a higher plane of living than that practiced by the world. Our life in the church is to emulate the loving behavior of our Lord. Be sure students recognize that we cannot do this, however, by our own power. In the previous chapter (**3:14–21**) Paul had prayed that God would strengthen them through His Spirit.

2–5. Choose any or all of these questions to apply the truths this lesson has brought out on Christian unity. Encourage students to volunteer their opinions.

Conclude with the prayer, spoken in unison. If time permits, sing or speak the hymn stanzas together.

Session 47: Trying to Be Wiser than God

BIBLE BASIS
1 Cor. 1:18–2:5

CENTRAL TRUTH
The world attempts to know God through human philosophy and has contempt for the message of Christ's death on the cross. God, however, puts the world's wisdom to shame by revealing His own wisdom and power in the crucified Christ.

OBJECTIVES
By the grace of God students will
1. identify how the world attempts to apprehend God through human philosophy and the eloquence of human wisdom;
2. affirm that the message of Christ's death on the cross is the wisdom and power of God for their salvation;
3. describe how God puts to shame the wisdom of the world by His own wisdom of the crucified Christ;

4. tell about the power and wisdom of God's plan of salvation in their own lives.

BACKGROUND

This lesson focuses on still another, and even more tragic, problem to which spiritual pride can lead. Paul wastes no time addressing himself to the problem of some of the Corinthians who were actually denying the cross of Jesus Christ. Bear in mind that the Corinthians had become vulnerable to a particular heresy popular in the Graeco-Roman world, namely, Gnosticism.

Gnosticism asserted that the ways of God could be known and apprehended through human wisdom (philosophy). The Greeks especially loved to demonstrate their wisdom through logic and rhetoric. Their culture was mentalistic (as ours is scientific) and was given to systematic argument based on lofty thought.

Paul was deeply upset to learn that many of the Corinthians were viewing Christ's cross as "foolishness." They had changed Jesus the Savior into a moral philosopher, a divine giver of knowledge. In other words, they had distorted the Christian faith into something amenable to their own culture.

The apostle reminds the Corinthians that the real power and wisdom of God can be found only in the cross. At the cross human sin is exposed, died for, and forgiven.

This topic is appropriate to our own culture in which human knowledge in the form of science also entices Christians to "water down" their faith in order to make it more palatable.

GETTING INTO THE LESSON (Objective 1)

Use the opening section to lead into the lesson. Have the students discuss the narrative about the United Nations chapel and the questions that follow. Point out that chapels and churches use symbols to indicate important truths about God and His essence. Such symbols tell us whether God's revelation in Christ is being referred to or whether the truths being expressed are based only on human speculation about God. Have the students explain what the United Nations chapel symbols are saying (or are not saying) about the God revealed to us in Jesus Christ.

Can Human Philosophy Lead Us to God?
(Objectives 1, 2, and 3)

1. Make certain the students understand how the Corinthians were reinterpreting the message of Christ's cross and thus distorting it. Use the background portion of this lesson to touch on the subject of Gnosticism and the Greek love for philosophy. Point out the common human error in religious matters: "trying to be wiser than God."

2) a. "Foolishness" to the Greeks was an indication of contempt.

b. Paul speaks of the cross as the power of God. This means that the message of Christ crucified is the means by which God Himself converts people and gives to them the gift of salvation.

c. Many people are offended at God's way of salvation because they lack the Holy Spirit. These verses show that the working of the Holy Spirit is necessary to open our understanding to our own need for God's forgiveness of our sins. Without the Holy Spirit we do not see the enormity of our sins and our need for God's grace.

d. Paul lays bare the pride of human wisdom and its feeble attempts to find God. Human wisdom is still operative today. The "clothing" is different, but the essentials are the same.

e and f. The judgment of God on human wisdom is decisive. When it poses as a way for humanity to find God, it will be destroyed.

The Way to God: The Crucified Christ
(Objectives 2 and 3)

1. Note the present tense of the verbs Paul uses: **"those who are perishing"** and **"those who are being saved."** Note the opposite directions—toward "perishing" and "being saved." Those who are perishing see the cross of Christ as nonsense.

2. Emphasize how "very important" Paul makes the message of the cross. It is nothing less than God's power.

3. Many things might be included here. Mary was a poor maiden, not a palace queen, when she was called to give birth to Jesus. The "cross" itself was the most despised symbol of shame in the Roman Empire.

4. This refers back to questions 2e and 2f of the previous section. God Himself mocks the wisdom of the world and declares it bankrupt in seeking to find the way to God.

5. God puts down the kind of human wisdom that seeks the glory of salvation for itself. That would make faith rest on a human work. But our faith rests on God's power. Therefore, we boast only in the Lord.

Sharing God's Plan of Salvation with Others
(Objective 4)

1–2. Paul does not attempt to use human logic and polished rhetoric to convince people of their need for salvation in Jesus Christ. Although such techniques are not wrong in themselves, they have no power to change the sinful human heart. Paul turns his readers' attention to the truth that Christ died on the cross for their sins. The Holy Spirit works through this message, convicting people of their sins and quickening them with faith to receive the gift of forgiveness and salvation.

3. This is an important question. Certainly Christians should use their intelligence in proclaiming Christ. Paul himself marshals a massive amount of evidence in disputing with unbelievers. But the techniques of preaching Christ should not be a substitute for the simple message of the cross itself. Paul used his intelli-

gence in turning people to gaze upon the crucified Christ and their need for Him.

4–5. Science, properly understood, is a gift of God to understand the natural phenomena of the world. When raised to a philosophy, it can be an arrogance as destructive as Gnosticism. Many scientists use science as a gift of God and are sincere believers. Other scientists use science as a philosophy of life and consider the Christian faith "foolish."

You may conclude this lesson with a prayer and by singing or speaking the hymn stanza in the Student Book.

Session: 48: The Pleasure Principle

BIBLE BASIS
1 Cor. 6:1–20

CENTRAL TRUTH
Christ died to make us His people and now lives within our bodies through the Holy Spirit. When we arrogantly insist on doing whatever we please, we dishonor Christ and our own bodies. Through Christ's grace, we are given strength to honor Christ in our bodily behavior.

OBJECTIVES
By the grace of God students will
1. describe how sinful pride leads them to rebel against God's will and to follow their own desires in bodily behavior;
2. affirm that they belong to Christ, not themselves, because He purchased them to be His own people;
3. acknowledge a desire to live responsibly as the temples of the Holy Spirit;
4. demonstrate ways they can honor Christ in their bodily behavior.

BACKGROUND
The Corinthian Christians carried their pride and conceit to an even more base level of sinful behavior. Because they falsely believed that they had attained the heights of spiritual wisdom (see session 47), they now reasoned that they had complete freedom to live physically as they pleased. Greek Gnosticism divided the life of the spirit from the life of the body. The Greeks felt that filling the mind with spiritual wisdom was the supreme goal of life. Matters dealing with the body had no relationship with the life of the spirit.

These people saw no contradiction in abusing their bodies or engaging in lewd sexual behavior and seeking spiritual enlightenment. Gnosticism asserted that only the spiritual was good; the world of matter or the body was of no eternal consequence.

The Corinthian Christians fell into this trap of dichotomizing the life of the spirit and the life of the body. They insisted that all things were lawful for them because they were now members of Christ's kingdom. Distorting the meaning of Christian freedom, they began suing their Christian brothers and sisters in courts of law and were pursuing sexual relations with prostitutes of the city.

Paul admonished the Corinthians for living life on their own sinful terms. He reminded them that Christ died for the whole person, the body as well as the spirit. He brought to their attention the fact that Christ's death put a claim on their bodies; in fact, their bodies were temples of the Holy Spirit. Loving Christian behavior honors God not only in the inner reaches of the mind. It must influence the way Christians treat and care for their bodies.

This lesson contains many truths that are applicable to life in the modern world. Living in a world that caters to the sensual appetites of the body (e.g., drugs, sexual freedom, and gluttony), Christians are motivated by Christ's love to pay special attention to how they can honor God in bodily behavior.

GETTING INTO THE LESSON
(Objectives 1 and 3)

Use the opening section of the Student Book to lead into the lesson. Have the students discuss the difference between the pleasure principle and the reality principle. Although this is a psychological model, it helps establish the theme of the lesson.

Teenagers wonder why society has so many rules. Their youthful exhuberance prevents them from a mature understanding of the need for guidelines in human behavior. Help students comprehend that if the pleasure principle is left unbridled (because it is dominated by our sinful nature), it would lead to societal chaos. Once you establish this point, you can point them to God's plan for bodily behavior in which the Holy Spirit guides the expression of our human nature.

Emphasize that God does not put a damper on human pleasure. He rather wants to elevate it to the highest expression possible.

Following the World's Pleasure Principle
(Objectives 1 and 2)

1 a and b. Paul refers to eating food offered to idols and sexual immorality. In **10:23–30** he discusses at length the matter of eating food offered to idols. Since both food and sex are major bodily functions (in all societies of the world food and sex are the focus of cultural taboos), the Corinthian disregard for any guidelines in these two activities reveals the depth of their rebellion and pride.

c. If students work well in small groups, consider using such an arrangement for this question. Then have volunteers share their findings with the entire class.

d. Greek society was permissive in all forms of sexual activity. Paul lists the most common forms of their sexual immorality and also other examples of sinful behavior to which the Thessalonians were exposed.

e. Emphasize the transforming power of Christ, who delivers us from the base passions of our sinful nature. The Holy Spirit gives us new power in our lives—a holy and meaningful perspective by which to live.

2. The topic of lawsuits and court cases can be a sensitive matter. In a society as litigation-conscious as our own, Christians are bound to meet other Christians in the court of law. However, we should not lose sight of the principle being discussed here. Christians ought to avoid any situation that might bring a scandal to the Gospel. It is better to suffer a wrong than to have unbelievers mock the sinful behavior of God's people. As Paul observes, God gives His church the gift of wisdom to resolve internal differences. Discuss contemporary examples of Christians whose behavior damaged the reputation of the Gospel.

3) a. God designed the body for sexual enjoyment and reproduction according to His purpose of establishing marriage and the family. Those who engage in sexual immorality sin against the purpose and design God has ordained for the body.

b. The body we possess today will one day be raised in glory. Paul is stressing the permanence of the body in God's plan of salvation. We have no right to abuse our bodies; these same bodies will be an essential part of our future life.

c. Be sure to emphasize that sexual coitus involves a responsibility to the other person; sexual coitus establishes the one-flesh relationship that is the essence of the marriage union. Among other things, sexual immorality perverts God's will by seeking the pleasures of the marriage relationship, but at the same time it refuses to accept the responsibilities of marriage.

Following God's Pleasure Principle
(Objectives 2, 3, and 4)

1) a. Just as God's presence dwelled in the Old Testament temple, so the Holy Spirit actually dwells within all believers (see **Rom. 8:9–17**). He not only seeks to control our behavior, but as our Counselor **(John 15:26; 16:12–14)**, He shows us how to follow the high calling of Jesus Christ. Because of the Spirit's presence within us, we should demonstrate care not to grieve the Holy Spirit through sinful behavior **(Eph. 4:30)**.

b and c. Christ has a claim on our bodies and everything we are because He died for our sins. Emphasize that Christ's redemption involved the totality of our being **(1 Thess. 5:23)**.

2–3. Spend some time discussing the positive use of the body as a means of honoring God. Point out the importance of God's design for the body as the positive dimension of human pleasure because it is centered on His will. Teenagers ought to be more exposed to a discussion of the positive benefits, rather than hearing only the negative aspects of the use of the body.

Conclude with prayer or by singing or speaking the hymn stanzas.

Session 49: To Marry or Not to Marry

BIBLE BASIS
1 Cor. 7:1–40

CENTRAL TRUTH
God gives us power to live our lives for Him whether we become married or remain single. Our decision to marry or to remain single should be based on how each of us may best serve God with our particular gifts.

OBJECTIVES
By the grace of God students will
1. explain that marriage and singleness are callings from God and depend on the particular gifts He gives to them;
2. affirm that the ultimate goal in their Christian lives is to live for God whether as married persons or as single persons;
3. describe the different ways they can serve God in their calling, and the problems and the challenges of their calling;
4. express their own feelings about their life's plans regarding marriage or singleness.

BACKGROUND
The church at Corinth had written the apostle about matters dealing with marriage and singleness. The entire seventh chapter of Paul's letter is an answer to their questions. Apparently the Corinthians were unclear about God's teachings concerning marriage and singleness as distinctive callings of God. They noted that Jesus Himself was not married; neither was Paul. Yet other apostles were married. No doubt there was confusion in the congregation. Some were wondering whether they should divorce their mates and become single or should remain married.

The matter of pride lay behind many of the questions about which the Corinthians had written. Their concern over sexual behavior may have been a masked desire to have unlimited freedom in this type of behavior. Paul instead gives them clear directions that according to God's will sexual activities are one of the essential aspects of marriage.

Perhaps the most pressing problem of the Corinthians was the mixed marriages of Christians and non-Christians. Most marriages at this time were, of course, mixed because of the small number of Christians. Paul's advice to seek marriage with a Christian partner (or if married to a non-Christian, to remain in that relationship) is still valid today.

This is an important lesson for young people today because they are asking similar questions. The church should attempt to make the truths included in this chapter as clear and as relevant as they were in Paul's day.

GETTING INTO THE LESSON
(Objectives 1, 2, 3, and 4)

The opening section leads into the heart of the lesson. Spend an appropriate amount of time developing the theme of marriage and singleness. Seek opinions from the class as to their feelings about the subject. Sociological research reveals that singleness is becoming an increasing option with many young adults: as many as 35 percent of all adults are single in America (this includes those divorced, widowed, and never married). Ten percent of all adults choose never to become married for various reasons. Many others, especially women, are delaying marriage for the sake of their careers.

This lesson is particularly important because of the changing face of the American family and the new alternative life-styles (including cohabitation) that are associated with it.

Marriage As God's Calling (Objectives 1, 2, and 3)

1. Gifts from God indicate that a person is "gifted" for a certain profession or calling. It speaks of God's creative activity in human life.

Many young people have never thought through the truth that marriage is not for everyone. The pressures for marriage until recently have been enormous: all socialization agents of our culture have assumed that only marriage is "normal." Paul points out that both marriage and singleness are gifts of God.

2) a. Sexual desires are not wrong in themselves and are a gift of God. When such desires are consummated in marriage, they honor God. Focus on this truth: sexual oneness can honor God.

b and c. Sexual activity outside of marriage (whether premarital or extramarital) sins against God's design for the sexual gift. People who cohabit should be lovingly dealt with, but their behavior should not be accepted. See **John 8:10–11.**

3) a. Marriage means sexual, social, and emotional unity. Partners in the marriage pact agree to this unity and must honor it. Insisting on personal "rights" destroys the unity on which marriage is based. Sexual separation should be by agreement.

b and c. The commitment to marriage is a lifelong commitment and should be entered into with that understanding. Even the state assumes this principle, or there would be no divorce laws. Divorce, except for adultery or desertion, is not acceptable to God. It breaks asunder the relationship God intended for the lives of the persons involved.

4 a and b. For the nonbelieving partner of a mixed marriage, there is the potential blessing of Christian love and peace received from the believing partner. The children of this union may be blessed by the sharing of God's Word and the Christian behavior in the home. Conversely, there is also the potential problem of conflicting attitudes, values, and goals which may erode the very foundations of the marriage, and children may become confused by the differing religious values of their parents.

c and d. Because marriage is such an intimate unity, it is advisable to marry a Christian person. Premarital counseling can reveal a person's aptitude for marriage, lead to discussion of significant issues, and build the foundation for a lifetime of open communication.

Singleness As God's Calling (Objectives 1, 2, and 3)

1. Paul's decision to remain single was clearly for the purpose of committing his entire life for God's service. Jesus suggests that remaining single is right only for those who have been given that gift.

2) a. Some of the "troubles" of married life include communication problems, lack of privacy, complicated schedules, and the need to provide time for the spouse and children.

b. Distractions of married life include all of the responsibilities that love for another person embrace. It is the difference between "thinking for two" and "thinking for one."

c. Single people may become lonely, but that situation need not exist. Many fill their hours with deeds of service to the needy and to the work of God's kingdom.

d. Before entering marriage, persons should ask themselves whether they are gifted to be responsible spouses and parents.

e and f. These are important questions. Encourage the students to remember that Christ's death and resurrection have fitted them for a high calling in this world. Both singleness and marriage should relate to this calling of service. Both are callings blessed by God.

Thinking about My Life's Decision (Objective 4)

Have the students apply the truths learned in this session to their personal lives. Time spent here is a good investment in their future.

Do not require anyone to share what she or he has written or thought about, but do provide the opportunity to do so.

Session 50: When Temptation Strikes

BIBLE BASIS
1 Cor. 10:1–13

CENTRAL TRUTH
We are constantly tempted in our daily lives to rebel against God and His will for us. But God empowers us in times of temptation to resist the temptation and to overcome it.

OBJECTIVES
By the grace of God students will
1. express how spiritual pride makes them vulnerable to temptation and to rebellion against God;
2. describe the universal occurrence of temptation and how Jesus Himself endured temptation in His mission of redemption;
3. explore their own feelings about temptation, the problems and the challenges;
4. relate how God rescues them in times of temptation and gives them strength to resist and overcome.

BACKGROUND
This lesson, as the others in this unit, focuses on the spiritual pride of the church at Corinth. Because of their emphasis on wisdom and philosophy, the Corinthians believed that they were impervious to falling into sin and to God's judgment.

Paul warns the Corinthian Christians that they were especially susceptible to temptation. He shares with them the example of ancient Israel, who experienced the same wondrous gifts of grace. Yet Israel rebelled against God and fell fictim to His judgment. The apostle's lesson is clear: pride comes before the fall.

As always, Paul presents God's grace as the means by which God comes to the rescue of His people. Even in temptation He is there, never allowing it to become too overwhelming, and showing us how we can resist and overcome.

This lesson provides the essential spiritual truths for young people to learn about the problems of temptation. More importantly, it keys their vision to the Lord, who overcame temptation in His own earthly ministry, the same Lord who walks hand in hand with them now.

GETTING INTO THE LESSON (Objective 3)
Use the opening section as a lead into the lesson. Write the word *temptation* on the board and ask the students what they think it means. Get them to express themselves freely on the topic before proceeding with the exercise. Make the following truth clear: *temptation itself is not sin;* the sin is falling or giving into the temptation. Falling into temptation is the rebellion against God to which this lesson pertains.

As the class participates in the exercise, try to discover where they are with the topic of temptation. This will give you an indication what parts of the lesson deserve more analysis and study.

Pride Comes before the Fall (Objective 1)
1. Be sure to point out how spiritual pride makes a person especially vulnerable to temptation. Frequently, proud people feel as if they have a special insurance against temptation to sin. Trusting as they do in their own strength, they are all the more deflated when the inevitable fall occurs. Some of Aesop's fables focus on the same truth that this passage highlights.

2) a. Paul refers to the Exodus from Egypt as a *baptism.* In the "cloud" and the "sea," God was graciously acting for Israel's salvation, just as He does in Holy Baptism today.

b. The reference to the "supernatural food" and "supernatural drink" that God provided the Israelites can be compared to the Lord's Supper of the Christian church. Paul is making it clear that the Israelites were beneficiaries of God's grace and salvation. They were richly blessed by His presence. The reference to "the Rock is Christ" affirms that wherever God is at work saving His people, Christ is present. Even the promises of the old covenant find their culmination in Christ.

c. The fact that ancient Israel enjoyed such rich blessings was not a guarantee against sin and rebellion.

d. Students can find the record of Israel's pride and rebellion to which Paul referred in **Num. 14:29–30; 11:4, 34; Ex. 32:4–6; Num. 25:1–18; 21:5–6;** and **16:30–49.**

e. This passage makes clear that humans themselves carry within themselves the seeds of their rebellion against God. Even Satan cannot make us sin; he can only tempt.

f. The warning to the Corinthians is clear: pride is fertile ground for temptation.

Understanding Temptation (Objectives 2 and 3)
1 a and b. No one ought to feel as if he or she is being singled out for temptation or for a particular type of temptation. All temptations possess the same basic essence: they present opportunities to rebel against God.

c and d. All believers may receive comfort from knowing that God Himself through Jesus Christ participated in the pains and agonies of human life. He experienced the most severe temptations on our behalf and overcame them all. In order to be true man, it was necessary that He endure our temptations. In order to be true God, it was necessary that He be sinless.

2. Use the Self-Discovery Exercise as a way for the students to understand that temptations come in

many forms or types. The types listed certainly do not exhaust the possibilities. It would not be unusual for teenagers to suppose that temptations of the flesh are the most severe or the most common for teens. While it may seem that every age in life has its special pressures, it is probably more accurate to state that all of the listed types of temptations affect us at every stage of life.

Try to impress upon the students that temptations come at them from *every angle*. They may seem to resist well in one area, only to succumb easily in another. How much we need to live by God's power and grace!

Dealing with Temptation (Objective 4)

1–3. Spend some time on these two promises of God: (1) He will not allow us to be tempted beyond our ability to bear it; (2) in every instance of temptation He will supply us strength to resist and overcome. These are the kinds of promises that make a difference in Christian decision-making. Behind the promise stands the faithful God who never deserts His children in the face of evil.

4. This section focuses on the Word of God as a resource against the temptations of Satan. God's Word is not a "magic charm." The Holy Spirit, however, works through the Word to strengthen the faith of His people.

5–6. If time permits, discuss the application of this lesson.

The session may conclude with prayer or the reading of the words of **Ps. 46** in the Student Book.

Session 51: Worship That Does More Harm Than Good

BIBLE BASIS
1 Cor. 11:17–34

CENTRAL TRUTH

Christ shares His forgiveness with us, as well as His body and blood, in the Lord's Supper. When we treat our fellow Christians with contempt during worship, we sin against Christ's body and blood, because we do not really acknowledge His loving presence in our midst.

OBJECTIVES

By the grace of God students will
1. describe how spiritual pride leads to contempt for other Christians and mocks the purpose of worship;
2. explain how Christ is really present in the Lord's Supper to offer us His presence and forgiveness;
3. identify those spiritual attitudes that demonstrate how Christians are to worship in a worthy manner;
4. tell how God blesses worship that acknowledges His presence and that also honors Christian fellowship.

BACKGROUND

The theme that dominates this lesson is closely correlated with the theme of the first lesson of this unit. The divided factions in the church at Corinth were making a mockery of Christian worship by their quarrelsome and arrogant behavior. Because of their contempt for one another, they were especially sabotaging the meaning of the Lord's Supper.

Some Bible scholars believe that the early Christians sought to emphasize the close fellowship of the Christian faith by celebrating a common meal or "love feast" prior to the celebration of worship through the Lord's Supper. The Corinthians violated both aspects of this bond of fellowship. Some of the members had already eaten their meals before other members had arrived for the common meal. In such an unloving atmosphere, the unifying presence of Jesus Christ in the Lord's Supper had completely lost its meaning. By their behavior the Corinthians were denying the Real Presence of Christ in His body and blood.

Other Bible scholars believe that the Christians at Corinth celebrated the "love feast" as a part of the Lord's Supper celebration.

Paul's point remains the same in both interpretations. He warns the Corithnians that their unloving approach to Christian worship was doing them more harm than good. He tells them that God brings judgment, not blessing, on those who treat fellow Christians with contempt during the worship service. He counsels them to examine their behavior before coming to worship and to recognize that Jesus Christ is in their midst, bringing them all into a common and intimate fellowship with Himself.

This lesson stimulates us to review our own worship attitudes as Christian believers. We should be prompted by Christ's love to develop worship attitudes that bring God's blessing and solidify the unity of God's church.

GETTING INTO THE LESSON
(Objectives 1 and 4)

Use the opening section of the Student Book. Encourage the students to look at Christian worship from God's perspective. What does God see going on in the assembly of believers on a typical Sunday morning? You might put two columns on the blackboard with the following headings: "Worship from God's Perspective" and "Worship from Human Perspective." Ask the students to volunteer their opinions about what God expects in our worship and also their opinions about how humans actually do worship. Try to highlight the truth that worship is not a casual performance to be entered into lightly. It can be an experience that brings great blessings. It can also be dangerous—if our attitudes toward fellow Christians are unloving.

The Danger of Going to Church (Objective 1)

1. Both of these worship narratives are examples of loveless behavior toward other people. Such worship is *hypocritical* because it seeks God's love for itself but denies God's love to others.

2) a. The divisions within the church at Corinth especially manifested themselves when people were forced to interact at worship. We can imagine the members snubbing one another and making negative comments about fellow believers.

b. The common meal or "love feast" (cf. **Acts 2:42, 46; 2 Peter 2:13; Jude 12**) might be compared to a modern potluck dinner in which food is contributed and then shared. The unity intended by this meal was blatantly dispelled by some members who went ahead and ate the food they brought before others arrived. The poorer members consequently had nothing to eat.

c. The apostle accuses the Corinthians of despising God's people who *are* the church of God.

d. This description of showing favoritism toward those who were affluent and finely clothed offers still another example of how Christian worship is distorted. The oneness shared in Christ must not be divided by human distinctions such as social class and the like (cf. **Gal. 3:28**).

e. Underscore this important truth. Worship is fellowship with God and fellow believers. You cannot have fellowship with God when you are out of fellowship with a Christian brother or sister. See **1 John 4:19–21**.

Worshiping in a "Worthy" or an "Unworthy" Manner (Objectives 1, 2, 3, and 4)

This section on the Lord's Supper will be more comprehensively treated in session 89 in this course. You might deal with this subject in a more general manner now and in a more particular manner in that session. Today's lesson focuses on the doctrinal emphasis of the unity Christians share as they fellowship with Christ in His holy Supper.

1) a. Jesus clearly taught that His body was present in the bread ("This is My body . . . ") and His blood present in the wine ("This is the new covenant in My blood . . . "). (See also **Matt. 26:26–28; Mark 14:22–24; Luke 22:19–20**. Refer also to a brief summary of the doctrine of the Real Presence in the Augsburg Confession, Article X.)

b. Be sure to emphasize this passage. It indicates the participation of Christ's body and blood with the bread and wine. It is essential to underscore the truth that Christ is really present in the Sacrament.

c. We remember Christ's *death* on the cross in which His body was sacrificed and His blood shed for the forgiveness of our sins. This remembrance brings with it the assurance of God's salvation. As Luther reminds us, "Where there is forgiveness of sins, there is also life and salvation" (SC VI 6).

d. Such eating and drinking portrays our confession of faith that Christ died for us and that He is truly in fellowship with us now as Lord. It also points to the future fellowship we will have with Him in the coming Kingdom.

2) a. "Unworthy" refers to the sinful behavior that acts as if the Lord Jesus was not present in the Lord's Supper or that His body and blood did not bind believers together in unity. **Verse 27** makes this distinction clear. Failure to recognize the presence of Christ in this Supper makes mockery of the holiness and meaning of this meal. It thus reveals impenitence and unbelief.

b. "Worthy" includes faith in Christ's promise of forgiveness, the recognition of His loving presence in the Supper, and love for the fellow Christians who share this Sacrament together. (See the discussion on "worthy" and "unworthy" guests in the Formula of Concord, Epitome, Article VII, 6–20.)

c. The purpose of a spiritual examination relates both to the need to recognize Christ's presence and the need to approach the Lord's Supper in penitence and faith.

d. The judgment of God on those who sin against Christ's body and blood is a disciplinary and corrective action. It was meant to create repentance, not to instill fear. Those who suffered sickness and death by virtue of their actions brought such judgment on themselves by their loveless behavior; that is, lovelessness has accompanying physical consequences.

e. The deepening of our faith in Christ and the growth of our love for God and one another are examples of His blessings.

Worship That Honors God (Objectives 3 and 4)

1. Emphasize the need to reach out to the fellow Christian and to build up the faith of those who are fellow believers. Worship is not a "solo" act.

2–4. Use these examples and students' responses to them as exercises to bring home in a concrete way the major theme of this lesson.

Conclude this lesson by having the class pray in unison the prayer in their books.

Session 52: Concluding Activities for Unit 5

STUDENT BOOK ACTIVITIES

Several activities have been included in the Student Book to help review the sessions of this unit. Let your decision about which activities to use be guided by your perception of student needs. You may want to use all the class time for further discussion of one or more of the sessions. For example, the students may want to speak at greater length about marriage or about the problem of temptation. Use your discretion about how best to reinforce the truths garnered from these sessions.

If you plan to make use of the skits, assign the groups a day or so ahead of time.

ESSAY TEST

If you must administer a formal test, consider preparing a series of essay questions over the things you emphasized during the unit. Following are some possible questions that you may use.

1. Discuss quarreling among Christians. Think of issues as: What causes Christians to quarrel? How can quarrels be resolved? prevented?

2. Compare human wisdom and the wisdom of the cross.

3. Tell what it means to you that your body is a temple of the Holy Spirit. How does it affect the things you do from day to day? Where do you get the power to live that way? How can you live with yourself and with God when you feel like you "let the Holy Spirit down"?

4. Discuss God's attitude toward marriage, toward singleness, and toward sexuality.

5. Discuss the relationship of temptation, sin, Satan, and God.

6. Describe the blessings you, as an individual believer in Christ, receive from the Lord's Supper. Also describe the blessings you and other Christians receive collectively from that Sacrament.

UNIT 6: FAITH USES GOD'S GIFTS

BIBLE BASIS: 1 COR.12–15

The writer and editor of this unit do not know you. Nor do we know your students. But we know something about all of you. We know that you have received marvelous gifts from God.

As a child of God, you have received one or more spiritual gifts to use for His glory and the good of His church. Your students who have faith in Jesus likewise have spiritual gifts. God has given very specific directions to use your gifts in love.

At times in church we conduct ourselves arrogantly or disorderly. God provides directions for us to live peacefully and orderly.

Because Jesus rose from the dead, we can be certain that we, too, shall rise. After the resurrection all believers in Christ will live with Him in heaven, bestowed with spiritual bodies that will be like His glorious body.

During the sessions of this unit you will have opportunities to examine these gifts in greater detail, with an emphasis upon using those gifts. Read the central truths and objectives of all the sessions to identify more completely the direction taken with these topics.

Ask students to read in advance the portion of **1 Corinthians** suggested for each session. If you assign homework, consider following the suggestions given in this guide to introduce unit 5.

Session 53: Finding My Spiritual Gift

BIBLE BASIS
1 Cor. 12:1–31

CENTRAL TRUTH

Just as every part of the human body has a useful function, so every member of God's church has a necessary and useful gift to contribute for the church's benefit. The Holy Spirit has called us to faith in Christ and has given each of us a spiritual gift to use for the common good of the church.

OBJECTIVES

By the grace of God students will
1. declare that God has called to them to faith in Christ and by Baptism has made them members of His church;
2. describe how the Holy Spirit has given them a spiritual gift to use for the common good of the church;
3. explain how the church is like the human body in terms of the diversity of its members but also in terms of the unity of its function;
4. seek to discover their spiritual gifts and become active in the ministry of the church.

BACKGROUND

The apostle Paul went to great lengths explaining the doctrine of spiritual gifts (*charismata*) to the Corinthian Christians. Nearly one-fifth of his letter is spent describing the nature and purpose of these gifts and their role in the life of the church (**chapters 12, 13, and 14**). Paul delights in showing how the Holy Spirit dispenses many gifts and blessings within the context of the church. He does not in any way minimize the doctrine of spiritual gifts.

The Corinthian Christians certainly prized the Spirit's gifts and sought after them eagerly. However, they perverted the divine function of these gifts by failing to use them for the edification of the church. As will be made clear in the next two lessons, the Corinthians were appropriating the gifts for their own gratification; they were seeking those spiritual gifts that more easily brought attention to themselves rather than the building of God's church. In summary, the Corinthians had frustrated God's plan for the unity and harmony of the church.

In this chapter Paul sketches God's plan for spiritual gifts by comparing the church to a human body. Every member of the church is to contribute his or her gift for the effective functioning of Christ's Body just as every part of the human body works in harmony with the rest of the body. Paul's basic theme is this: God provides diversity in the church, but above all, there is unity.

This chapter contains the most comprehensive listing of spiritual gifts in the New Testament. Other New Testament books, however, mention additional gifts, so we cannot state the exact number or actual list of all the Spirit's gifts.

This lesson is especially appropriate for young people who seek a more active role in their congregations. It challenges the students to express their faith through contributing their gifts to the church. By the same token it warns them not to make their individually appointed gifts more important than the mission of the church.

GETTING INTO THE LESSON
(Objectives 2 and 4)

Use the opening section of the Student Book to lead into the lesson. You might ask the students what they already know about spiritual gifts. Seek to perk their interest in this topic by pointing out that every believer has been appointed a spiritual gift. The work of the church will suffer if some believers fail to contribute their particular gift to the church's mission. Emphasize that young people as well, because they have the fullness of the Holy Spirit within them, have gifts to share for the common good. Throughout the lesson try to keep the focus on the *church* rather than on an individualistic appropriation of gifts.

As you discuss this lesson, you need not make any reference to the charismatic movement. Likely such discussion would only detract rather than add to the Scriptural foundation presented in this lesson. If the subject is brought up, simply refer to the fact that the term *charismata* refers to spiritual gifts. Remind the students that the study of spiritual gifts for the edification of the church is the objective of the lesson.

What Are Spiritual Gifts? (Objectives 1, 2, and 4)

1) a. This refers to the phrase, **"I do not want you to be ignorant" (12:1).**

b. Faith in Jesus Christ is God's working within us through the Holy Spirit. The Spirit calls us to faith through the Gospel. The passage from **1 Cor. 2:12–15** makes it clear that we cannot understand spiritual truths without the Holy Spirit's intervention.

c. This refers to the many different types of Christian service that must be performed within a Christian congregation. God's plan involves everyone in the congregation, not just a privileged few. The vast variety of gifts allows every believer to participate.

d. The text clearly states, **"He gives them to each one."** God mentions no exceptions. The Spirit's selection process is equally clear, **"just as He determines."** As to the question whether some believers have more than one spiritual gift, the answer is affirmative. Paul had several of the spiritual gifts he mentioned in his letters.

e. Make a strong emphasis of this truth. All spiritual gifts have but one purpose: the edification of God's church—**"for the common good." (Chapters 13 and 14** of **1 Corinthians** were necessary for Paul to write because the Corinthian Christians were not using their gifts for the common good.)

2. Do not spend too much time on the interpretation of the spiritual gifts enumerated in this chapter and listed in the Student Book. They are included in the Student Book so that the students may obtain a "feel" for what these gifts involve.

Much of the interpretation of these spiritual gifts was taken from *The Charismatic Movement and Lutheran Theology,* a report of the Commission on Theology and Church Relations of the Lutheran Church—Missouri Synod, January, 1972 (pp. 19–20).

Several of the spiritual gifts listed in the Student Book are identified in portions of Scripture not studied in this session. Following is a more complete listing of gifts mentioned elsewhere:

- **Rom. 12:** Prophecy, service, teaching, exhortation, giving, mercy, leadership
- **Eph. 3:** Missionary
- **Eph. 4:** Evangelism, prophecy, pastoring, teaching
- **1 Cor. 7:** Celibacy
- **1 Cor. 13:** Martyrdom, voluntary poverty
- **1 Peter 4; Heb. 13:** Hospitality

3. These suggestions for discovering one's spiritual gifts are a consensus of persons who are active in the ministry of spiritual gifts. If your students are interested in pursuing this topic, provide resources (such as inventories) used in congregations that support your school. Encourage students to become involved in their congregations' spiritual gifts programs.

How the Body of Christ Works (Objectives 1, 2, 3, and 4)

1) a. Paul points out that many different types of people have been called into the fellowship of God's church and have been molded into a unity. This unity is possible because the Holy Spirit who has called them is one. He further has called them through the Sacrament of Baptism in which all of them received the fullness of the Spirit at the time of their baptism.

Emphasize that the New Testament teaches only one baptism, namely, water baptism. The phrase, **"and you will be baptized by the Holy Spirit,"** ordinarily refers to the receiving of the Holy Spirit and His gifts through the preaching of the Gospel (the Word and the Sacraments). The modern Pentecostal belief that one is first baptized into Christ and then into the Holy Spirit is foreign to the New Testament. See **Eph. 4:4–5.**

b, c, and d. These passages teach a major truth about the doctrine of spiritual gifts. God provides a *diversity* of gifts in the church. By the same token, He gives the gifts for the *unity* of the church. Paul's analogy of the human body aptly illustrates this important truth. Problems with spiritual gifts occur when one or more members move out of the fellowship of Christ's body and seek to do "solo acts" with their gifts.

2) a. Answers will vary. As a part of the body of Christ, God will move us to "be alive"—to identify the spiritual gift through which we can provide special service to Him and the rest of His body.

b. Many in the Corinthian church (as will be expounded upon in **chapter 14**) were seeking those gifts that enabled them personal gratification. For this reason the most important gifts, those gifts that were more vitally involved with building the faith of the members, were often bypassed by the self-seeking Corinthians. The gifts of apostleship, prophecy, and teaching are listed as more important than the others because they are more involved with faith-building.

c. The gift of tongues does little, if anything, for the edification of the church. Apparently for this reason it is listed last.

d. Believers should be open to any of the gifts of the Holy Spirit. The love of God, however, should make them so concerned about the faith of others that their desire is for those gifts that build faith.

3. Use this question to provide a forward-looking

conclusion to this session. Discourage discussion that dwells upon controversies around spiritual gifts, and encourage comments related to the blessings that can occur when we use our gifts for the glory of God and the good of the rest of the body of Christ.

Session 54: Using My Spiritual Gifts in Love

BIBLE BASIS
1 Cor. 13:1–13

CENTRAL TRUTH
God fills us with His love so that our ministry of spiritual gifts benefits others in His church. His love, which will never cease, sustains us in our ministry now and will be the foundation of our life with God in the world to come.

OBJECTIVES
By the grace of God students will
1. declare that God's love in them is necessary to direct and make fully effective their ministry of spiritual gifts;
2. describe how Christian love is Christ-like; it seeks the good of others instead of trying to gratify our own sinful human nature;
3. explain how God's love will never cease, but will be with them in their life with God in the world to come;
4. reaffirm that God's love in Jesus Christ is God's greatest gift of all.

BACKGROUND
The famous 13th chapter of **1 Corinthians** is actually a commentary on the proper use of spiritual gifts in God's church. Paul reaches the heights in showing how God's love must direct and motivate the Christian ministry of gifts.

True to their pattern of spiritual pride, the Corinthian Christians had appropriated the Spirit's gifts for their own selfish gratification. Rather than unity and fellowship, the members were engaged in a charade of individualism, each one seeking to out perform the other. As a result, they failed to use the Spirit's gifts for the purpose He had given them—for the edification of the church.

The apostle reminded the Corinthians that God's gifts must be used with Christ-like love, because only God's love can transform sinful human nature. When God's love controls us, we will show concern for the good of others and will use God's gifts for their intended purpose. God's love in the life of Christians both now and in the life to come is so important that Paul insists that God can give no greater gift. Spiritual gifts will cease when their purpose on earth has come to completion, but God's love will remain forever. This love is the empowering principle that makes both faith and hope possible.

GETTING INTO THE LESSON (Objectives 1 and 2)

Use the opening section of the Student Book to lead into the lesson. Discuss the implications of the story with the students. Try to get them involved by volunteering similar situations in which human pride claims God's gifts as its own. You might point out that one of the major differences between the Christian life and paganism is that Christians see all of life as God's gift to them. We have this view because God's love has changed our perception of life itself.

The Most Excellent Way (Objectives 1 and 2)
1) a. The gong or cymbal represents a sound that signifies noise—or nothing.
b. This refers to the gift of martyrdom. Even this heroic gift is without value if not done in love.
c. Any gift performed without love has no value for the body of Christ. It is only for show. It is like a tree with magnificent foliage but no fruit.
2) a. All of the qualities of love mentioned by Paul are exemplified in the life of Jesus Christ. Use as much time on this question as you feel is necessary to make this truth indelible.
b, c, and d. Be sure to apply these qualities to the daily life of the students. Make certain they realize that God's love goes against the grain of their natural inclinations. Neither can they manufacture this love on their own. God's love is His gift to us through faith.
e. The love God poured out to the world in Christ's sacrificial gift is the same love bestowed on us today through the Holy Spirit.
f. Emphasize that love is open to God and to all of His promises. Love makes faith and hope possible. That is why love is greater than faith and hope (see **v. 13**).

Love Never Fails (Objectives 3 and 4)
1) a. Spiritual gifts have been given to Christians as a special blessing for the good of the church until the end of the age when Christ returns to earth. They are important funtions for the spiritual life of believers at the present time. In the life to come when we are face to face with God, we will not need spiritual gifts.
b. We will attain perfection in the life God has designed for us in the world to come; it includes the resurrected body.
c. Spiritual gifts seem childish when compared to the glory of heaven.
d. It is difficult for us to imagine being face to face

in God's presence, but this is what God promises. Our sinful nature prevents us from seeing Him except by reflection now.

    2. See the note on 2f above.

    3. Spend some time with these situations or any others you wish to pose. Note that a designated driver (e) may contribute to chemical abuse, including enabling action toward dependency.

    Close with a prayer or sing together the hymn verses.

Session 55: A God of Peace and Order

BIBLE BASIS
1 Cor. 14:1–40

CENTRAL TRUTH
God desires that our life together in His church be patterned after the way of peace and order. He shares His love with us and equips us to conduct our ministry of spiritual gifts and worship in an orderly and edifying manner.

OBJECTIVES
By the grace of God students will
1. affirm that God's plan for their life together in the church is the way of peace and order;
2. explain how they should use their spiritual gifts to edify others in the church;
3. describe how every aspect of ministry in the church, including worship and the roles of men and women, should reflect the way of peace and the building up of God's church;
4. tell how God's love motivates them to seek the way of God's peace.

BACKGROUND
In **1 Cor. 14** Paul sums up his comments about the proper use of spiritual gifts and an orderly worship life. He once again underscores the truth that all aspects of the church's life be directed toward the edification and spiritual growth of the members of Christ's body.

The apostle argues that life in the church must be peaceful and orderly because God Himself is a God of peace. This admonition became necessary because of a disregard for the common good within the church at Corinth. The Corinthians had overprized the gift of tongues, the least edifying of the Spirit's gifts. True to their flair for individualism and self-gratification, their desire for self-edification via tongues had brought spiritual poverty to the congregation. This was especially reflected in a disorderly and devisive worship life that produced an unwholesome witness to unbelievers at these services.

The edification of the Corinthian church was also disrupted by their disregard for the proper roles of men and women in the church. Because of their belief that they had freedom to do anything they pleased (see **chapter 6**), women were usurping the authority of men in meetings and in worship. Paul reminds the Corinthians of God's design for the role of woman, calling her to be in submission to her husband. The scope of activities for women to take part in in the church is vast. Spiritual gifts are bestowed on women as well as men. God, however, vests the authority of the public ministry on men, not women.

The issues raised in this lesson—speaking in tongues and the role of women in the church—are sensitive issues. Approach them as Paul approached them, not in legalism but in the love of Christ. Only through the eyes of God's love can we understand and follow after God's design for peace and unity in the church.

GETTING INTO THE LESSON
(Objectives 1 and 4)

    Use the opening section of the Student Book for a lead into the lesson. Have one of the students read the parable aloud. Involve the class in a discussion on how disorder in the church so easily arises when members go their own way without regard for the common good. Ask the students to volunteer examples from their own experience. Try to emphasize that disorder is the normal experience of our life together because of our sinful disposition to have our own way. Point out that God not only calls the church to live together in peace but also gives us the power, namely, His love in Christ Jesus, to accomplish this task.

Seek to Edify the Church, Not Yourselves
(Objectives 1 and 2)

    1) a. The gift of tongues is addressed only to God, not to others. Contrariwise, the gift of prophecy **"speaks to men for their strengthening, encouragement, and comfort"** (v. 3). **Note:** The definitions of *tongues* and *prophecy* have been included in session 53.

    b. Tongues edify others only when their content has been interpreted either by the speaker or by someone who has the gift of interpretation.

    c. Tongues sound unintelligible to those who hear them. Like hearing a foreign language, one hears sounds without meaning.

    d. Those who pray in tongues do not mentally understand what they are praying; only God does. Praying with the mind edifies others because the speaker is thinking thoughts that can be understood when verbalized.

    2) a. Paul is concerned about the spiritual life of others, the major truth he focuses upon in this chapter.

b. "Will they not say that you are out of your mind?"

c. The Holy Spirit works through the gift of prophecy (the message of the Law and Gospel) to convict hearers of their sin and turn them to Jesus Christ.

d. Paul does not forbid tongue-speaking, but urges believers to seek spiritual gifts that build the church. Take note of **verse 20** and Paul's scolding of the Corinthians for overprizing tongues. As so often is the case, those who are compulsive about tongue-speaking are like children seeking attention. Paul views tongues as a gift that can be used privately and simply to God's glory.

Strive for Orderly Worship Objectives 1, 2, and 3)

1. The picture described in **verse 26** suggests mass confusion, similar to the opening parable.

2. Paul is interested in the spiritual edification of the congregation. Too many speakers turns worship into a contest.

3. Those who are speaking God's will to the congregation should be clearheaded and responsible. They especially should be sensitive to the need for wholesome order or peace.

4. This seems to be a good exercise to allow the students to discuss the concept of meaningful and orderly worship. Spend some time exploring how the entire liturgy draws out and blends the spiritual gifts of the members into a unity of praise and worship. Perhaps for this reason the liturgy of the church must be changed from time to time.

The Role of Women in the Church
(Objectives 1, 3, and 4)

1) a. Paul often uses the term *Law* to refer to the revelation of the Old Testament. In the order of creation God places the woman in a subordinate position to the man **(Gen. 3:16)**. The New Testament upholds the order of creation in every instance where the relationship of the two genders is mentioned.

b, c, d, and e. Emphasize in this study the same things that Scripture emphasizes. Paul is talking about headship and authority in the church. Concepts of superiority and inferiority are psychological concepts; they deal with the topic of the self-worth of the person. Such concepts have no bearing on the discussion of the topic of complementarity: the authority of the man and the submission of the woman. God's design establishes wholesome order in the relationship of the two genders. Understood through the eyes of God's love, this design does not frustrate the spiritual gifts of men and women, but guides them into their best possible expression.

Translated into the life of the church, this means that women may not hold positions involving the distinctive functions of the pastoral office or any other office that may usurp authority over men.

2–3. Balance the discussion of the woman's role in the church with an emphasis on the vital and wide-ranging activities in which women are involved. Spend some time discussing the important functions that women played in the New Testament church. As in all topics that deal with the life of the church, focus on the unity and edification of God's church.

4. Make certain that the students understand that God's love is essential in the use of spiritual gifts and our life with others. You may want to refer to this section from time to time as you proceed through the lesson.

Session 56: We Shall Be Raised from the Dead

BIBLE BASIS
1 Cor. 15:1–34

CENTRAL TRUTH

By means of the resurrection of Jesus Christ, God guarantees that our sins have been forgiven and that we too shall be raised from the dead. We live in faith and hope made more certain by that resurrection promise.

OBJECTIVES

By the grace of God students will

1. affirm the truth of the Gospel and the certainty of the resurrection of Jesus Christ;
2. explain how the resurrection of Christ guarantees that their sins have been forgiven;
3. explain how the resurrection of Christ guarantees their own resurrection from the dead;
4. describe the hope that the resurrection promise brings to their lives.

BACKGROUND

All that characterized the spiritual pride of the Corinthian church as we have discussed in these past lessons finds its culmination in the denial of the resurrection. Some of the members of the congregation were denying that the dead could be raised. Paul responds by stating that a denial of the resurrection of the dead meant also a denial of the resurrection of Jesus Christ—consequently, this meant a denial of the Gospel itself!

The truth of the resurrection is tied to the truth of the Gospel and the promise of salvation. For this reason Paul begins his discussion of the resurrection by establishing the importance of the Gospel. If there is no resurrection, there is no Gospel, and all is lost.

In this chapter Paul goes to great pains to show

the necessity of the resurrection for the Christian faith. He marshalls argument after argument in order to prove that the dynamic of the Christian life is linked inextricably to the fact of the resurrection of the dead. In his entire discussion of the topic, Paul always links together the resurrection of Christ with the resurrection of God's people. Christ's love is so great that He would never desert His own. *Because Christ lives, we live!* This is the basis of our resurrection hope.

This lesson is extremely important in showing the relationship of the resurrection to the power of the Gospel and to the validity of our Christian faith. A careful examination of the text is an investment that knows no price tag.

GETTING INTO THE LESSON
(Objectives 1, 3, and 4)

Use the opening section as a lead into the lesson. Emphasize the radical nature of the Christian Gospel as it challenged the fatalistic beliefs of the ancient world. Try to correlate this same challenge with the fatalism of the modern world which attempts to mask its fear of death by hiding from it. Seek to involve the students in a discussion of the hope that the resurrection brings to their faith and life. **What difference does the resurrection make?** This is the theme that runs through the entire lesson.

The Resurrection Gospel (Objectives 1 and 2)

1. The Gospel is the proclamation of the death of Christ for our sins and of His resurrection from the dead. It assures us that our sins have been forgiven. This redemptive work of Christ is rooted in history and based on fact. The Gospel is the news of what Christ has done for us.

2. Through the Gospel God offers us salvation. He freely offers this gift to all who will receive it by faith. The Gospel is the heart and center of the Christian faith. Remove the Gospel, and nothing remains except a lifeless shell.

3. The eyewitnesses were important to verify the resurrection of Jesus. But more than that, Paul here rooted the Gospel in historical fact and removed it from the genre of mythology. He will not allow anyone to spiritualize the resurrection away, as the agnostics were wont to do.

4–5. Paul claims to be an eyewitness of the resurrected Christ, but through very exceptional circumstances. Nevertheless, he sets forth the claim that he has the credentials for the apostolate.

The Necessity of the Resurrection (Objectives 1, 2, and 3)

1) a. Certain Christians were denying that Christ was raised.

b. The truth that Christ's resurrection and our resurrection are indissolvably linked is based on the fact that Christ has made Himself one with us. We are *His* people and the recipients of all His gifts. In **Rom. 6:4–5** Paul states that through Baptism we have become united with Christ.

c. No martyr's death can assure the forgiveness of sins. Without the resurrection the cross is emptied of its power **(1:17)**. Our faith in Christ is not based on his example. We believe in Him because He has released us from sin's bondage and because His power rules our lives.

d. If the resurrection was a falsehood, Paul and the other apostles would be accused of lying.

e. Without Christ's resurrection those who have died would be lost forever.

f. In **verse 19** Paul means that we would be living a hoax. Everything we would consider as important and meaningful would have no basis of truth.

2. Paul states that he takes great risks with his life. The certainty of the resurrection causes Him to be unafraid of what people can do to him. If there is no resurrection, the philosophy of the Epicureans **(vv. 32b–33)** is as good as any to follow.

The Hope of the Resurrection (Objectives 3 and 4)

1) a. Paul draws the illustration of firstfruits from the Old Testament. It refers to the first fruits of the harvest. The remainder of the harvest would be gathered during the days and weeks that follow.

b. The terms first Adam and last Adam provide a useful paradigm to explain the reason for death and the promise of the resurrection.

c. When Christ returns on the Last Day, He will bring a completion to His mission of redemption. All that has been broken will at last be healed. All the enemies of God, including death, will be vanquished. Christ will present His completed work to the Father.

d. Death is an enemy in the sense that it has disrupted God's creation and broken what God has made. Only in the sense that death is the means by which we shall be changed at the resurrection, can it be said to be a friend.

2–4. Use these exercises as opportunities for the class to apply the truths learned in the lesson.

Close with prayer or speak or sing the hymn stanzas.

Session 57: We Shall Be Raised with Spiritual Bodies

BIBLE BASIS
1 Cor. 15:35–58

CENTRAL TRUTH
In the resurrection God will raise us with spiritual bodies that will be like Christ's glorious body. He gives us power to live confidently in the hope of the resurrection, when we shall share His victory over death.

OBJECTIVES
By the grace of God students will
1. describe how God will give them new bodies at the resurrection;
2. explain how their new bodies in the resurrection will be like Christ's glorious body;
3. explain the distinction between their earthly bodies and the spiritual bodies God will give them at the resurrection;
4. tell how the hope of the resurrection gives them confidence to live their lives in victory.

BACKGROUND
This lesson continues the study of the chapter of the resurrection, **1 Cor. 15.** In the last half of this chapter Paul deals with the nature of the resurrected body itself.

One issue—the question concerning the type of body God will raise—may be Paul's cynical response to the attitudes of the resurrection held by some of the Corinthians. On the other hand, Paul may be answering one of the many questions the Corinthians addressed to him (see **1 Cor. 7:1**). At any rate Paul considered such questions as foolish, a denial of the power of God to create life.

Paul's description of the resurrected body is a comparison of the earthly body we now possess and the spiritual body with which we shall be equipped in the resurrection. Once again the apostle links together the resurrection of Jesus Christ and the resurrection of the dead. Our bodies in the resurrection will be like Christ's glorious body, equipped with honor, power, and imperishability. The day of resurrection, in which Christ will defeat death forever, will signal the victory promised ages ago. We live by this promise now. The resurrection power floods our lives with a faith and confidence no enemy can overcome.

GETTING INTO THE LESSON
(Objectives 1 and 2)

Use the opening section of the Student Book to lead into the lesson. Allow the students opportunity to express their own questions about the resurrection body. What speculations have they lived with all their lives? What questions and concerns do they still harbor in their hearts and minds? Encourage them to express such concerns before entering the lesson proper, inasmuch as the Biblical answer will raise them to a much higher level and provide much more satisfaction. Underscore the truth that *all* questions of faith and life for the Christian find their answer in the knowledge and wisdom of Jesus Christ.

The Resurrection Body (Objectives 1 and 3)

1. Paul considers the skeptical attitude to be foolish. See the "Background" section for more discussion.

2. Paul compares our bodies to a seed and the plant that ultimately proceeds from it. It may be well to have an actual seed and plant in the classroom to visualize this important distinction.

3. Emphasize this truth of a transformation from one body to another. Ordinarily, death provides the catalyst for this transformation. Even those who will not pass through death on the day of Christ's return (the "living" in the Apostles' Creed) will go through a change (see **v. 51**).

4. Paul's argument is straightforward. There is no distinction between the power of God that created our present forms of life and the power that will create the new resurrected body.

"In the Likeness of the Man of Heaven"
(Objectives 1, 2, and 3)

1) a. It is difficult to say exactly what the term *spiritual* connotes. This term can also mean supernatural. Clearly, Paul seems to be saying that our bodies will be animated by a life-giving spirit **(v. 45).** It may also designate a body which is a perfect dwelling place for the Holy Spirit (cf. **6:19**).

b. Make certain the students are clear on the difference between a spiritual being and a spiritual body. In the resurrection we will not be free-floating spirits or angels. We will possess the clothing of a spiritual body **(2 Cor. 5:4).**

c and d. Our resurrected bodies will be impervious to death or any weakness whatsoever. In the Luke reference Christ mentions that there will be no marriages in the resurrection. Obviously this means that there will be no need for procreation in heaven. Marriage and family life are earthly blessings. Our life in the resurrection will be face to face with God.

2) a. These passages make clear that our resurrected bodies will not be fashioned like the perfect body of Adam before the Fall. We will not be returned to a pristine state of existence. Rather, we will be fashioned after the last Adam, even Jesus Christ.

b. Our resurrected bodies will be equipped with

glory, honor, power, and imperishability. The Philippians reference contrasts our present lowly existance and our exalted existence to come. All this is due to God's grace.

c and d. Emphasize that our earthly bodies are dominated by and contaminated by the power of sin. Fashioned as they are by flesh and blood, they are vulnerable to death. Such bodies are not equipped to live with God in the glory of the Kingdom to come.

Sharing in the Victory to Come
(Objectives 1, 2, 3, and 4)

1) a. See the note under 1c in the previous section

b. Our bodies will be imperishabile and immortal.

c. The victory of Christ over death is traced back to Adam's transgression which brought to the human race the guilt of sin and the consequence of death. Sin is the sting because sin gives death power over humanity **(Rom. 5:17)**. The Law is the power of sin because sin grows more powerful when confronted by the Law **(Rom.5:20)**.

2–4. Use these exercises as opportunities for the class to apply the truths learned in this lesson.

Close with prayer or speak or sing the hymn stanzas.

Session 58: Concluding Activities for Unit 6

STUDENT BOOK ACTIVITIES

Several activities have been included in the Student Book to help review the sessions of this unit. Let your decision about which activities to use be guided by your perceptions of student interests and needs. If you discuss one of the more controversial issues (such as charismatic gifts or the role of women in the church), be sure to thoroughly study the issue on your own before class. You may be able to receive guidance from a study document prepared by the Commission on Theology and Church Relations of The Lutheran Church—Missouri Synod, 1333 South Kirkwood Road, St. Louis, MO 63122-7295.

If you work on one or more banners, divide the class into groups in advance. Provide time for them to meet to plan the banners, assign responsibilities, and secure materials.

ESSAY TEST

If you must administer a formal test, consider preparing a series of essay questions over the things you emphasized during the unit. Prepare your own questions or use those that follow.

1. Describe a plan a congregation can follow in using the spiritual gifts of its members. Include discussion about how to deal with problems that may occur, such as apathy or the use of a gift for self-gratification instead of for the common good.

2. Discuss the relationship between love and spiritual gifts. Illustrate how members of a congregation may demonstrate love toward one another.

3. Discuss the roles of men and women in the church.

4. Suppose the Christian father or mother of one of your classmates died suddenly. Write a letter to that classmate in which you describe the hope God gives us through Christ's resurrection.

5. Contrast the way a Christian and a non-Christian face death.

UNIT 7: FAITH POINTS US TO SERVICE

BIBLE BASIS: 2 CORINTHIANS

The situation that prompted Paul's second letter to the Corinthians found a congregation far more receptive and repentant than previously. In Paul's first letter he scolded the Corinthians for their spiritual arrogance and pride. After that letter he sent Timothy and Titus to visit the congregation. The situation worsened because a group within the congregation opposed Paul's authority and claimed the authority of spiritual guidance for themselves. Paul felt compelled to visit the troubled congregation himself (in addition to sending yet another letter now lost; cf. **2 Cor. 2:4**). Probably no congregation gave Paul greater heartbreak than Corinth.

When Paul wrote this second (the last) letter to the church at Corinth, the major problems of the congregation had been resolved. With such concerns settled, the apostle turns his attention to the urgent task of spreading the Good News of Christ. This letter contains some of the richest expositions of New Testament evangelism. The spirit of love in the apostle's writing overwhelms us, especially when we consider the pain and the grief both he and the congregation endured.

The sessions in this unit follow this theme: faith points us to service.

God's new covenant with us empowers us to witness mightily to those around us.

God's power works through even our weaknesses to advance the Gospel message. Therefore we need not lose heart.

God reconciled us to Himself and thus also made us ambassadors to the world.

God's generous love for us empowers us to contribute liberally to the needs of others.

God works through our hardships and weaknesses to strengthen our faith in Him and to empower us to minister more effectively for Him.

The statements above summarize the content of this unit. Read the central truths and objectives of all the sessions to identify more completely the direction taken with these topics.

Ask students to read in advance the portion of **2 Corinthians** suggested for each session. If you assign homework, consider following the suggestions given in this guide to introduce unit 5.

Session 59: The Glory of the New Covenant

BIBLE BASIS
2 Cor. 3:1–4:6

CENTRAL TRUTH
God calls us to be ministers of the new covenant and empowers us with the sufficiency to accomplish this task. God's old covenant came with glory, but the glory of the new covenant surpasses it in every way. God makes us bold in our faith and will use our witness to advance the Gospel.

OBJECTIVES
By the grace of God students will
1. declare that God has called them to be ministers of the new covenant in Jesus Christ and supplies them with power for this task;
2. explain how the Holy Spirit breathes new life into people through the ministry of the new covenant;
3. describe how the glory of the new covenant far surpasses the glory of the old covenant of Moses;
4. express confidence and boldness that God will use them mightily to witness for the Gospel of Christ.

BACKGROUND
This lesson introduces the students to the important teaching of the new covenant and the privilege of all Christians to share in this ministry. Paul sets forth the theme of the splendor of the new covenant by comparing it with the old covenant. Whereas the old covenant, fashioned on tablets of stone, condemned the sinner, the new covenant offers life with God. In the new covenant, in which the Holy Spirit brings the Gospel of forgiveness to human hearts, God shares His glory with us in a manner that pales the glory of the old covenant. We are indeed privileged to minister to this new covenant and to share our faith with others in word and deed.

GETTING INTO THE LESSON (Objective 1)
Use the opening section of the Student Book to lead into the lesson. Review the narrative to demonstrate how our Christian influence is one of the most effective ways by which we can share the Gospel. People take note of what we say and how we behave in certain situations. The repercussions of our total life are vast and either affirm the Gospel or negate it. In such a manner parents witness of Christ to their chil-

dren, friends witness to friends, and spouses to spouses (cf. **1 Peter 3:1**).

Preaching the Gospel doesn't have to be showy or spectacular. Such a false impression of witnessing many dampen the enthusiasm of young people. They may feel intimidated and, as a result, not witness at all. You might make a distinction between witnessing for Christ and being gifted with the gift of evangelism **(Eph. 4:11).** Not every believer has the gift of evangelism (the ability to disciple a person so that he or she becomes a Christian). But all of us have been called to be witnesses for Christ in word and deed.

In sum, the aim of this lesson is to have the students warm up to the topic of sharing the Gospel and to feel a privilege in doing so.

We Are Ministers of the New Covenant
(Objectives 1 and 2)

1. The term *minister* means *one who represents another* or *one who serves*. It certainly applies to all believers, not just the pastor. The pastor, however, serves in special ways as the shepherd to his flock. For instance, He preaches the Word and administers the Sacraments.

2. The competency refers to the working of the Holy Spirit within us who uses us as channels by which the power of the Gospel is proclaimed. We need not question how the Spirit uses us. We only need to be open to His leading.

3. The chart assists in quickly assessing the differences between the two covenants. This activity assumes that the students have some background in the old covenant. Nevertheless, you may want to review **Ex. 19:3–6.** References for the new covenant include **Luke 22:20; 1 Cor. 11:25; Heb. 8:8–10; and 10:16.**

4–5. As the old covenant condemned the sinner by its legal demands, the new covenant offers God's life, that is, God's free gift of forgiveness which inwardly renews the person and inspires in him or her a will that is in harmony with God's will. The new covenant was secured by Christ's sacrifice on the cross by which He shed His blood for our sins. We celebrate the new covenant at every occasion of the Lord's Supper.

6. This important passage declares that the new covenant will be written in the hearts of people wherein the Spirit of Christ resides within us.

7–8. This again refers to the truth that every believer possesses Christ's life. Christians have Christ's love and forgiveness written in their hearts, minds, and behavior.

The Glory of the New Covenant
(Objectives 1, 2, and 3)

1. The people of Israel could not bear to look upon the brightness of God's glory that shone from Moses' face. For this reason he wore a veil.

2. The new covenant not only offers the "righteousness" of God in Christ but, unlike the old covenant, possesses a glory that will never fade away.

3. When the law of Moses is read, those who follow the old covenant cannot understand that the real significance of the law is to witness to the righteousness of the Gospel, which has been revealed (cf. **Rom. 3:21**). In Christ, this veil is removed.

4. The Holy Spirit shares with us his many gifts and blessings, all of which are aspects of God's glory.

We Witnesss for Christ Boldly (Objectives 1 and 4)

1) a. We avoid all such shameful tactics that are not motivated by God's love and that do not bring honor to Christ.

b and c. God promises to give power to His Word as it is spoken by us. We cannot claim that promise, however, if we veil His Word in any way, such as when we speak innaccurately or when we fail to speak.

d. Our boldness to preach Christ openly and without fear stems from the truth that the new covenant is filled with God's power and glory.

2) a. The god of this age refers to Satan, one of the many appellations given to his evil activity by the New Testament writers.

b. Compare the parable of the sower **(Luke 8:11–15).**

c. Our testimony about Christ should focus on Him and His saving activity for our new life with God.

3. Discuss aspects of a life of witnessing. Obviously, it includes showing love to those in need and refraining from activities that God forbids. Note that sometimes we need to show tough love—we need to point out sins or act in a way that causes people to suffer consequences for certain actions. At other times we demonstrate God's love by forgiving one who has sinned against us.

Close with prayer or sing or speak the hymn stanzas.

Session 60: Don't Lose Heart

BIBLE BASIS
2 Cor. 4:7–5:10

CENTRAL TRUTH

Although we are frail jars of clay, God has placed the transcendent power of Christ within us. God's power works through our weakness to advance the Gospel message. That power enables us not to lose heart in our sufferings, but to live by faith that Christ will make us whole at the resurrection.

OBJECTIVES

By the grace of God students will
1. describe how the transcendent power of Christ shines through their human frailty;
2. explain how their own frailty demonstrates that the power of the Gospel comes from God;
3. tell how they live by faith and do not lose heart in times of trouble;
4. express their desire to please Christ, who will make them whole at the resurrection.

BACKGROUND

In this section Paul describes how suffering for the cause of Christ has taken its toll on his physical life. Yet he rejoices that the power of Christ shines through his mortal body, and this encourages him to preach the Gospel all the more. When others hear the Gospel testimony, even in view of his infirmities, they are led to praise God for His grace.

How does Paul continue with such optimism despite the physical distress and mental discouragements he constantly encounters? He fixes his vision on God's promise of the resurrection at which time the Lord will make him whole and clothe him with a heavenly dwelling. Indeed, he longs for that reality now. Nevertheless, until that day of restoration, he will do all he can to please Christ with a life of faith.

This lesson presents a powerful motivation to those who are losing heart because of the setbacks of their ministry. At such times we must all the more walk by faith and come to learn that God's power is at work in us in a mighty way.

Treasures in Jars of Clay (Objectives 1, 2, and 3)

1) a. "Jars of clay" characterize fragility, inasmuch as clay pots are so easily broken (as an archaeologist will attest!). By the same token, they are not easily destroyed. Paul's commentary in **verses 8–9** illustrates these qualities.

b. The "treasure" refers to all Christ is. Paul is especially referring to the power of the Gospel by which Christ rules in human lives.

c. The very fact of our fragility makes clear that the power of our ministry is from God. By virtue of being afflicted, persecuted, and struck down, ministers of the Gospel demonstrate that a power beyond themselves is being manifested in their weakness.

d. God's Gospel brings the new life of Christ.

e. Paul quotes from **Ps. 116:10**; he must speak what he believes. He is not afraid of the consequences of this commitment, because he is certain that Christ will raise him from the dead at the resurrection.

2 a and b. When examined from the perspective of eternal life, our earthly troubles are insignificant and only momentary. Looking at life in this manner is a spiritual key that deserves our attention.

c. Faith enables us to rely on evidence that is not provable to the senses. Such faith relies on a reality that is eternal and that demands our total commitment.

We Live by Faith, Not by Sight (Objectives 2 and 3)

1 a, b, and c. Since the topic of the resurrected body has been comprehensively discussed in session 57, you need not dwell on this subject. Paul's focus in this section is somewhat different. Here he emphasizes how believers seek the new clothing of the resurrected body rather than the nature of the new body itself.

d. Judaic thought—in contrast to Greek thought—could not conceive of a person existing without some type of bodily clothing. Paul's comments emphasize the absurdity of the spirit being "naked." Other religions, including animism, Hinduism, and Buddhism, conjecture the immortality of the soul, which loses all personality and uniqueness.

e. This important truth should be underscored.

2 a and b. Living by faith—not by sight—draws together all the truths contained in this lesson.

c. Spend some time discussing the nature of the judgment seat of Christ. The Student Book contains the basic points for discussion. The works to which Paul refers in **verse 10** are the fruits of faith. They have nothing to do with justification. The **1 Cor. 3:10–15** passage discusses how the fruits of faith will be rewarded with glory in the life to come.

The Lutheran Confessions talk about this matter thusly:

"For when good works are done on account of right causes and for right ends (that is, with the intention that God demands of the regenerated), they are an indication of salvation in believers **(Phil. 1:28)**. It is God's will and express command that believers should do good works which the Holy Spirit works in them, and God is willing to be pleased with them for Christ's sake and he promises to reward them gloriously in this and in the future life" (FC SD VI 38).

Close with prayer or sing or speak the hymn stanzas.

Session 61: Ambassadors to the World

BIBLE BASIS
2 Cor. 5:11–6:2

CENTRAL TRUTH

God has reconciled the world to Himself through Jesus Christ, who died for the sins of all. Through His love for us, He compels us to live our lives for Him as His new creation. God also calls and empowers us to be His personal ambassadors and to share this message of reconciliation with others.

OBJECTIVES

By the grace of God students will

1. tell how Christ's love compels them to live for God as a new creation in Jesus Christ;
2. explain how God has reconciled the world to Himself through Christ's sacrificial death;
3. describe how God has called them to be His ambassadors for the purpose of sharing this message of reconciliation;
4. declare themselves ready to respond to the urgency of proclaiming the message of the Gospel.

BACKGROUND

In this section of 2 Corinthians Paul attains spiritual heights in describing the liberating power of Christ and the redemptive task of the Christian community to proclaim it. He clearly shows the Corinthians how much the love of Christ compels his behavior. If at times his moods seem strange or should he ever behave as if he were beside himself, they must understand that his only goal is to live for Jesus Christ, not himself.

Perhaps because Paul sensed that some of the Corinthians who heard the Gospel had not been regenerated by it and were seeking to achieve their own salvation, he seeks to remove all such delusion by setting forth the content of the Gospel precisely. What God has done, explains Paul, has been nothing less than to reconcile the lost world to Himself through the sacrificial death of His Son. God Himself brought about this reconciliation; we had nothing to do with it. His love made possible the friendship that now exists between heaven and earth; Jesus took upon Himself the sins of the whole world. Those who accept this free gift of salvation become a new creation.

Such a Gospel must be proclaimed before it can be accepted. Therefore God ordained the ministry of reconciliation. He calls his new creation to proclaim the urgent message. Those privileged to hear the word of the Gospel are faced with the inescapable duty of receiving it in faith or rejecting it. But they cannot put it off. *Now is the day of salvation.*

Very few lessons probe the Gospel more deeply than this one. The challenge upon us to be God's personal ambassadors cannot be dealt with blithely.

GETTING INTO THE LESSON
(Objectives 3 and 4)

Use the opening section of the Student Book to lead into the lesson. Emphasize the opportunities God places before us to share Christ with others. Discuss the topic of opportunities. How do students recognize an opportunity to speak about their faith if such an opportunity came their way? Conversely, how do they recognize when the time is not ripe for proclaiming Christ? What do they consider to be the optimum moment or the God-given opportunity for sharing?

Many who are experienced in mission work state that the optimum moment is when a person is in need. Such a person is seeking help and guidance. When people reach out to us, the most golden opportunities present themselves. At such times one can freely speak about the Lord and His love without feeling pushy and artificial.

Christ's Love Compels Us (Objectives 1 and 2)

1) a. Paul talks about making his life plain for everyone to see. He considers his mission in life to persuade people to accept God's offer of salvation in Christ. The "fear of the Lord" refers to Paul's permanent awe and reverence of Jesus Christ as the Lord of life.

b. Not all Bible scholars agree on the interpretation of these phrases. Paul's point, however, is clear. No matter how he may appear in the eyes of his hearers, his motives are to serve Christ. Certainly God can use the full range of our temperment, emotions, and mental faculties. There is no ideal personality type for the Christian faith. God pours His love into all types of personalities. This explains the rich diversity by which we live out our Christian lives.

c. This phrase may be threatening to students who don't feel as if there is very much of Christ's love in their lives. Keep the emphasis on the positive. Affirm the things they are doing well and encourage them to feed upon God's Word, through which they *will* receive power!

d. This refers to the mystical union of the believer and Jesus Christ. We experience Christ's death, burial, and resurrection, as the Romans passage points out.

2) a. Paul states that no longer does he judge people according to external considerations. Through the eyes of faith he seeks to see people from God's point of view. The John passage helps explain this.

b. Emphasize how Christ changes everything about us because He is now the nerve center of our existence. The old values and goals (which the power of sin drives us to follow) have been replaced with a new perspective. By faith we live in a new world. We march to the beat of a different drummer. What God has begun in us, He will complete at the resurrection.

c, d, and e. Spend some time discussing the problems of translating Christ's new life into the lives of the students. This exercise can help them reflect on their growth as Christians and the particular values of the world with which they are struggling. You might work on (e) in small groups before you identify the concerns as a class. If you use this process, invite students (*but only if they wish!*) to share some of their thoughts from (d) during the small-group discussion.

The Ministry of Reconciliation (Objectives 2 and 3)

1. Point out that the world had alienated itself from God because of rebellion. Sinful people were God's enemies. Left to their own devices, sinners could never bridge the chasm their sins have created. It was essential that God initiate the act of friendship.

2. Christ bore the sins of the human race upon the cross in order to take upon Himself the punishment that all people deserved. In this manner He appeased the wrath of God against sin. In a word, Christ built the bridge by which God could freely offer forgiveness to the world through faith in Christ. **Rom. 3:21–26** has a fuller discussion of this truth.

3. Because of Christ's vicarious sacrifice for us, God does not count our sins against us anymore. The Lutheran Confessions state this clearly: "We receive forgiveness of sin and become righteous before God by grace, for Christ's sake, through faith, when we believe that Christ suffered for us and that for his sake our sin is forgiven and righteousness and eternal life are given to us" (AC IV).

4. Ambassadors do not act on their own authority. They communicate what they have been commanded to say, and not their own opinions. As Christ's ambassadors, we represent His authority.

The Urgency of Our Task (Objectives 3 and 4)

1) a. God desires that Christian witnesses be winsome and loving, but they must also be honest. They must firmly but lovingly state even to members of their family that salvation is not a matter to be put off. We dare not give the impression that people can respond to God's offer at their own convenience.

b. The Christian Gospel challenges a form of existence in which many people think *they* are in control.

c. As it was true at Corinth, so it is also true in congregations today. We dare not suppose that all who bear the title of Christian have become regenerated by the Holy Spirit. Paul even stated in **5:20, "Be reconciled to God."** The matter of salvation must always be central in our preaching and teaching.

Close with prayer or speak or sing the hymn stanzas.

Session 62: God Loves a Cheerful Giver

BIBLE BASIS
2 Cor. 9:1–15

CENTRAL TRUTH

Through the generous love God bestows on us, He empowers us to give generously and cheerfully to those in need. When others see God's generosity in us, they are encouraged to praise God for His grace.

OBJECTIVES

By the grace of God students will
1. describe how God's grace prompts them to give generously and cheerfully;
2. explain how God responds to the generous gift they give to the needs of others;
3. tell how generous giving encourages others to thank and praise God for His mercy;
4. express thanks to God for enriching their lives through His grace in Christ Jesus.

BACKGROUND

One reason Paul wrote the Corinthians this second letter was to remind them of the offering being collected for the saints in Jerusalem. **Chapters 8 and 9** are fully devoted to this topic of the worldwide offering being gathered by the churches of Greece and Asia Minor to assist the impoverished Christians of the mother church in Jerusalem.

Paul had already brought this matter to the Corinthians and had given them instructions on setting aside funds for the collection **(1 Cor. 16:1–4)**. Some time—perhaps a year—had passed and delegates, carefully chosen from the churches to gather the offering **(2 Cor. 8:16–24)**, were ready to come to Corinth as promised. The apostle is anxious that the Corinthians, who were the first congregation to volunteer for this project, and about whom he had boasted **(9:3)**, would be prepared when the delegates arrived. He therefore encourages their generosity and even seeks to stimulate their giving by commending the example of generosity displayed by materially poor Macedonians.

In this lesson Paul sets forth the fact that God loves a cheerful giver. Giving generously is God's own nature, and He responds to generosity by causing His grace to abound in the lives of those who give cheerfully. Not only does God grant a generous spirit to those people, but He makes possible the resources for the outpouring of such gifts. When others see Christians sharing so liberally of their possessions, they become encouraged to praise God for the gift of Jesus Christ who touches people's hearts with His saving love.

You may need to correct the erroneous notion that one gives generously in order to receive material blessings from God. Such thinking turns everything topsy-turvy and provides a flesh-induced motive. We give generously because God's love fills us; we may give as a response to that love or because our hearts are filled with compassion for those who are suffering want. He promises in return to give us what we need to reap generously. To "reap generously" may mean that God will provide abundant temporal blessings, but it also may mean that He causes us to feel content—happy with the gifts He has given us.

See session 33 of *God's Old Testament People*, another course in the Lutheran High School Religion Series, for discussion about offering our firstfruits to God. You may also receive stewardship education materials from Department of Stewardship and Financial Support, The Lutheran Church—Missouri Synod, 1333 South Kirkwood Road, St. Louis, MO 63122-7295.

GETTING INTO THE LESSON
(Objectives 1 and 3)

Use the opening section of the Student Book to lead into the lesson. Write the word *generosity* on the chalkboard. Ask the students to volunteer what thoughts come to their minds when they think of this word. Jot down their suggestions on the board. Ask them if they can remember the most generous deed they have ever rendered. What prompted them to be generous in that situation? Discuss with them the Christian goal of living with the attitude of giving rather than getting.

Warm up to the lesson by talking about the intense concern Christians have for the needs of the whole person. Discuss the need for assisting those who are impoverished and victims of disasters. Emphasize the truth that our giving represents the hands of Jesus Christ to those who have no other resource and no other hope.

The Collection for the Saints (Objective 1)

1–2. The church at Corinth had been the first of the churches to participate in the offering and from the outset were enthusiastic about the collection for the Jerusalem saints. Their example prodded the poorer Macedonian Christians to be extremely generous in their gifts for the saints.

3. Paul is concerned lest the Corinthians fail to match their professed enthusiasm with deeds. Even today many pledge with an outward show of eagerness, but actually contribute little or nothing.

4. **2 Cor. 8:12** is a key passage in interpreting Paul's understanding of generosity. Paul interprets generosity as the willingness to give, not in the size of the offering. A person giving a smaller amount is more generous if the amount is given willingly than a richer person giving a larger amount unwillingly. How much left for one's self enters into the concept of generosity (see **Luke 21:1–4**).

Sow Generously and Reap Generously
(Objectives 1 and 2)

1–2. Ask volunteers to paraphrase the quotes from **Proverbs, Luke,** and **James.**

3. The blessings of God on His people are wholistic. That is, they include both material (**"increase your store of seed"**—receive more so that you may sow more) and spiritual (**"enlarge the harvest of your righteousness"**—of people praising God for your deeds). As you discuss these blessings, you might point out the relationship between motive, action, and blessings. See the "Background" information for this session.

4. The grace of God so changes the perception of believers that they find resources from God of which they were not aware previously. Because they see all of life as a gift from God, they take note how God increases these resources day after day. This causes believers to be stimulated to increase their generosity as a thank offering to God.

5. Obviously, the widow gave selflessly and cheerfully, trusting God to provide that which she needed.

Give Cheerfully As God Gives
(Objectives 1, 2, and 3)

1. This statement refers back to **2 Cor. 8:12.** Paul is speaking about the loving willingness of believers to give to others as Christ's servants. This basically is what cheerful giving is all about.

2. Discuss various reasons people give. These reasons include a hope to get something in return, a hope to avoid punishment, a desire to receive praise, and a genuine compassion rooted in human kindness rather than in the love of God.

The only acceptable gifts flow from faith. God's grace is the motivating power in the Christian's life. We are prompted to do all things because of grace. Grace means God's unmerited favor. One aspect of grace is His love toward us. Emphasize the **2 Cor. 8:9** passage. Christ's voluntary poverty for the sake of our spiritual richness perfectly illustrates God's grace.

3. Whenever the giver is unwilling to give, but gives anyway, the motivation does not come from grace. Such gifts, says Paul, are not acceptable and should not be solicited.

4. Paul desires equality within the church. Those who have the abundance should share with those who do not.

5. Though sacrificial giving entails denying one's self, it does not necessarily mean that one becomes destitute. Rather, it means a willingness to share liberally with others at our own expense and to trust God to supply what we need. Sacrificial givers are not afraid to give and to let go.

Thanks Be to God for His Gift
(Objectives 1, 3, and 4)

1) a. "By their fruits you will know them." People do evaluate our spiritual life by our willingness to give. We find evidence of this truth in the praises to God such people render when they observe our generosity.

b. Generous giving is not the only test of our commitment to the Gospel. Paul mentions other examples in **2 Cor. 8:7**. He does, however, urge the Corinthians to also excel in the grace of giving. Thus, the statement is true, but be sure to point out that other evidences of our obedience to Christ also show evidence of our commitment to the Gospel.

c. Paul states that those who are encouraged by our generosity add us to the prayer list.

2. There is some question whether Paul is referring in this passage to God's grace or to the sacrifice of Jesus Christ for our sins. The latter seems more likely, inasmuch as Christ's sacrifice undergirds our entire understanding of God's grace.

3. Emphasize this study of **Matt. 25** and the theme of putting our Christian love out in the world where people are hurting. Focus also on God's concern for the total person. These actions demonstrate our faith in Jesus—the faith by which we are judged. Note that the rewards listed in these verses are given to those who serve without thought of reward. Jesus speaks of giving blessings out of grace, not debt.

4. Assure students of God's love, but also take some time to discuss our sinful condition. Because we continue to sin during our lifetime, our desires and actions reflect that sin which still lives in us. Only by the power of God, working through the means of grace, can those desires change. By God's grace we also receive forgiveness for those selfish thoughts.

5. Seek to get the students involved by applying this lesson to a concrete situation.

Close with prayer or by singing or speaking the hymn stanzas.

Session 63: When I Am Weak Then I Am Strong

BIBLE BASIS
2 Cor. 12:1–10

CENTRAL TRUTH
God lovingly permits hardships to come to our lives for the purpose of drawing us closer to Him. He renews us in our weaknesses by His gift of grace. We can be confident that God's power is at work in our weaknesses so that we become stronger in faith and more effective in our ministry.

OBJECTIVES
By the grace of God students will
1. describe how God allows Satan to subdue them with afflictions, but at the same time God preserves His children;
2. explain how God uses afflictions to lead them to a greater dependence on His grace;
3. tell how weaknesses can be the means by which God will make them stronger in their faith and more effective in their ministry;
4. express a desire to live by God's grace in every situation of their lives.

BACKGROUND
We can describe this section of 2 Corinthians as Paul's defense of his apostleship in Jesus Christ. The Corinthians had been so easily led astray by false apostles who boasted of their superior spiritual gifts. These men were challenging the authority of Paul.

In fashioning his debate against such arrogant usurpers of his authority, Paul reminds the Corinthians that if he wanted to boast of his gifts, he would be more than equal to these imposters. He states, however, that he will not argue on these terms. He will rather base his apostolate on the countless trials and hardship he has endured as a true soldier of the Lord. If he must boast, he will boast in his weaknesses.

Because of what he has personally suffered as a minister of the Gospel, this should be proof enough that he is God's true apostle. No one has been made to endure greater deprivations and physical abuse in the defense of the faith than has he.

Paul points out that there is great gain spiritually in being buffeted by the afflictions that Satan sends. We are stripped of our pride and conceit. Because we can turn to nothing except the everlasting arms of God's grace, we are renewed. God's power surges into the weakened vessel. This explains the divine paradox, "When I am weak, then I am made strong."

This lesson focuses on one of the most faith-strengthening truths a young Christian can experience. Afflictions can be opportunities for spiritual growth because they reveal our need to live by God's grace.

GETTING INTO THE LESSON (Objective 3)
Use the opening section of the Student Book to lead into the lesson. After reading the story, involve the students in a discussion of the paradox that is the theme of this lesson: our weaknesses can become our strengths. Mention that some people would never achieve their valued goals except through the crucible of affliction and weakness.

Ask the students to volunteer some examples of

their own. Get them comfortable with the thought that good things can come out of hardships. Challenge them with the truth that God's grace is the key. Whenever we are open to God's grace, His power creates possibilities that go beyond any of our dreams.

When "Thorns in the Flesh" Come into Our Life
(Objectives 1 and 2)

1) a. Paul states that the Gospel was revealed to him directly from Jesus Christ, and that he was neither taught it nor did he learn it.

b and c. These references to heaven signify that God Himself, whose abode is heaven, is the author of those things the writers are communicating.

d. Paul explains that his knowledge and wisdom have been revealed to him by God Himself. His letters are not human opinion or dissertations of his own scholarly research. They are God's words.

2 a and b. As Paul states, his affliction was sent so that he would not fall victim to spiritual pride (**"conceited"**—v. 7). Afflictions sober us to the realization that we can do nothing without God's grace. Pain has a way of bringing us back to this reality.

c, d, and e. Emphasize that sickness was not part of God's design. Satan breaks down what God has created and is the power behind all sin and sickness. On the other hand, God permits the activity of Satan in our lives. Thus, God permits sickness in order to bring about His own divine purpose in dealing with people.

f. Many scholars, including the earliest fathers of the church, believe Paul's affliction was physical. Reformation scholarship, on the other hand, interpreted Paul's thorn in the flesh as those enemies of the apostle who frustrated his ministry (for example, the faction in the church at Corinth who opposed Paul).

Strength through Weakness (Objectives 3 and 4)

1) a. By means of affliction believers are stripped of any human power and are led to depend upon Christ's grace. Affliction becomes in this sense a valuable learning experience. We are led to appreciate the truth that God's grace and love are of inestimable value.

b, c, and d. God's power is more effective in our weakness in the sense that we don't get in the way. When we are stripped of things that cause pride, God moves us to rely upon Him and His power. Paul's initial experience with his thorn in the flesh (it appears to have been permanent) prepared him for the all of the deprivations he was to suffer as God's apostle. No wonder Paul exults in his weaknesses. He can now see clearly how effective God's power has been revealed through his sufferings.

2. Spend some time working through the stories of the Biblical personalities. Make certain that God emerges as the Hero!

3. There are no right answers to these hypothetical situations. We do not know exactly how the person's strength will appear, except that it will through the Lord's guidance.

Close with prayer or by singing or speaking the hymn stanza.

Session 64: Concluding Activities for Unit 7

STUDENT BOOK ACTIVITIES

The Student Book contains some activities to help review the sessions of this unit. Let your perception of student needs guide your decision of which activities to use. You may want to use all the class time for further discussion of one or more sessions.

Be sure to make plans and assignments in advance so students can complete the letter or collage during this session.

ESSAY TEST

If you must administer a formal test, consider preparing a series of essay questions over the things you emphasized during the unit. Following are some possible questions that you may use.

1. Describe the role of high school students as ministers of Jesus Christ.

2. Compare and contrast a potter working with clay and God working with the people in His church.

3. Explain the relationship between Christ's work of redemption and the way we live our new life in Christ.

4. Suppose the chairperson of your congregation's stewardship committee asked you to summarize the teachings of Scripture regarding stewardship. In less than 100 words, write a summary that could be used in a congregational mailing.

5. Write a letter to someone who is struggling with some kind of "weakness"—an illness, alienation of friends, poverty, etc. Use the theme, "when I am weak, then I am strong," to bring hope and comfort to this person.

OTHER ACTIVITIES

Film on Mission and Ministry

Secure a thought-provoking film on mission work, one that sets forth the challenges and rewards of being God's ambassadors. Consider a film on David Livingstone or Adoniram Judson, one from the This Is the Life series, or order a current film from Mission Education, The Lutheran Church—Missouri Synod, 1333 South Kirkwood Road, St. Louis, MO 6311-7295

Handicapped Student Appreciation Day

Invite a student with a handicap to address your class and to discuss the problems and challenges of having a handicap.

A blind student or one with very limited mobility might have experiences or insights that would be especially relevant to highlight this topic. If possible, choose a student close to the same age as the class members.

UNIT 8: THE JOY THAT PROCEEDS FROM FAITH

BIBLE BASIS: PAUL'S LETTER TO THE PHILIPPIANS

The congregation at Philippi, to whom Paul addresses this letter, was established by the apostle early in his second missionary journey (see **Acts 16:11–40**). The Philippian church was the first Christian church Paul founded in Europe, and it forever remained close to his heart and personal concern. Philippi itself was a Roman colony in Macedonia. It was settled principally by Roman soldiers, who found the area agreeable and easily accessible to Rome by sea. Since there was no synagogue in Philippi, Paul and his helpers (Silas, Timothy, and Luke) preached in the area set aside for prayer within the city.

One of Paul's first converts at Philippi was a wealthy and generous woman by the name of Lydia. Her home may have been among the first meeting places of the fledgling congregation (**Acts 16:14–15**). Perhaps because of Lydia's example, the Philippian church became known as a generous, congregation, liberal in its financial giving. It was an example to all other congregations of Christendom (see **2 Cor. 8:1–5; 2 Cor. 11:8**). So self-giving were the Philippians that they sent one of their members, Epaphroditus, to minister to Paul while he was in prison in Rome **(Phil. 2:25)**.

In this letter to the Philippian Christians, Paul gives them counsel to remain faithful to the Gospel despite the recent persecutions they were enduring. He himself had been persecuted and imprisoned at Philippi for preaching the Gospel. But God triumphed through that suffering and the Gospel was advanced; the jailer and his household became converts to the Lord (see **Acts 16:25–40**).

Troubles came to Paul, and troubles come to us. But the troubles need not wear us down, because God lifts us up. Therefore we can face each day with joy.

We receive joy from God because we can see that He works through us to advance the Gospel.

We live that joy as we follow the perfect model provided by Jesus, whose sacrifice makes all this possible.

We rejoice because the power from God enables us to strive for the goal of attaining a personal relationship with Christ (a gift of His grace) and thus receive the prize—life with Him now and eternally.

God's boundless love enables and empowers us to rejoice in the Lord always.

During the sessions of this unit you will have opportunities to examine this joy in greater detail. Read the central truth and objectives of all the sessions to identify more completely the direction taken with each session's topic.

Ask students to read in advance the portion of Philippians suggested for each session. If you assign homework, consider following the suggestions provided in the introduction to unit 5.

Session 65: Joy in Advancing the Gospel

BIBLE BASIS
Phil. 1:3–29

CENTRAL TRUTH
God often changes the trying circumstances of our lives into opportunities for advancing the Gospel. We can rejoice in suffering for Him because He works through our lives to preach the Gospel of Christ's love to those who are in need.

OBJECTIVES
By the grace of God students will
1. affirm that their mission in life is to witness of Christ's love even when this entails suffering for the Gospel;
2. explain how God can use persecution and imprisonment as opportunities to advance the Gospel;
3. rejoice that their lives are secure in Jesus Christ, whether in life or in death;
4. tell how God gives them strength to triumph while being persecuted and tested for their faith.

BACKGROUND
Even as Paul writes this letter to the Philippians, he is in jail, most probably at Rome, awaiting his trial before Caesar. Yet God is working mighty things through his imprisonment, and Paul is filled with joy for that very reason. He urges the Philippians to experience this same joy, which comes from walking faithfully in the Gospel of Christ's love.

This lesson reminds us that faithfulness to the Gospel can bring severe testing of our faith. But we are assured that God can use such trials to build bridges to those who live without the power of the Gospel.

GETTING INTO THE LESSON
(Objectives 1 and 2)

Use the opening section of the Student Book. Encourage the students to understand that some of the most renowned saints of the Scriptures were prisoners at one point in their lives. In addition to those mentioned in the Student Book, you might mention Joseph in Pharaoh's prison, David as an outlaw, fleeing King Saul, and God's people, the Israelities, as captives in Babylon.

Ask the students if they can add to this list. Emphasize that God is not bound by human prisons or even by human labels. Ask the students to explain how a prison might become an ideal location for the preaching of the Gospel. If you know of people (whether incarcerated for just or unjust reasons) who carry out an effective ministry while in prison, share information about this ministry with your class. (Thomas Bird, the Lutheran pastor featured in the TV movie *Murder Ordained,* conducts regular Bible study classes in a Kansas prison as this is being written in 1987.)

Christian Joy: As a "Prisoner for Christ"
(Objectives 1, 2, and 4)

1) a. Paul is joyful because the Philippians especially share the same vision of proclaiming God's love in Jesus to others. Those who share this vision are "partners" in the Gospel.

b. As mentioned in the unit introduction, Paul felt a special closeness to the Philippians. More than others, they seemed to be serious about witnessing to the Gospel and sharing their faith.

c. Try to impress upon the students that all Christians are partners in witnessing to Christ in their lives. This witness is not only verbal. Much of our witness is behavioral.

d. A prayer for lives lived in Christ is a prayer that Christian lives will bear witness to Him. Prayer does advance the Gospel, whether we pray for those who do not know Christ or whether we pray for those who are actually preaching the Gospel (e.g., evangelists, pastors, missionaries).

2) a. Probably the recipients of Paul's preaching were the soldiers and slaves who attended him in his palace prison.

b. Some Christian preachers were encouraged to speak the Gospel more courageously. Persecution often has this effect on people with conviction. The more they are oppressed, the more fearless they become.

c. The power of the Gospel lies in the Gospel itself, not in the motivations of those who speak it. The same is true for the practice of the Sacraments. (See the Augsburg Confession, Article VIII, "What Is the Church.")

d. Paul was assisted by the prayers of fellow Christians and also by the help of the Holy Spirit. Confidence gives rise to joy in such a situation, because one is assured that God is personally at work.

Christian Joy: Whether Dying for Christ or Living for Christ (Objective 3)

1) a. The Greek word for "eagerly expect" means that Paul actually couldn't wait to see what God was going to do with his life, so confident was he that God would be exalted, no matter what his fate.

b and c. Death for the Christian means the liberation of our sinful flesh and an even closer fellowship with Christ. This is based on Christ's promise that at death we are brought into His presence (**John 14:1–3**; see also **2 Cor. 5:1–5** and **1 Cor. 13:12**). Allow the students to talk freely about this topic. At the same time encourage them to find joy and hope in the Gospel promises. These promises about our future with Christ are valid, because they are based on the power of Christ's resurrection.

d and e. Emphasize that life for the Christian means ministry in Christ's service, no matter what that ministry may entail. Paul felt a need to continue his ministry and was confident he would see the Philippians again. Our days on earth should focus on this ministry of love to which God calls us. Even a high school student has a "ministry." Have students discuss what their "ministry" may be.

Christian Joy: Facing Troubles in My Own Future

1. Christians are to face persecution without fear, with firmness of faith, and with the realization that God will bring judgment on those who seek to oppress the Gospel. The privilege of believing in Christ carries with it the privilege of suffering for Him.

2. This exercise may sharpen the students' perceptions that persecution has not ended, nor will it ever cease. In some of the countries listed, persecution may come because of political reasons; in others, because of a rival religion.

3. This aspect of suffering for Christ may speak to the students' needs concretely and personally.

4 and 5. Reaffirm the theme of the lesson through these exercises.

Have the class sing or speak the hymn stanzas together as a closing devotion.

Session 66: The Ultimate Role Model

BIBLE BASIS
Phil. 2:1–16

CENTRAL TRUTH
Even though He was the Son of God, Christ took on the nature of a humble servant and obediently died on the cross for our sins. His servant attitude is the same attitude we should imitate, because we are united through faith in Him. God's love empowers us to do this.

OBJECTIVES
By the grace of God students will

1. describe how Jesus, the Son of God, voluntarily took on the nature of a humble servant;

2. affirm that His humble servant attitude led Him to obediently die on the cross in order to secure their salvation;
3. explain how they are to emulate Jesus by imitating His servant attitude in their relations with others;
4. tell how God's love strengthens their faith to live as humble servants in this world.

BACKGROUND

There is a distinct tone to Paul's letter to the Philippians. Besides radiating the theme of Christian joy, this letter overflows with encouragement.

Paul can be likened to a coach who spurs his team to reach its true potential. Not satisfied that the Philippians had grown in faith and demonstrated this fact to the world, the apostle encourages them to become even more like Christ. He challenges them to take on the servanthood role of Jesus Christ as their very own.

This section in **Phil. 2,** dealing with the humility and exaltation of Jesus Christ, is one of the most familiar in the New Testament. Many scholars believe that **2:5-11** represents an ancient Christian hymn which the Philippians knew and sang at worship. This section also has an important doctrinal emphasis—the doctrines of Christology and Jesus' humanity. Students must be exposed to these cardinal doctrines.

Teaching the concept of servanthood as a Christian ideal is not an easy task in our modern world, especially in a culture that does not prize humility highly. Humility as a virtue goes against the grain of a "me first, get all I can get" mentality. Some spiritual maturity (such as the Philippians displayed) would seem to be a prerequisite today in order to grasp the nature of self-giving love. This lesson, therefore, represents an important step in the development of young Christians who should be challenged to have "the same attitude as that of Christ Jesus."

GETTING INTO THE LESSON (Objective 3)

Use the opening section in the Student Book. Have the students take the self-test and generate some discussion about qualities they admire in other people. Spend some time with the second self-test in which they select a quality of Jesus Christ that describes His mission of salvation. Try to find out their perception of humility and self-giving love. How highly do they rate this quality? Do they know what it means to live in a "servant role" in order to minister to others? Do they know of any other people who exemplify this quality? Help the students develop a better understanding of the concept of humility so that they will better understand this lesson.

Am I a Humble Person? (Objective 3)

1) a. Paul sets the theme for living a humble and self-giving life by introducing the standard of Christian love. Christians are to love one another because Christ first loved them. The Holy Spirit urges us to practice tenderness and compassion toward one another.

b. Living in a competitive society and seeking to win does not necessarily conflict with Christian humility. In the Christian perspective, we seek to honor God through our efforts. "Selfish ambition" is concerned only with the "self."

c. Christian love is concerned about the interests of the other person more than about self-interests. This desire for the other person's welfare is the essence of God's love and provides a background for understanding what Christian humility is all about. Christian love is even prepared to die for the other person's welfare. See **John 10:11-13.**

2. Spend some time discussing how secular culture sets itself against the practice of Christian humility. The emphasis on "me first" and "self before others" is antithetical to the standard of love. Emphasize that humility is not allowing oneself to be a "doormat." Point out that Christian self-giving for others requires courage and fortitude.

3. This exercise will assist the student in assessing his or her need for growth in Christian humility. It provides a good lead-in to the next section on Christ's modeling of humility.

The Ultimate Model of Humility
(Objectives 1, 2, and 3)

1) a. The cardinal Christian doctrine of Christ's Godhead is expressed clearly in this passage. Other key passages include **John 1:1** and **John 8:14-18; 54-58.** The Nicene Creed states Christ's divinity as follows: "the only-begotten Son of God, begotten of His father before all worlds, God of God, Light of light, very God of very God, begotten, not made, being of one substance with the Father, by whom all things were made."

b. The doctrine of Christ's humanity is contrasted with His divinity by the expression, "made Himself nothing." As a true human being, Jesus participated in our world by taking on Himself the role of a "servant." See **Heb. 2:5-12; 5:7-10.**

c. Jesus' role as God's Suffering Servant can be observed from His conception until His death on the cross. Throughout His earthly ministry He freely gave of Himself in a ministry of love that frequently brought a response of hostility and pain. Jesus' humility is exemplified by the supreme shame of His dying as a criminal even though He was without sin. **Heb. 2:14-18** provides an excellent commentary on **verse 8.**

d. God's love for the world provides the essential understanding of sending His Son to take on the humble role of a servant. Jesus' love for the world moved Him to accept that role.

2) a. These verses dramatically describe Jesus in His active role as the Suffering Servant. His mission of redemption met hostile opposition from the kingdom of evil.

b and c. The death of Jesus on the cross for the sins of the world was ordained by God as the way by which God reconciled the world to Himself. Jesus knew that His mission to the world included the shame of the cross, and He voluntarily and lovingly submitted His life to this mission.

3) a. The exaltation of Christ refers to the glory due Him as the faithful Son of God who has reconciled the world to the Father. His status as "sitting at the right hand of God the Father Almighty" **(Heb. 1:3; 12:2)** means that He is accorded the highest place of honor in the universe. Christ deserves this honor and adoration because He has healed the brokenness of the universe **(Col. 1:17–20)**.

b. The name of Jesus tells us who He is to distinguish Him from all others. He is the One through whom God has revealed His plan of salvation to the world. Compare **Heb. 1:2–3.**

c. In the New Testament there is no other title that sums up the significance of Jesus as does the term *Lord*. It tells us that He possesses power and authority over everything.

4. True servanthood means to imitate the ministry of Jesus Christ who walked the road of humility. Only the humble will be exalted as Jesus declared, **"For everyone who exalts himself will be humbled, and he who humbles himself will be exalted" (v. 11).**

Shining As Stars (Objective 4)

1) a. "Working out our salvation" must be understood in the sense of expressing **"our faith through love" (Gal. 5:6),** not in an attempt to earn God's grace but rather to demonstrate God's grace through works of love. All that we produce through our faith depends on the power of God working within us.

b. When we understand how God works through a life devoted to servanthood, He empowers us to live above complaining and self-pity. Be sure to emphasize this point: We don't possess the power to make ourselves humble. Only God can do that for us.

c. Being faithful to the will and way of God through Christian servanthood differs so much from the depraved way of the world that such a life-style "shines" and reflects God's glory for all to see. Compare **Matt. 5:16.**

2. You might want to use this exercise as a way of demonstrating that each of us, no matter what our skills or personal qualities, can live the "servant life." The key is to have the same attitude as that of Jesus Christ.

Conclude the lesson by singing or saying together the hymn stanzas in the Student Book.

Session 67: Strive for the Goal and the Prize

BIBLE BASIS
Phil. 3:7–21

CENTRAL TRUTH

Christ gives us the power of a new life so that He alone becomes the purpose and goal of our lives. Through faith in Him we are empowered to seek after the goal of living closely with Him and to strive for the ultimate prize of our resurrection from the dead.

OBJECTIVES

By the grace of God students will

1. affirm that the goal of the Christian life is attaining (through faith) a personal relationship with Jesus Christ;
2. explain the need to put aside earthly advantages in order that Jesus Christ and His righteousness becomes the priority in their lives;
3. express their feelings about the race of faith which leads to God's promise of the resurrection of the dead;
4. relate how Christ gives them the power to run this race of faith.

BACKGROUND

This lesson focuses on the subject of life's values as compared with the supreme value of a personal relationship with Jesus Christ. Paul insists that nothing in life compares with a life lived in faith in Christ. He warns the Philippians about people who pride themselves on having valued earthly credentials. Such a distorted sense of values not only robs Jesus Christ of His rightful glory but it also turns people from the most valued goal of all, namely, a living faith in Christ.

Paul speaks from personal experience. He himself once possessed superb human credentials. (Compare **Phil. 3:4–6.**) But now that he has Christ, he considers all such earthly values as "rubbish." Paul believes that the things that seem to matter to people are ultimately a waste of time and energy, not because they are wrong in themselves, but because they cannot compare with the one thing that truly matters, the supreme goal of knowing Christ. He pictures the life of the Christian as a race in which the prize at the goal line is the promised resurrection of the body and life eternal with Christ.

This is a valuable lesson because it gives purpose and direction to the Christian life. It also emphasizes what the goal of the Christian life is all about.

GETTING INTO THE LESSON (Objective 3)

Use the opening story in the Student Book. Choose a student who reads with flair and feeling to read the story aloud. Ask the students if they had heard of this dramatic event or if they had experienced something of a similar nature.

What Is Life's Supreme Goal?
(Objectives 1, 2, and 3)

1. Briefly discuss the questions that summarize the opening story. Try to set the theme of "running the race of faith" firmly in the students' minds.

2) a. "Knowing" Jesus Christ means to be in a personal relationship with Christ through faith. This term emphasizes a *total* relationship; it goes far beyond a simple intellectual understanding of Christ.

b. Paul is attempting to make a dramatic contrast here in order to emphasize the primacy of knowing Christ. In his previous status as a Jewish Pharisee, he possessed credentials of the highest order. These were totally unimportant to him now.

c and d. Point out that the Christian lives by faith. This means living with a dependency on God for the blessings of life. The Matthew passage illustrates that faith looks to God first and does not fret or worry about the needs of life. In this context of faith the Christian monitors his or her earthly desires and ambitions.

e and f. The phrase "to gain" Christ means essentially the same thing as "knowing" Christ, that is, the believer enters into a personal relationship with Christ through faith. Make clear the truth that faith in Christ is God's gift to the believer. We enter into such a personal relationship because God in His grace offers us the righteousness of Jesus Christ as a free gift. We cannot establish this relationship through our own efforts nor by "deciding" for Christ. The phrase "and be found in Him" states clearly that our salvation is initiated by God's love for us.

3) a. God finishes what He begins. Our resurrection with glorified bodies like Christ's body is essential to salvation. To believe in Christ only for this life limits God's power and frustrates His design for the future.

b. Christ Himself will raise our bodies from the graves because He possesses the power of life over death. See **Rev. 1:17–18.**

c. God's promise is clear. Our bodies, though lowly now and susceptible to infirmity and death, will be made glorious in the resurrection to come. They will be modeled after Christ's glorified body.

Pressing On toward the Goal (Objective 3)

1) a. Paul makes clear the truth that our sanctification in Christ grows in greater depth the more we apply ourselves to following after Him. This is our goal—to daily grow closer in our faith relationship with Christ. There is no room for the arrogance of "Christian perfectionism," as some religions teach.

b. Christians are future oriented, always looking ahead to the day of resurrection when God's promise of eternal life will be made complete. This truth provides the foundation of the Christian life-style.

2) a. The self-inventory exercise can help to put this lesson into a personal perspective for the students. Let the students deal with this exercise personally. Point out, however, that the race of faith depends upon the resources that God gives us, and not on our personal strength.

3. Use this important reference as a means to demonstrate that personal discipline is needed in our faith-life. Likely Paul himself observed an ancient Greek "Olympics" and applied this concept of training and discipline to the Christian life.

The Power behind Our Performance (Objective 4)

1) a. Athletes who watch their coach for instructions and encouragement have the advantage over those who seek to go on their own. Christians keep their eyes focused on Christ and their future life with Him in heaven. As they do so, God's power strengthens them to run the race in assurance and joy and to resist the temptations that seem so much greater when we let our eyes dart to and fro. You might ask students to give examples of this. For example, the eyes fixed on Jesus may lead to a night of homework, while eyes that dart to and fro may lead to telephone chatter planning a Friday night party that includes alcohol and other drugs.

b. Those who are "enemies of the cross" look to their own feeble resources and their own earthly credentials.

c. Make as indelible as possible this truth that our promised "future" with Christ in the resurrection determines how we live our "present" with Him.

2 and 3. Focus on the promise of God that our destiny is with Christ in heaven, that He will raise our bodies from the dead, and that we will live with Christ forevermore. This assurance is based upon the grace and power of God who is working out His plan in our lives.

Conclude by singing or speaking together the hymn stanzas in the Student Book.

Session 68: Rejoice in the Lord

BIBLE BASIS
Phil. 4:4–13

CENTRAL TRUTH

God gives joy to our lives of faith by assuring us that He is with us now and in our future. Because He continually demonstrates His power and peace in our lives, we are people who continually rejoice in Him.

OBJECTIVES

By the grace of God students will
1. affirm that Christian joy is the assurance that their lives are linked to Christ through faith;
2. identify the various ways God demonstrates His power and peace in their lives;
3. explain how God's continual care gives them reason to constantly rejoice in their faith;
4. celebrate the joy of faith through thanksgiving and praise to God.

BACKGROUND

The fourth chapter of Philippians ranks among the most joyful chapters in the Scriptures. Paul had introduced the theme of joy in the opening verses of this letter. Throughout the epistle he liberally makes use of this term as he describes the life of faith. Now, like a bird in song, he opens up the fullness of his feelings about joy. Paul states that Christians should continually rejoice because God blesses them with His care now and always.

In Paul's understanding of the term, Christian joy is the distinguishing mark of a deep, inner faith that links the believer to Christ. It is no temporary, will-o'-the-wisp feeling. Rather, it is a cheerful attitude so dominant in its expression that it is on constant public display. No matter what the setback of life may do to the Christian believer, Christian joy shines its happy face.

We have good reason for this attitude. God's power and peace are evident day after day, so much so that the natural response of the thankful Christian is to break out in joyful praise. In contrast, those who are not good advertisements of Christian joy are people who are experiencing faith-problems or who are struggling with sin.

This is an important lesson for maturing Christian students. The theme of joy is a necessary dimension in the development of their faith.

GETTING INTO THE LESSON (Objective 1)

Use the opening section of the Student Book. Spend some time with the class experiment in which the students seek to identify symbols of joy in the church. Make this a positive experience rather than a negative one.

Some people attack a formal liturgy as being anti-joy when, in reality, formal worship can be a most joyful experience. On the other hand, hand-clapping and shouting in worship may not always indicate joy and can at times border on being disrespectful—or it can become as ritualistic as a formal liturgy. Seek a balanced discussion on this topic.

The Secret of Christian Joy (Objectives 1 and 2)

1) a. Other words for joy might include "being glad" (which is closest to the original Greek), "being happy," or even "being cheerful." Caution should be exercised in equating Christian joy with simple "happiness," which is situation based. Christian joy is based on eternal truths. You might compare "joy" with the term "blessed," as Jesus used it in the Beatitudes **(Matt. 5).** The joy we receive from God empowers us to feel happy on the inside even when a boyfriend or girlfriend is dating someone else.

b. Christian joy is a gift of God. It comes through faith in fellowship with Him. Joy is possible because God dwells within us. It is a fruit of the Holy Spirit.

c. Jesus preached a message of faith in a loving Father. That was a radically new message in His times. Jesus invited people into the kingdom of God where love and joy reigned. He proclaimed the forgiveness of sins and the promise of salvation. These were themes the people heard "gladly."

d. The word *gentleness* **(v. 5)** is perhaps better understood as being gracious to others. It connotes a cheerful spirit, quite in contrast to the divisiveness and cruelty more common in Paul's day.

2) a. Christian faith is personally experienced by the totality of the believer. It reaches into the affective and emotional domains as well as the cognitive. Certainly we are emotionally involved with our salvation.

b. We must not avoid the subject of personal feelings when talking about faith. Make it clear, however, that the experience of God and the attendant feelings of joy are a *result* of the working of the Gospel. This can be a problem area when people focus more on their feelings than on the power of the Gospel. This takes the glory away from God and centers it on the person. Also point out that everyone has distinctive emotional responses to the working of the Gospel. Psychologically, different people will express their joy in different ways. Let us be happy that there is variety.

What Is Joy Like? (Objective 3)

1) a. Paul prescribes that the anxious believer (1) pray about the problem in dialog with God; (2) petition or request that the problem be solved; and (3) offer thanksgiving to God. This is a "complete" prayer because it praises and honors God, depends on God, and gives thanks to Him.

b. To "petition" means to make an actual request that God intervene and bring a solution to the problem. Thanksgiving in prayer causes us to "remember" how God has solved such situations before. Such remembering brings comfort and defuses the anxiety.

c. God protects the anxious heart with "peace." This can be translated "wholeness." It means that God is at the center of the person's existence. Philippi was a base for Roman soldiers, and Paul was saying that Christ's peace is better protection than the greatest army of the world.

2) a and b. Each of these types of godly thoughts reflects upon God's goodness and the existence of His goodness in the world. No matter how sinful and ugly people become, a multitude of good and healthy things occupy the mind. Just as with prayer, God gives His gift of peace to those who focus on godliness.

c and d. Students may suggest various ways to respond to those who tell dirty jokes or off-color stories. At times we may want to confront the individual (privately); at other times we may walk away or just ignore the person and think about other (*truly* joyful) things—things that make us joyful in the Lord.

3) a. Paul knew the problems that come to people who become too emotionally involved with material goods. They reflect the highs and lows of life's euphoria and life's despair. Paul's approach was contentment—to be truly free of dependency on material things and to live by God's grace.

b. This passage powerfully describes what it means to live by grace. God will provide for Paul's needs by giving him the strength to face each and every situation of life.

3 c, d, and e. Worry paralyzes the anxious person so that the problem cannot be constructively solved. Faith in God frees the person to set about finding ways in which God will provide. Both poor and rich find joy in the God who is working out His grace in their lives.

Celebrate the Joy of Faith (Objective 4)

Use the class activity in the Student Book or devise an activity of your own. If your class enjoys a particular hymn or a song, this would be an appropriate time to sing it. Whatever you do, let this time truly be an illustration and affirmation of Christian joy!

Session 69: Concluding Activities for Unit 8

STUDENT BOOK ACTIVITIES

Several activities have been suggested in the Student Book to review some of the concepts studied in this unit. Choose the activity or activities that best meet the needs of your students. Note that the banner-making project will require some advance planning. Groups will need to be selected in advance, and needed materials will have to be gathered.

Instead of those activities, you may want to continue discussion of one or more lessons that prompted considerable interest on the part of the students.

TEST

Should you wish to review the material in a more formal way, you might consider adapting the following questions.

Multiple Choice

Choose the best answer:

1. The main theme of St. Paul's letter to the Philippians is Christian
    a. faith.
    b. love.
    c. hope.
    d. joy.
2. Our best example of true Christian joy is
    a. Paul.
    b. the Philippian Christians.
    c. Jesus.
    d. a smiling Christian friend.
3. Christian joy is the result of our faith. It comes to us when
    a. we pray for it.
    b. we try hard to be joyful.
    c. we receive it from God.
    d. someone makes us happy.
4. The ultimate goal of the Christian life is
    a. being a perfect person.
    b. always being happy.
    c. personal faith in Jesus.
    d. resurrection from the dead to eternal life.
5. We should be humble like Jesus so that
    a. we will be better people.
    b. people will like us better.
    c. people will see us as faithful witnesses to Christ.
    d. we can be proud of our humility.

Essay

1. Tell what it means to you that you are to be a joyful Christian.
2. Tell what it means to rejoice in suffering. What makes this possible?
3. Describe the characteristics of Jesus that make Him the ultimate role model. Tell what a high school student who exhibits these same characteristics would be like.
4. Compare the Christian life with running a race.

UNIT 9: FAITH EXPRESSED BY HOPE

BIBLE BASIS: 1 AND 2 THESSALONIANS

The church at Thessalonica seemed naturally fitted to be a missionary center for the apostle Paul. It was the capital of the Roman province of Macedonia and was commercially important as a harbor city and a communications depot for the Roman government.

Paul arrived in Thessalonia on his second missionary journey with his companions, Silas and Timothy **(Acts 17:1–15)**. As was his custom, Paul first visited the local synagogue and proclaimed Jesus to be the Christ. His success in attracting some of the Jews and a large number of Gentiles provoked jealousy in the Jewish community. After a stay of only a few months, during which the Christian community flourished, Paul became the focus of a riot. It appears that he and Silas were forced to leave Thessalonia primarily to protect his friend, Jason, at whose house Paul had stayed **(Acts 17:5–9)**. Timothy remained with the Thessalonian Christians.

The congregation at Thessalonica seems to have been composed mainly of Gentiles **(1 Thess. 1:9; 2:14; Acts 17:4)**. It was a vigorous group, noted for its faithfulness to the Gospel despite severe trials and persecution. The intense hope by which they looked forward to the coming of Christ at the Last Day marks the faith of the Thessalonians. Indeed, the theme of the Second Coming dominates the discussion of both 1 and 2 Thessalonians, letters in which Paul attempts to clarify the confusion of these Christians about the sequence of events surrounding the Day of the Lord.

Paul did not veil his words about that day with a feeling of dread, however. Rather, he emphasized the hope with which we, as children of God, may face that day.

The hope we have in Christ empowers us to live each day to please God.

The certainty that the Day of the Lord is coming also provides a certainty that all believers in Christ will be raised again to live with Him in eternal glory.

The fact that the Day of the Lord will come suddenly should bring fear to those without faith, but believers in Christ can live joy-filled lives, because we know the return will bring glory to us, also.

Though antichrists attempt to take our faith from us, God gives us the certain hope that He will work through Word and Sacrament to keep our faith strong.

As we wait for Christ's return, our hope in Him enables us to live active and productive lives.

During the sessions of this unit you will have opportunities to examine these topics in greater detail. Read the central truths and objectives of all the sessions to identify more completely the direction taken in each session.

Ask students to read in advance the portion of Thessalonians suggested for each session. If you assign homework, consider following the suggestions given in this guide to introduce unit 5.

Session 70: Living to Please God

BIBLE BASIS
1 Thess. 4:1–12

CENTRAL TRUTH
God has redeemed us through Christ and has called us to lead holy lives in order to please Him. The Holy Spirit guides us to conduct our lives with proper sexual behavior. As we live out God's will for our lives, we influence and win the respect of unbelievers.

OBJECTIVES
By the grace of God students will
1. tell how God calls them to abstain from sexual immorality and to conduct themselves honorably;
2. affirm the power of the Holy Spirit, who guides them to live lives of holiness;
3. describe how their daily behavior should demonstrate a Christian witness to unbelievers;
4. express a willingness to let God's love shape their behavior more and more.

BACKGROUND
This lesson focuses on the problem of sexual immorality, which Timothy had reported to Paul on his return from Thessalonica. Like other pagan groups who had no future hope in life, the Thessalonicans indulged in gross sexual sins. This was affecting the Christians of Thessalonica, and Paul writes to them in pastoral love and firmness. He reminds them that they are to live to please God, because they do have a future hope. In fact, Paul urges them to influence the unbelievers by the loving quality of their Christian lives. How appropriate this theme is in our modern era of sexual permissiveness!

GETTING INTO THE LESSON (Objective 1)
Use the opening section of the Student Book to lead into the lesson. Have the students discuss the story, especially focusing on the power of the Gospel to deliver those caught in the grip of sexual immorality. Prostitution is but one aspect of sexual immorality, but because of its tight organization, it is one of the most

difficult sexual habits to overcome. Many prostitutes commit suicide by the age of 30.

A Gospel victory over prostitution symbolizes victories over other forms of sexual immorality as well. Discuss how a person's view of their future destiny is strongly correlated to how he or she behaves presently. Point the students to the Gospel's future perspective: the coming of Christ in glory. They are to live "blameless lives" in anticipation of His coming glory. **(1 Thess. 3:13** is a key verse for this lesson.)

The Call to Holy Living (Objectives 1 and 2)

1) a. Sexual immorality is a perversion of God's intended purpose for the gift of sex. Sexual behavior was created for the purpose of bonding a husband and wife together in unity and for the procreation of children. The way we use our gift of sex reflects our relationship to Jesus Christ and our relationships with others. A responsible use of this gift displays the effect of the Holy Spirit within us, and a perverted use of this gift displays irresponsibility and a lack of faith in Christ, who is coming again to receive us to Himself.

b. Those engaged in passionate lust view their bodies as instruments of pleasure. God calls Christians to view their bodies as **"temples of the Holy Spirit" (1 Cor. 6:18–20).**

c. Simply reflect on the language of those who "use" people sexually. They "score," "make out," etc. This is not treating others as bearing the image of God.

d. God can punish sexual immorality in many ways, including physical disease. Often we also see psychological implications, such as a sense of shame and worthlessness. The worst consequences are spiritual: it is an act of unfaith and grieving of the Holy Spirit.

2. This exercise is intended to make the students aware of how our culture parades sexually explicit activities and influences the thoughts and attitudes of young people. Use it as a discussion piece to dramatize this point.

3. Encourage debate on this issue. If no one takes the side of sexual signals being overrated, take up that side yourself temporarily. Reactions to such an attitude may strengthen students' recognition of the dangers of such signals.

4. This is a subtle temptation of our culture. Many use affection for another person as a rationalization for sexual passion. They quickly forget the *responsibility* that sexual cohabitation involves **(Gen. 2:24).**

The Power at Work within Us (Objectives 2 and 3)

1. The Holy Spirit guides us in the will of God, which is holiness (or wholeness). Holiness is to be like God.

2. A powerful force in the search for freedom from any addiction lies in learning to love others and to live for others, following the example Christ gave us and using the power He supplies.

3. Love gives us the capacity to see others as made in God's image. We begin to see them as total persons: body, mind, and spirit, and not as mere sex objects.

4. Love for others grows out of our love for God. Such love relies upon His power to preserve us from immorality. God causes that love to grow as we feed upon the means of grace—Word and Sacrament.

Influencing the World around Us

1) a. By doing such activities in earnest joy, unbelievers will see that we live for a cause beyond ourselves, namely, for the glory of God.

b. Answers will vary for this one. Encourage students to give very specific examples.

c. By being dependent on God we show that we have a resource that supplies all our needs. Also, by giving rather than getting from others, we display a motivation that brings respect and admiration.

2. A person who lives with principles usually earns more respect than one who follows the crowd.

3. Our eyes being focused upon future glory influences us to live *today* in the same manner that we will want Christ to see us when He comes in glory.

Conclude with prayer or by singing or speaking the hymn stanzas.

Session 71: The Coming Day of the Lord

BIBLE BASIS
1 Thess. 4:13–18

CENTRAL TRUTH
Because Jesus died and rose again for our salvation, He gives us the sure hope that we also will be raised from the dead on the Last Day. On that day Christ will return in glory to this earth and will gather all believers to live with Him forever.

OBJECTIVES
By the grace of God students will
1. affirm that believers in Christ live with the sure hope of the resurrection and Christ's Second Coming;
2. explain how Jesus' death and resurrection provide the basis for this sure hope;
3. describe how Jesus will return in glory to this earth and give to all believers the fullness of eternal life;
4. tell how God's promise of their future with Him supplies them with encouragement and joy in their present walk in faith.

BACKGROUND
Both of Paul's letters to the Thessalonians deal extensively with the teaching of the Parousia—the return of Jesus Christ at the Last Day. Nowhere do we

find this teaching so clearly expressed as in this lesson. The teaching of the Parousia can be attributed to Christ Himself, who promised that He would return to the earth one day in triumphal glory (see **Matt. 24:23–44; 25:1–13; Mark 13:28–37; Luke 21:5–36**). On that day, which will come suddenly and without warning, He will raise the dead and usher in His eternal kingdom. Believers are to demonstrate their faith by being watchful and alert as they prepare for His coming.

Speculative questions about the Parousia, especially the sequence of events surrounding Christ's coming, have often been raised by immature and overimaginative believers. This was certainly the case with the Thessalonian Christians who imagined that all the dead in Christ would miss out on Christ's kingdom of glory when He returned. They somehow had falsely drawn the conclusion that the Parousia was only for those alive on the Day of the Lord.

Paul reassures these Christians of God's grace and His promise of the resurrection. When Christ returns, He will raise the dead, and together with all the saints, He will be with His elect forever. **"And so we will be with the Lord forever" (1 Thess. 4:17).**

Doctrinal aberrations about the Parousia usually emerge when people speculate about God's "timetable" regarding the Day of the Lord, rather than focusing their faith on the promise of the resurrection. In our own times we are familiar with such aberrations as the rapture and the millennium, popular teachings of certain groups who distort the clear understanding of the Parousia and lead believers into confusion and doubt.

This lesson is designed primarily to give encouragement to the faith of young Christians—faith that turns to the promise of Christ, who will raise them from the dead and give them eternal life.

GETTING INTO THE LESSON (Objective 1)

Use the opening section of the Student Book to lead into the lesson. Spend some time talking about the anticipation of the early Christians for the imminent return of Christ, and tell why this hope was somewhat influenced by the intense persecutions meted out against the tiny band of Christians.

Discuss the background material for this lesson and introduce the theme of the Parousia. Point out how this teaching is especially subject to overspeculation on the part of some sectarian bodies who lead people to concentrate on the wrong things. The students should proceed into the lesson with the understanding that the purpose of Christ's return is to raise the dead, bring judgment to this world, and share the glory of His eternal kingdom with the elect.

Living with a Sure Hope (Objectives 1, 2, and 3)

1–2. The New Testament uses the term "fallen asleep" to show a contrast with the Greek understanding of death—which connoted hopelessness. Death as "sleep" in the Christian perspective looks forward to God's promise of eternal life. Because of God's power over death through the resurrection of Jesus Christ, death is only an interlude before the resurrection to come.

3. On the day of His coming, Christ will bring back to earth with Him the spirits of those who have died in faith.

4. The Thessalonians, who were so concerned about the dead missing out on Christ's return, are assured that the dead will meet Christ even before those who are alive at His return.

5–6. Christ's death and resurrection provide the basis for our Christian hope. Because Christ has power over the enemies of sin and death, we can share a future with Him.

The Day Christ Returns (Objectives 1 and 3)

1. Jesus clearly stated that He would come again to the earth and that in His Second Coming He would come in glory and in judgment. The Hebrews passage speaks about the "Second Coming" to contrast it with the first coming, when Christ was born of a woman.

2. On the day of His coming, Christ's appearance will be announced by the trumpet. He will bring with Him to the earth those who have died in faith. Christ will raise the dead and then gather those who are alive with Him in the air. It will be a time of full communion with Jesus Christ and all those who loved Him through faith.

3–4. The angels of God will accompany Christ in His glory and will assist in the triumph of this day. The "cry," the "voice," and the "trumpet" are all ways of saying the same thing; they symbolize God's power and majesty.

5. Those who are alive will be changed physically according to God's promise.

6. Christ will return to fulfill God's promise of eternal life. We have Christian hope and can look forward to Christ's coming because we will "be with the Lord forever."

Tell the World about It (Objective 4)

1–3. Plan to spend some time applying the lesson to the practical situations mentioned in the Student Book.

Conclude with prayer or by speaking or singing the hymn stanzas.

Session 72: The Suddenness of That Day

BIBLE BASIS
1 Thess. 5:1–18

CENTRAL TRUTH

Christ has redeemed us to be children of the light. As we wait for His return in glory, His Spirit empowers us to live joy-filled lives of faith and productivity. The suddenness of Christ's coming will not surprise us but will bring God's wrath upon those who live in darkness.

OBJECTIVES

By the grace of God students will
1. relate how they have been made children of light through the grace of Jesus Christ;
2. describe how children of light live alertly and in anticipation of the sudden return of Jesus Christ;
3. explain how the suddenness of that Day will surprise those who live in darkness and confront those people with God's wrath;
4. tell how they can live joyful and productive lives as they wait for Christ's return.

BACKGROUND

This section is a theological addendum to the previous section on the Parousia. Because the Thessalonian Christians had been overly concerned about times and dates of Christ's return, they were becoming slack in their own Christian behavior. Paul had to gently turn their attention to the proper way to live out their Christian hope.

As to the date and hour of Christ's return in judgment, the apostle reminds the Thessalonians that it will take place suddenly and without warning (cf. **Matt. 24:36–44**). It will be a day of wrath for those who live in darkness (the spiritually dead), but for the children of light (God's elect people), the day of Christ's coming will be the fruition of their anticipated hope.

Paul's language in this section is apocalyptic, that is, it is a perspective of the world in which the dualistic forces of God and Satan are locked in a mortal combat. Metaphors such as light and darkness dominate the action. Satan and his evil kingdom seek to destroy the small band of Christians who are nurtured by the Gospel. Although darkness may seem to dominate the life of the world now, the day will come when God's kingdom of light shall triumph. On the day of the Parousia, Christ will destroy Satan and his kingdom. The children of light shall then share in Christ's triumphant glory.

Paul urges the Thessalonians to prepare for the Day of the Lord by living as true children of the light. Christian behavior is exemplified by alertness, self-control, and productive hard work, not by living as the drunken and self-indulgent children of darkness.

The application of this truth to young people today is certainly appropriate. How do we best live in a world that so willingly caters to evil? By living in steadfast faith and patiently waiting for the triumphal return of Jesus Christ, our Lord.

GETTING INTO THE LESSON (Objective 2)

Use the opening section of the Student Book to lead into the lesson. Try to engage the students in a spirited discussion of how they would spend their last day on earth. Their answers will likely reveal their understanding of what constitutes spiritual readiness for the coming of Christ. Spend some time on Luther's approach to spiritual readiness. He focused on faith and confidence in Christ. In brief, set the mood for how Christian believers anticipate Christ's coming by living faithful lives today.

Don't Be Unprepared (Objectives 2 and 3)

1. The phrase, "times and dates," may refer to many things, including a belief that world history has been carved out into certain eras ordained by God. An active belief in many groups today claims that the numbers mentioned in the apocalyptic books of Daniel and Revelation can be deciphered to reveal the cosmic clock God is working with. Paul, however, dismisses this entire subject summarily.

2. The apostle reminds the Thessalonians of the truth about Christ's coming, which he had taught them, namely, that Christ would come suddenly as a thief in the night, the very words Jesus Himself had used.

3. These figures of speech emphasize the suddenness of the Day of the Lord. It will come at a time people least expect it.

4–5. The issue here is faith in God's promise. Faith trusts that Christ will come, even if He does not reveal the exact date. Knowing the date would remove a challenge to faith, since we then would not need to live in a state of readiness.

Live in the Light, Not in the Dark
(Objectives 1, 2, and 3)

1. Darkness and light are metaphors that refer respectively to the spiritually dead and God's elect people in Christ. These metaphors reveal opposite qualities in the human spirit and human behavior (cf. **John 1:4**). The behavior of those who live in darkness (e.g., sleeping and drunkenness) is especially described in **verses 6–7**. Becoming a child of the light is God's gift of grace through Jesus Christ, who gives salvation to all who will receive it through faith.

2. Those in darkness will be surprised—that is, caught unaware—in a life dominated by slavery to sin. On the other hand, those who live by faith anticipate Christ's coming.

3. Faith and unfaith in Christ's coming are dem-

onstrated by behaviors that are diametrically opposed. Faith lives alertly and in self-control because it seeks its Object, the coming Savior. Those without faith live only for themselves and as captives of their own passion.

4. The parable emphasizes the quality of readiness in faith. Believers seek the completion of their redemption in Christ, in which they will live with Him forever in glory.

5. Those in darkness will receive the wrath of God because judgment for sin is the due consequence of those who have not heeded the call of the Gospel (cf. **Matt. 25:41–46**). On the other hand, God's elect will receive their appointed salvation.

6. Christ's sacrificial death has made us God's children of light.

Faith Prepares Us for Christ's Coming (Objective 4)

1. Paul here refers to pastors and teachers who shepherd God's people and equip them with the Word of Life to live faithfully for Christ.

2–4. Work through these Christian expressions of love carefully. Challenge students to understand how faith in Christ calls them to walk the higher road.

5. These phrases refer to the quality of the Christian life-style, rather than a measure of quantity. They reflect the motif of a person's daily walk with Christ.

Conclude with prayer or by singing or speaking the hymn stanzas.

Session 73: The Appearance of the Antichrist

BIBLE BASIS
2 Thess. 2:1–17

CENTRAL TRUTH

Before the Day of the Lord comes, God will allow the Antichrist to appear in the world as a sign that His judgment on evil is to follow. We thank God that He has called us through the Gospel and saved us to be His own. Through His power we can stand firm against all evil as we wait for the glory of God to appear.

OBJECTIVES

By the grace of God students will
1. demonstrate knowledge of God's plan of bringing judgment to the powers of evil;
2. explain how the power of evil in the form of the Antichrist will precede the coming of Christ in glory;
3. describe how believers in Christ are to grow in faith and stand firm against the forces of evil as they wait for Christ's coming;
4. express thanksgiving to God for calling them through the Gospel and empowering them to live strong lives of faith.

BACKGROUND

The situation in the church at Thessalonica had become tense and unsettling. Not only were these Christians undergoing intense persecution for their faith, but they were also being torn asunder by a vicious rumor that the Day of the Lord had already come **(2:2)**. This distortion of the teaching of the Parousia was particularly faith destroying; if true, it meant that their Christian hope was utterly in vain.

In his second letter to the Thessalonians, Paul addresses this heresy head on. He states that the Day of the Lord will not come until the man of lawlessness is first revealed. This is a reference to the Antichrist, the representative of Satan, who will bring terrible grief to God's church prior to Christ's return.

Jesus Himself predicted the appearance of the Antichrist in His description of the last times of the earth **(Matt. 24:15–25; Mark 13:14–26; Rev. 13:1–8)**. While posing as God to be worshiped himself, the Antichrist is the true God's mortal enemy and will use every type of sign and wonder to deceive the people of the earth. These days of the Antichrist will be characterized as rebellion against the people of God, a time alotted by God until the day of the Parousia when Christ will destroy the man of lawlessness and the kingdom of darkness.

We do not teach about the Antichrist to merely speculate about his identity or his location in history. Rather, we wish to encourage God's people to live faithfully even when it appears that the powers of darkness have triumphed. We also wish to remind Christians that God's promise is sure. The Antichrist is a sign that God will surely come to judge and to destroy the power of evil.

This lesson, as well as the others in this section, brings comfort to young Christians. We thank God for calling us into His kingdom and sharing His grace. He gives us strength to live in hope, no matter how evil the day may be.

GETTING INTO THE LESSON
(Objectives 1, 2, and 3)

Use the opening section of the Student Book to lead into the lesson. Discuss the theme of the conflict between good and evil. Encourage students to provide examples of their own. You might emphasize the deadly nature of such conflicts. Especially draw attention to the reality of evil in our world. Set the stage for the introduction of the teaching of the Antichrist and the warfare to come in the last days. Survey the students' awareness of this teaching. Point out that the Antichrist is the final sign before the coming of Christ in glory when He shall bring judgment to all evil.

The Appearance of the Antichrist
(Objectives 1 and 2)

1) a. We do not know the exact origin of this rumor. **Verse 2** mentions some possibilities. It appears that the rumor was quite upsetting to the congregation.

b. Those who are firmly grounded in the Scripture are less apt to be disuaded by the opinions of those who present an opposing point of view.

2. Proceed point by point through this Scriptural study so that students can grasp the entire corpus of the doctrine of the Antichrist. Have them examine the Scriptural references and use the Scripture as the basis for any questions they might have. The appearance of the Antichrist is the final "showdown" between God and Satan, the concluding battle of the warfare that has been waging since the beginning of creation. It is a necessary sequence in the events that will culminate in the coming of Christ in glory.

Exercise caution in attempting to locate the Antichrist in time and space. Speculation as to the identity of the Antichrist often sidetracks believers from the more important truth of standing firm against every evil they must endure, even the evil of the present age.

However, the prophecy that the Antichrist will set himself up in God's temple **(v. 4)** is remarked upon in the Lutheran Confessions:

"The kingdom of the Antichrist is a new kind of worship of God, devised by human authority in opposition to Christ. Thus the kingdom of Mohammed has rites and works by which it seeks to be justified before God, denying that men are freely justified by faith for Christ's sake. So the papacy will also be a part of the kingdom of the Antichrist if it maintains that human rites justify" (Ap XV 18).

3) a. The counterfeit miracles, signs, and wonders are a diabolical smokescreen to blind people to the evil intent of Satan's kingdom. In a similar way Hitler hypnotized millions with spectacular displays of power and force.

b. The oppressive rule of the Antichrist and the success of his campaign seem to almost blot out the remnant of God who remain faithful.

c. The Antichrist might be an incarnation of Satan or a specially chosen representative. At any rate, he expresses the Satanic intent of destroying the church of God.

d and e. Point out that God desires all people to be saved. He must, however, execute judgment on all who persist in rebellion against Him. The Antichrist in this sense is an instrument of God whereby evil will be judged on the day that Christ comes in triumph to the earth.

f. Emphasize that God will destroy the Antichrist and all evil on the day of Christ's coming.

Stand Firm in Christ (Objectives 3 and 4)

1. God has chosen those who are the heirs of salvation by drawing them to Himself through the work of the Holy Spirit. Through faith they believed the Good News of salvation.

2. Encourage free discussion of the benefits of prayer. Correct impressions (if given) that prayer is a means of grace. Emphasize that we really do receive blessings from God through prayer; God really does answer prayer.

3. God always works through the power of the Gospel, which transforms people to a new life in Christ.

4. Our faith draws strength from the promises of God in Holy Scripture and from the spiritual encouragement of fellow Christians.

Conclude by prayer or by singing or speaking the hymn stanzas.

Session 74: In the Meantime Live by Faith

BIBLE BASIS
2 Thess. 3:1–16

CENTRAL TRUTH

God calls us to serve Him with active and productive lives before He returns in glory. Through His power and love, our faith can triumph over the Evil One and persevere in deeds of love to one another.

OBJECTIVES

By the grace of God students will

1. affirm that they do not need to fear the power of the Evil One because they belong to Christ;
2. tell how God strengthens them to live faithfully despite the evil powers that persecute them;
3. explain how they are to serve God, not in idleness, but with active and productive lives;
4. relate how work is a calling from God in which He leads us to serve Him by using our aptitudes and skills.

BACKGROUND

In this concluding section of 2 Thessalonians Paul urges these Christians to continue in their walk of faith. He gives them assurance that God is faithful in His promise to protect them from the Evil One.

Paul also leaves the Thessalonian Christians an admonition about working hard and leading productive lives. Apparently a few members of the congregation had drawn the false conclusion that they need not work for a living if the Parousia was imminent. Consequently, they had become a burden to the community in the sense of being freeloaders. Besides not earning their own bread, they had become busybodies in the affairs of others.

The apostle makes it clear that such behavior is not acceptable to the high calling of Jesus Christ. Those who truly love Christ never tire in working for His glory and doing good deeds in His name. Paul cites himself as an example of a person who refused handouts from others, but rather worked with his own hands (cf. **1 Cor. 9:1–23**). He wanted his behavior to bring respect and honor to the cause of the Christian Gospel.

Be sure to use this Scripture correctly. Some erroneously see here a Christian philosophy of economics. Such false interpretation can lead to a self-righteous attitude toward people in poverty and a distorted view of those on welfare. The deeper truth is the spiritual one; our Christian behavior should always reflect our love for Christ and seek to advance the cause of the Gospel.

Young Christians need the wise counsel of this section as they begin thinking about their vocational careers. A proper use of the spiritual truths in this lesson can enrich their understanding of work and of the Christian response to serving Christ through it.

GETTING INTO THE LESSON
(Objectives 3 and 4)

Use the opening section of the Student Book to lead into the lesson. Begin with a discussion about jobs and careers and the attitudes of the students toward work.

Emphasize how work involves much more than simply earning money and is an essential aspect in the development of one's self-image. For example, many of the unemployed possess negative self-images and are victims of a failure syndrome. Research also reveals that those who are forced to retire from their work often lose a sense of purpose in their lives and succumb easily to illness and death. Explore the extremes of the workaholic and the idler in an effort to see where the students are in their understanding of work as a calling of God. You may also explore gender role distinctions regarding work to determine if there is a potential problem in this area.

Don't Be Afraid of Evil
(Objectives 1 and 2)

1–2. Underscore the need to pray daily for the success of the Gospel in overcoming the powerful forces of evil that seek to prevent its acceptance. Even Jesus prayed that His disciples would be protected from evil **(John 17:15–21)**.

3. God's faithfulness means that He never changes in His love and favor toward us. We can live with confidence in His promises; He will give us every resource we need to be strengthened in our warfare with Satan.

4–5. The human heart is either controlled by God's love or by the torment of fear. When God's love fills us, our lives show much less concern for the threats and taunts of evil people. See **1 John 4:18.** Missionaries often say that the Gospel of Christ's love delivers people from the fear of the spiritual world in dramatic ways. After being converted to Christ, they now laugh at the spirits that once intimidated them.

Make Each Day Productive (Objective 3)

1. By avoiding the idle person, we shame that person into an awareness of his or her selfish and destructive ways. Idlers hurt the unity of the congregation. Exiling from Christian fellowship for a time leads them to understand their sin.

2. Idle people tend to be burdens by virtue of their parasitic need to be supported by those who work. Not only do they drain the resources of others, they also disrupt the productivity of workers by their busybody attitudes.

3. Review the remarks on this passage in the background section. Paul is concerned about the unity of the congregation and the potential harm to the congregation's fellowship that the idlers are causing. We must admonish such a disruptive influence. Paul speaks firmly about how the congregation must handle this problem.

4–5. Paul always supported himself by his own labor wherever he preached the Gospel. He was sensitive to any criticism from unbelievers that might deter the spread of God's saving Word. Paul felt a need to make special sacrifices in areas where the Gospel was being newly introduced. However, he strongly defended his right to be supported by the Gospel by contributions from those to whom he preached. See his exhaustive argument in **1 Cor. 9:3–18.** Paul certainly did not expect ministers of the Gospel to abide by the same pattern he modeled on the mission field.

6. This entire section focuses on the need for members of the congregation to work together and to serve Christ in harmony and unity. We certainly can assume from the text that each member of the congregation ought to contribute his or her fair share according to the gifts God has given to each.

Be Busy at Your Work and Serve the Lord
(Objectives 3 and 4)

1. Paul prescribes that believers be responsible ("earn the bread they eat") and faithful ("doing what is right") in their approach to their work. We are representatives of Jesus Christ in whatever vocation to which we have been called.

2–3. Through Christ God empowers us to do everything in this life in the name and for the sake of Jesus Christ. Christ's love motivates us as much in the place where we work as in the church where we worship.

4. Spend some time having the students discuss possible choices of a future career. Emphasize that all vocations should be considered in terms of God's calling. Be sure students understand that God's calling to a certain vocation is related to their own aptitude and

skills for such a position and not necessarily to the prestige or rewards of the position. Also point out that all vocations, no matter how humble, are equally honorable to God if we can serve Christ through them.

5–6. Stress the importance of serving Christ rather than ourselves in the working world.

Conclude with prayer or by singing or speaking the hymn stanzas.

Session 75: Concluding Activities for Unit 9

STUDENT BOOK ACTIVITIES

Several activities have been suggested in the Student Book to review some of the concepts studied in this unit. Choose the activity or activities that best meet the needs of your students. If you use the class debate, assign students to teams in advance. Encourage them to meet, perhaps during some class sessions of this unit, to plan their strategies.

Instead of those activities, you may want to continue discussion of one or more lessons that prompted considerable interest on the part of the students.

TEST

If you administer a formal test, consider preparing a series of essay questions over the things you emphasized during the unit. Following are some questions you may use.

1. Discuss the relationship between sexual behavior and our life in Christ. What tensions do teenagers face in this area? How can Christian teenagers deal with those tensions? Why are sexual relationships such an important aspect of our lives?

2. Think of someone you know who has lost a close Christian friend or family member through death. Write a letter to this person, using the theme, "The coming day of the Lord." (If you don't know a person to whom to write, address your letter to a hypothetical friend.)

3. Compare the way children of light and of darkness look forward to the coming day of the Lord.

4. What messages for your life do you find in God's teachings about the Antichrist?

5. Explain the relationship between work and your life as a child of God.

UNIT 10: KNOWING WHAT WE BELIEVE: STUDIES IN LUTHER'S LARGE CATECHISM

During the first nine units of this course students have examined Scripture and drawn doctrine from those studies of Scripture.

The first four units provided a verse by verse study of Romans. Units 5–9 examined selected portions of 1 and 2 Corinthians, Philippians, and 1 and 2 Thessalonians.

During this final unit students will study Luther's Large Catechism. This approach is designed to help them tie together in a systematic way the teachings of units 1–9. It will also provide a review of doctrines many of the students learned from Luther's Small Catechism during their years of confirmation instruction.

Each student will need a copy of Luther's Large Catechism. (*The quotations from the Large Catechism in this unit are from the translation by F. Samuel Janzow published by Concordia Publishing House. You may order the Janzow translation from Concordia. Its order number is 14-2021.*)

Session 76
Basic Christian Teachings Revisited

CENTRAL TRUTH

Pastors and heads of households should study the main teachings of the Christian faith daily and teach them to the children entrusted to their care. We need to study these chief articles of our faith to know what we believe, to drive away the devil, and to give us guidance for our lives.

OBJECTIVES

By the grace of God students will
1. affirm the need to study the main teachings of the Christian faith as presented in Luther's Large Catechism;
2. identify the many opportunities they have to study these teachings;
3. explain why it is so important that we study the main teachings of our Christian faith.

BACKGROUND

Luther originally wrote his Large Catechism as a book of instructions for fathers to use in instructing their families in the basic teachings of the Christian faith, as his preface of 1528 states. He wrote his second preface (in 1530) to pastors, not to fathers. This indicates that Luther expected his catechism to be used as the basis for instruction not only in the home but also in the church.

Luther's Large Catechism is still an important book for us today. It can provide for us the basis for studying basic Christian teachings and for putting those teachings into practice in our lives.

GETTING INTO THE LESSON
(Objectives 1 and 3)

Begin by having students read the introduction to unit 6 in the Student Book. Then have them read the opening paragraphs of this session. Talk about how important it is for us to continually review the basic teachings of our Christian faith and to increase our understanding of those teachings. Point out that we don't, however, create faith in ourselves as we attain such knowledge. Rather, the Holy Spirit works through the Word (including explanations of that Word) to create and sustain faith.

A Model for Studying Basic Christian Teachings
(Objectives 1–3)

1 a and b. The Israelites were to take God's commandments to heart, teach them, talk about them, tie them on their hands and foreheads, and write them on their door frames and gates. They were to be constantly reminded in these ways of how they were to serve the Lord who had given them these commandments.

c. As the Israelites were to be constantly teaching and talking about God's commandments, so God wants us to daily study the basic teachings of our Christian faith, teach them, and talk about them with others.

2. Luther says the head of the household should teach the catechism to his children. Luther considered this important because he felt these basic teachings were the very least a Christian should know and still be considered a Christian. Christians should certainly have this basic knowledge of their faith, even though faith in Jesus Christ as their Savior is sufficient for salvation. Certainly Luther would define knowledge of the catechism as knowledge of the truths therein contained rather than knowledge of the catechism in and of itself.

3 a and b. Luther addressed this preface to pastors who were obviously not spending much time studying Christian teachings. Today he might write his

preface to all of us, since few, if any, of us study our catechism daily.

c. Luther suggests that the canonical hours formerly observed by the priests would provide a good opportunity for pastors to study their catechism. Opportunities today might be just before going to bed or after doing homework. Such opportune times for studying the catechism daily will vary for each person.

Reasons for Studying Basic Christian Teachings
(Objectives 1 and 3)

1 a and b. Studying basic Christian teachings helps you resist the devil and evil thoughts in two ways, according to Luther: neither will come to you when you are so occupied, and the Word of God is the best weapon against them.

c. Besides studying the catechism, we should put into practice what it teaches.

2. We are to resist the devil by standing firm in our faith. This again implies that we must study basic Christian teachings, for only in that way can we know what we believe.

Putting Basic Christian Teachings into Practice
(Objective 3)

Let students struggle with this one. The main thing you want to look for is the idea that we are to live a Christian life in response to what God has done for us. We do not live by Law. We live by grace. The Holy Spirit gives us both the desire and power to live out that response.

Session 77: What Makes God God?

CENTRAL TRUTH

The true God becomes our God through the faith He gives us. We are to trust in God alone, look to Him, and expect to receive nothing but good things from Him. God threatens to punish those who do not keep this commandment, and promises to bless those who do keep it.

OBJECTIVES

By the grace of God students will
1. explain that it is only through faith that the true God becomes their God;
2. describe some false gods people worship today;
3. explain what it means that everything good comes to us from God;
4. identify the threat God makes against those who do not keep this commandment and the promise He makes to those who do keep it.

BACKGROUND

Luther wrote his Small Catechism in 1529, but a year before that, in 1528, he wrote his Large Catechism. The Small Catechism, then, is really a summary of the Large Catechism, which Luther had originally intended those who instructed children to use.

This explanation of the First Commandment, like all of Luther's Large Catechism, is a masterful piece of writing. Written in language simple enough for children to understand, it presents profound theological truths. This lesson will seek to apply those truths to the everyday lives of high school students today.

GETTING INTO THE LESSON (Objective 2)

Begin with the first section in the Student Book. Give students a few minutes to fill out their personal checklists. Talk briefly about what occupies important places in their lives and what really occupies first place. If they claim that God occupies first place, challenge them with questions (e.g., whether they really spend more time thinking about God than about anything else). This section is not designed for students to come up with answers, but to move them to think seriously about the subject matter.

What Makes God Number One?

1 a and b. There could be a long list of things that people look to "for any good things." That list might include horoscope, lottery, a good job, friends, parents, grandparents, stores—the list could go on and on. These things become "gods" when you look to them as the primary source of good things and begin to trust in them for your welfare instead of trusting in God.

c. In a sense, you can keep these things from becoming your "gods" by realizing in some cases that they are not really a source of good things and are therefore not from God and in other cases that these are means through which God gives His good gifts. In a greater sense, however, "you" can't keep anything from becoming your god. Only the Holy Spirit, working through Word and Sacrament, can keep you (or anyone!) from making gods out of things besides the true God.

d. Today people turn to many places for help in times of need, depending on what the need is—doctors, friends, the government, social agencies, psychiatrists, marriage counselors, etc. This may become idolatry if you trust in these people or institutions instead of trusting in God, and do not see them as means through which God gives His good gifts.

2) a. The false gods people have worshiped throughout history have included Jupiter and the whole array of Roman gods, the Roman emperors, the saints, devils, and many others.

b. Idolatry "does not consist simply in setting up an image and worshiping it; it takes place primarily in the heart, which looks elsewhere than to the one God, seeks help and comfort in created things, in saints, or in devils" (LC, p. 31).

2 a and b. Worship of the true God can include idolatry if we trust in our act of worship to give us good things. Good things do not come to us because we go to church, but because God gives them by His grace. We can guard against such idolatry by trusting in God alone as the Source of all good things, realizing that He gives them to us out of His grace and not because of what we do.

Our Good God

1. The Israelites had been delivered from slavery in Egypt. We have been delivered from our bondage to sin, death, and the devil through our Lord Jesus Christ.

2 and 3. Good things sometimes come to us through doctors, parents, and from many other natural sources. These sources are the "hands, channels, and means" through which God gives good things.

4. With the Spirit's power we can keep the good things God gives from becoming our idols by using them as we need them and then laying them aside.

A Threat and a Promise

1. These words are attached to the First Commandment because when the "head" is right, then the entire life will be right. If we make God our Head, then we will also strive to keep all His other commandments. God is a *jealous* God means that He will not share His first place position with anything or anyone.

2 and 3. Godless people may seem to prosper, but usually their prosperity is shallow. Even if they should prosper in this life, they will suffer in the life to come. The opposite of this is true for God's people who suffer. They are God's sons and daughters now and will prosper in life everlasting.

4. This is a hard question, with no simple answer. But there are still many good things in our world, and our faith tells us that God is still in control, ruling the world and our lives for our good.

5. If students are reluctant to share with the entire class, you might have them share in pairs or in groups of three or four.

Close with the prayer in the Student Book.

Session 78: How to Serve God

CENTRAL TRUTH

Through faith in His Son God has established a loving relationship with us. The Second Commandment tells how we will use God's name in such a relationship; the Third Commandment tells how we will use the Lord's Day.

OBJECTIVES

By the grace of God students will
1. explain what it means that we should not use God's name in order to support lies or any kind of wrong;
2. identify ways to use God's name properly;
3. explain how we are to sanctify the holy days;
4. identify some of those who violate the holy days;
5. describe how we are to observe the holy days.

BACKGROUND

The first three commandments comprise the First Table of the Law. These commandments tell us how we are to act in order to "love the Lord, your God with all your heart, with all your soul, and with all your mind."

The Second Commandment speaks about what we will *not* do if we are in a right relationship with God. We will not use His name to support lies or to deceive other people.

When we have identified how we are not to use God's name, we are then led to identify how to use it properly. We are not to be like some of the ancient Jewish people who so feared disobeying this commandment that they never uttered God's name at all. Rather, God wants us to use His name for swearing rightful oaths, teaching the true doctrine, calling on Him in times of trouble, and praising and thanking Him on good days or when He has been especially good to us.

As the Second Commandment speaks of what we are *not* to *say* as people in right relationship with God, so the Third Commandment tells us what we *are* to *do* as people who live in that relationship. We are to "sanctify the holy day." This means that we should lay aside one day a week for rest from our physical labors, Luther says. But more important, it means that we should use that day for learning God's Word, for, as Luther says, "the treasure that sanctifies all things is the Word of God."

GETTING INTO THE LESSON (Objective 1)

Start with the opening paragraphs in the Student Book. Point out that when Luther explains this commandment, he does not emphasize cursing. Rather, he puts his emphasis on swearing, lying, and deceiving by God's name. This does not mean that Luther condoned cursing. It simply means that was not the emphasis he saw in this commandment.

It's Only a Little Lie, for God's Sake (Objective 1)

1. Peter violated the Second Commandment by swearing with an oath that he did not know Jesus. This hurt Jesus, who had been betrayed by a close friend, but it hurt Peter more, because he had sinned against the One he had earlier declared to be "the Christ, the Son of the living God."

2–3. People use God's name in vain today in many, many ways. These include perjury, the use of God's name by television evangelists to amass fortunes for themselves, and the sale of Bibles or sacred music for profit only. At times the use of God's name in this way may lead to temporary temporal gain, but often it results finally in the loss of all such gain. If unrepented, it leads to eternal damnation.

Using God's Name for Truth's Sake (Objective 2)

You might give students about five minutes to work through this section in pairs. Then ask volunteers to share some of their responses with the entire class.

1–3. God wants us to use His name to worship Him, to praise Him, to pray to Him, to bring our needs before Him, and to thank Him for His goodness. All of this may be done in public or in private, aloud or silently. The important thing to remember is that God's name is to be used in the ways that He would have us use it.

Keeping God's Day Holy, for His Sake
(Objectives 3, 4, and 5)

1) a. Luther says the two reasons for observing a holy day are to rest from your labors and to have an opportunity to hear and study God's Word. The latter would seem to be more important, although you could argue that you can hear and study God's Word every day, while only Sunday provides a true day of rest.

b. People should go to church on Sunday primarily to hear the Word of God and to worship Him. Not going to church on Sunday is not a sin in and of itself; no commandment says we must be there. The important thing is that we regularly take the opportunity to hear God's Word and to offer Him our prayer and praise. Since the Holy Spirit works through Word and Sacrament, we starve ourselves when we stay away from that food.

2) a. Perhaps the greedy, the frivolous, and the drunkards violate the Third Commandment callously and willfully, while those who listen to God's Word as entertainment or out of habit believe they are doing the right thing. The latter behavior, however, could be more damaging, since the person seems less likely to feel a need for repentance.

b. A church service is certainly not a circus or a television show. It should entertain only inasmuch as this helps to focus people's attention on God's Word. Opinions expressed in response to this question will probably vary greatly.

As an outgrowth of this question, you might discuss your school's chapel services. Perhaps the faculty would welcome input from your class of ways to effectively focus students' attention on God's Word.

c. None of the things listed are really wrong, in and of themselves, to do on Sunday. The real question to consider is whether in some way those engaged in these activities are resting from their work—whether on this or another day—and listening to the Word regularly. Perhaps we should ask, before *any* activity, "What spiritual and physical rehabilitation will I be receiving?"

3. Luther did not touch upon this issue in the Large Catechism, but very likely some students will wonder why we observe other parts of **Ex. 20:1–17** and **Deut. 5:6–21,** but do not keep the Sabbath in the way prescribed there. Since the deliverance foreshadowed (Jesus' atoning sacrifice for our sins) has come to pass, both Jesus and Paul indicate that we no longer need to follow the Sabbath laws.

Close with a prayer asking God to help students use both His name and His day in ways that give Him glory.

Session 79: Honoring Parents and Other Authorities

CENTRAL TRUTH

God commands us to obey parents and other authorities as His representatives on earth. He promises a long and prosperous life to those who keep this commandment. The indescribable love God has shown us in Jesus provides us with the power to keep it.

OBJECTIVES

By the grace of God students will
1. affirm that they are to honor their parents as those placed over them by God:
2. explain how others in authority derive their authority from this commandment;
3. identify ways in which they are to keep this commandment in their daily living;
4. explain the special promise God attached to this commandment.

BACKGROUND

The Fourth Commandment is the beginning of the Second Table of the Law. The first three commandments exhort us to love God and tell us how that love will show itself. The other seven commandments tell us how those who love God will show love to their fellow human beings.

Note that the Fourth Commandment is the only commandment in the Second Table of the Law written in positive terms. All the others speak of things we should *not* do. Thus we have a special challenge to live in relation to our parents in conformity with God's will. And, as Luther indicates, this also applies to our relationship to others in authority.

The motivation for keeping this commandment, like the motivation for keeping all commandments, is our love for God. That love flows from God's love for us. As St. John puts it: **"We love because He first loved us" (1 John 4:19).** That love from God moves us to love others, and therefore, to obey the commandments contained in the Second Table of the Law **(1 John 4:19–21)**.

GETTING STARTED

Discuss some of the signs that show the breakdown of the family. These might include divorce, child abuse, child abandonment, and runaway children. Discuss the reasons for the breakdown of the family today. Have students read the opening paragraph in the Student Book.

The Special Place of Parents (Objectives 1 and 3)

1) a. "Honoring" someone means to hold that person in high esteem. Love is a prerequisite for honor; honor without love is really a charade. Jesus indicated that "love" is basic to keeping all the commandments **(Mark 12:29–31)**. The commandments spell out ways to show love. The command to honor also includes obedience **(Eph. 6:1)**.

b. God tells us to honor our parents because they are His special representatives on earth. He has given us our parents to train and instruct us in both physical and spiritual things.

c. We show that we honor our parents first and foremost by obeying them. We also honor them by showing respect for them and by loving them.

d. Children are to honor their parents, Luther says, even those who are not deserving of honor. This is fitting since God loves us, even though we do not deserve His love. This implication of the commandment may cause great agony to children of irresponsible parents. Be very sensitive to this. If some students seem overly agitated about this, talk to them privately, arrange for discussions with your school counselor, and if necessary, help them to get professional counseling.

Scripture provides examples of honor shown to authorities whose behavior did not merit honor. David honored King Saul **(1 Sam. 24:6; 26:9–12)**, and Paul honored the high priest **(Acts 23:2–5)**.

2) a. This question is a direct follow-up on the previous question. Children might find it difficult to honor parents who are abusive, alcoholic, or emotionally disturbed. Honoring such parents does not mean allowing them to ruin their children's lives. It includes getting help for them so they may improve their lives and so the relationship between parents and children may improve.

b. This is a most difficult situation, but in God's sight murder is wrong. This is one instance where honoring one's parent would involve disobeying her. That act shows more honor than does blind obedience.

At this time you could discuss other issues in connection with aging parents (e.g., placing parents into nursing homes; permitting parents to die instead of using "heroic" means to sustain life; honoring parents when children also have demands for raising *their* children).

The Special Gifts of Parents (Objectives 1 and 3)

1) a. We can show that we prize and value our parents by obeying them, speaking well of them, and doing things to please them. This includes simple things like remembering birthdays and other special days, and bigger things like caring for them when they are ill or infirm.

b. Parents can train us to do good works; they can provide an example for us, whereby we are the recipients of their good works; and, above all, they can nurture our faith in Jesus, through whom we receive the desire and power to do good works.

2. Answers to (a) and (b) will vary greatly and may include many things. The greatest gift parents can give to their children is to show them the way of salvation through faith in Jesus.

3. We grow in the desire and ability to keep this commandment—and *all* the commandments—through our faith in Jesus. Only God can empower us; on our own we would fail again and again. You might look at two passages by the apostle Paul in this connection, **Eph. 2:1–10** (especially **verses 3, 4, 5,** and **10**) and **2 Cor. 5:14–15**. This might also be a good time to point out that our sinful natures will cause us to live the new life imperfectly; we will sin against the Fourth Commandment. As children of God, however, He has forgiven all our sins, including these **(1 John 1:9)**.

On Being Parents (Objective 1)

1–2. The two main responsibilities of parents are to care for their children's physical and spiritual needs. They provide for children's physical needs by working to obtain food, shelter, etc., and by teaching them what they need to know to function in the world. They provide for their spiritual needs by providing training for them in the Word of God through family devotions, by taking them to Sunday school and church, and by setting a good example in their own life-style and conversations, etc.

3–4. If parents take these responsibilities seriously, the family will be strengthened, and the children will be well prepared for their life in the world. This would provide better-equipped people physically, mentally, emotionally, and spiritually, and greatly strengthen society. Discuss the ills in society that occur because parents have failed to follow through on these responsibilities. (Of course, some children still "turn out bad," but students probably know of instances where the bad behavior of children occurred primarily because parents failed in their responsibilities.)

Other Authorities (Objective 2)

People derive authority from various places: the government, the church, and the school, to name a few. Ultimately, however, all authority comes from God.

The Promise (Objective 4)

1–3. God promises that those who keep this commandment will have a long and prosperous life. This would seem to emphasize the special importance of this commandment. We cannot and should not, however, judge whether a child who dies early has not honored his parents. That is for God alone to judge.

4. Those who do not keep this commandment, just as those who disobey any of the commandments, are condemned to eternal death and damnation. But Jesus dies for sins against this commandment, too, and those who trust in His atoning death can be assured that their sins are forgiven.

Close this session by praying that we would honor our parents and asking God's forgiveness when we do not do so.

Session 80: Out Among Our Neighbors

CENTRAL TRUTH
The Fifth, Sixth, and Seventh Commandments command us not to sin against our neighbor's person, spouse, or property by thought, word, or deed. They exhort us rather to defend our neighbor from harm, honor the institution of marriage, and help our neighbor protect his or her property. Realizing our inability to keep these commandments perfectly, we turn for forgiveness to the suffering and death of our Lord Jesus Christ.

OBJECTIVES
By the grace of God the students will
1. explain what God forbids in the Fifth, Sixth, and Seventh Commandments;
2. identify the all-inclusive nature of the prohibitions in these three commandments;
3. describe the positive attitudes and actions required of us toward our neighbors by these commandments; and
4. realize their inability to keep these commandments, yet rejoice in the forgiveness that is theirs in Jesus Christ.

BACKGROUND
The first three commandments told us how we are to live in relationship to God. The Fourth Commandment told us how we are to live together within the confines of our homes and families. The next three commandments move us out of the home and tell us how we are to live in the world among both our Christian and non-Christian neighbors.

On the surface all of these commandments have as their purpose to command us to avoid sinful acts. But when you look at these commandments more closely, you realize that they are much more inclusive than that. They have to do with how we live in relationship with our neighbors as an extension of our relationship with God.

This is what we hope to share with students during this class session. Not only do we want them to be able to identify specific acts of wrongdoing that they are to avoid, we also want them to understand what it means to live in right relationship with other people. Such an understanding will help equip them for life among the realities of the world.

GETTING STARTED
Begin by having students read the opening paragraphs in the Student Book. Continue immediately with the section that follows.

Charting Your Required Relationships
Briefly discuss the model in the Student Book. Make sure students understand what they are to do. Have them work at this activity individually or in groups of two or three. At the end of the time you have allotted for this activity (about half of your class period), have a brief sharing session involving the total class.

Some of the charts for the Sixth and Seventh Commandments might look like this:

Thou Shalt Not Commit Adultery

	Forbidden	*Encouraged*
Thoughts, emotions	Sexual fantasies, lustful thoughts	Loving, caring, chaste thoughts
Words	Dirty jokes, sexual innuendoes	Words of love, especially important between spouses
Deeds	Adultery, sexual promiscuity, extramarital sex	Acts of love, faithfulness of spouses to one another

Thou Shalt Not Steal

	Forbidden	Encouraged
Thoughts, emotions	Conniving, scheming, to steal or defraud	Thinking of ways to help your neighbor defend his or her property
Words	Deceptive words that would defraud the neighbor	Words to protect the neighbor from being cheated by another
Deeds	Out-and-out stealing, cheating another out of what is rightfully his or hers	Helping another person improve or protect his property and business

2) a. We are to help people in their times of physical need. Not to do so is to violate the Fifth Commandment as surely as if we had murdered them.

b. The Sixth Commandment does not just forbid adultery. It forbids even any thought, attitude, or emotion that might lead to adultery or sexual promiscuity.

c. To defraud another of what rightfully belongs to him or her is to steal from that person and thus to violate the Seventh Commandment.

Some Practical Matters

Have the students read through the statements in the Student Book. Then go back through them one by one and use them as a basis for class discussion. Try to get the class to come to proper conclusions before indicating right and wrong responses. Below are some comments about each statement.

1. As far as the world is concerned, this is a practical reason for avoiding extramarital sex. The Sixth Commandment, however, tells us to avoid extramarital sex because God forbids it. You might also discuss **1 Cor. 7** (e.g., **v. 9**) in connection with this topic.

2. Technically, keeping such change is stealing. Usually one can find a responsible person (e.g., the manager of an area), but at times this will require considerable effort.

3. This is the way Christians are to respond. Otherwise, violence simply escalates. See also **Matt. 5:39.**

4. This is a true statement. The mutual love and respect spouses have for one another will keep them from committing adultery.

5. As Luther clearly indicates, this is a false statement.

6. This statement is not true. It does not take seriously Jesus' words in **Matt. 5:27–28.**

7. Students might debate this issue. As Luther points out, government actions are exempted from this commandment.

8. This statement is true in our day and age. Some of the greatest theft that occurs is the theft of time by employees for which they are being paid by their employers.

9. Luther says this is true. He says that in general all men and women should get married except those who are not equipped for married life and those "whom by means of a high supernatural gift He has released from it, enabling them to maintain chastity outside of marriage" (LC, p. 62).

10. God expects everyone to keep these commandments, even though He knows it is impossible for anyone to do so. Because we cannot keep them, He sent His Son Jesus to keep them for us and to die for our sins, so that through faith in Him we might be saved from His wrath and from eternal damnation and be restored to a right relationship with Him and with other people.

Close with the prayer in the Student Book.

Session 81: Don't Even Think It!

CENTRAL TRUTH

God's law does not just forbid sinful acts. It also forbids sinful words and sinful desires. The Eighth Commandment forbids slander and gossip, while the Ninth and Tenth Commandments forbid covetousness. These commandments show us, as do all the rest, that we cannot on our own be righteous before God.

OBJECTIVES

By the grace of God students will

1. describe what it means to bear false witness against another person;
2. explain the sin of covetousness and how this sin can destroy a person's life;
3. affirm that we cannot on our own be righteous before God and, therefore, need Christ's righteousness to be restored to a right relationship with God.

BACKGROUND

The last three commandments deal not with sinful actions, but with words and thoughts (that may lead to sinful actions). Note, however, that God does not forbid these words and thoughts because they may lead to sin, but because they are themselves sinful.

Bearing false witness against another person may be the most rampant sin today. Many people perjure themselves in the courtroom and do not give their lying testimony a second thought. Gossip occurs among all sorts of people in all kinds of settings, from a high school cafeteria to a sophisticated office building, and much of that gossip is deliberately malicious.

And when it comes to rampant sin, covetousness is not far behind. Many people envy those who have many material possessions and secretly wish that somehow they could get their hands on their neighbor's car or house. Coveting another's wife is, of course, very common. You don't have to look far from yourself—in fact, maybe only inside—to see lust for another person's spouse who seems more attractive or witty or, for some other reason, more desirable than yours.

In this lesson, then, we will help students identify the sins of false witness and covetousness. Then we will see how such sins can infect a person's life. Our ultimate goal will be to point them to their Savior so that they are moved to trust in the righteousness that is theirs in Him.

GETTING INTO THE LESSON
(Objectives 1–3)

Begin with the introductory section in the Student Book. Ask students to share some other instances—real or imaginary—of bearing false witness or covetousness that might happen in the life of a high school student. Spend only a few minutes at this. Then continue with the next section.

When Not to Speak (Objective 1)

1) a. As Luther points out, this commandment expressly forbids false witness in public courts, slander against Christians, and the sin of language that may harm or offend your neighbor. The most prevalent form of false witness is gossip— saying things intended to damage the reputation of another.

b. Those allowed to say bad things about another, Luther says, are civil authorities, preachers, and parents. All are called upon as God's representatives to correct evil and, therefore, must speak out against it when they see it.

c. Note Luther's emphasis upon a person's *reputation*. The test of whether or not to repeat something does not end with the question, "Is it true?" One should also ask, "Is it kind?" and "Does it build up the person?" You might take time to read **James 3:1–12** and to talk about the effects of gossip.

2. If someone sins against you, go to that person to tell him or her how he or she has sinned against you. If that doesn't work, you take one or two witnesses with you. If that doesn't work, you go to the congregation with the charge, asking that the person be declared outside the fellowship of the church, since the church is made up of *repentant* sinners. If the person is declared outside church fellowship, then that person is to be treated as "you would a pagan or tax collector." That means that the person is to be considered an evangelism prospect, not that he or she should be totally ignored and abandoned.

3) a. Luther says that if your neighbor's sin is public knowledge, there is nothing wrong with talking about it (LC, p. 74). Of course, he does not say we *should* talk about it, but that we *may*, because our conversation will not damage the person's reputation.

b. When someone else says something bad about someone, you should try to think of something good to say about that person. As the saying goes, "If you can't think of anything good to say about a person, don't say anything at all."

Forbidden Desire (Objective 2)

The case studies in this section could be answered in a variety of ways. Use them primarily as the basis for discussion.

1. This is a prime example of coveting, one that happens far too frequently. Such coveting destroys relationships between people.

2. It's difficult to know what one should do in this situation. The president of your company is guilty of coveting the services of an employee of another company. You probably should refuse to be a party to such covetousness.

3. Probably the most loving thing to do in this situation would be to offer to help Bob pay for his convertible. Let the class wrestle with other alternatives. They should recognize that God's commandments require just the opposite as the desires of our sinful natures and are, therefore, difficult to keep.

The Bottom Line (Objective 3)

1. Our obedience to every other commandment depends on our committing ourselves to the First Commandment. Only when we acknowledge that the God who gives the comandments is the true God, will we commit ourselves to obeying His commandments. Our relationship with God determines how we relate to other people.

2. The commandments serve three purposes: First, they serve as rules of conduct. Second, they show us how far short our righteousness falls of what God requires; as we see that our righteousness falls short, God points us to our Savior, whose righteousness covers our sins. Third, the commandments provide guidelines for God-pleasing behavior for those whose faith in Christ causes them to want to please God.

Close this session with a prayer asking God's forgiveness for our offenses against these commandments and thanking Him for sending His Son to be our Savior.

Session 82: The Father of Us All

CENTRAL TRUTH

The Apostles' Creed tells us about everything for which we must look to God. In the First Article we learn that God the Father is the almighty Creator. He has created each of us, provides us with the necessities and comforts of life, protects, and defends us. In response, we are to love, praise, thank, and serve Him.

OBJECTIVES

By the grace of God students will
1. explain the purpose of the Apostles' Creed;
2. affirm that God is their Maker and the Creator of all things;
3. respond with love, praise, thanks, and service.

BACKGROUND

The Apostles' Creed is the earliest of the ecumenical creeds of the church. This creed was not formulated by councils of theologians but grew spontaneously out of the needs of the early church. It was not written by the apostles but is the formulation of the apostolic faith.

In this session we will not concern ourselves with the history of the Apostles' Creed; rather, we will deal with its content. The creed contains a concise summary of all the basic teachings of the Christian faith.

The First Article deals with creation. In explaining this article, Luther does not address the subject of how God created the world. He simply acknowledges that God is the Maker of everything that exists and what this means for our lives. He then tells us how we are to respond to our Creator God.

Your students, however, live in a world with different aberrations than those that existed in Luther's day. They are impacted by forces that speak of evolution, abortion, gay rights, and other abominations. You will not have time to do an in-depth study of any of these issues during one session. Attempt, however, to provide at least a summary of Scripture's position on each of them.

Session 3 of the Teachers Guide for *God's Old Testament People*, another course in this series, provides additional material about creation and evolution.

GETTING INTO THE LESSON

You could begin today by reading responsively **Ps. 8**. Without comment, move into the introductory paragraphs in the Student Book. Reinforce responses that indicate how God's Word provides knowledge beyond that which we find in nature and thus enriches our understanding and appreciation of what we see there. Students will undoubtedly be able to add to the list of marvels of God's creation.

Introducing the Apostles' Creed (Objective 1)

1. Luther says the Apostles' Creed shows us everything for which we must look to God and helps us know thoroughly what God is like. It also helps us to do what we should be doing according to the Ten Commandments, since we cannot keep the commandments of ourselves; we need God's power to do so. Furthermore, the Ten Commandments show us our sin; the creed shows how God rescues us from that sin.

2) a. The First Article tells us that God the Father is our almighty Maker. The Second Article tells us that God the Son, true God and true man, is our Redeemer. The Third Article tells us about God the Holy Spirit and about how God's Spirit works in the world.

b. Some of the teachings in the Apostles' Creed are creation, the humanity of Jesus, the divinity of Jesus, Jesus' virgin birth, the atonement, Jesus' descent into hell, the resurrection, Jesus' intercession for us at His Father's right hand, the work of the Holy Spirit, the doctrine of the church, bodily resurrection, and everlasting life.

c. Expect students to readily acknowledge that they can trust God the Father to take care of them; that they receive peace of mind because they know they have salvation through Jesus; and that they depend upon the Holy Spirit to keep them faithful to God and to do works that please Him. You may want to push them to express strong "gut-level" implications. After students respond, ask questions like: "So what?" "What do you mean by that?" "Did that *really* make a difference to you today? How?" "You know that's what I expected you to say. Now, what's your *real* feeling?"

The Almighty Maker (Objective 2)

1 a and b. God is almighty. He has the power to create, to supply all our wants and needs, and to protect and defend us in times of danger. Our Creator also loves us. He desires to supply the wants and needs of us who are His creatures and to protect and defend us from harm and every evil. You might discuss the impact of these facts as students walk along the street, ride in a car, face unemployment, see approaching storm clouds, feel the earth quake, etc.

c. The act of creation by the Father was not just a one-time act at the beginning of the world but is an ongoing activity throughout time. Because this is the Father's work, He continues to care for us throughout our lives. He also continues to care for His creation. Because it is His creation, we have a duty to relate to it responsibly. This includes care for our body and being responsible with and responsive to environmental concerns.

2) a. Encourage lots of sharing here. If you have access to a school newspaper, you might encourage

individuals, groups, or the class as a whole to prepare their adaptations of **Ps. 104.**

b. If the science teachers in your school deal with the creation versus evolution issue, you need not spend lots of time with it here. Perhaps two or three students could summarize the Scriptural position as it has been presented. Since Scripture is without error in all its parts, our faith in God will cause us to believe what God caused Moses to write in **Gen. 1–2.**

c. This discussion could get into areas of marriage, reproduction, and homosexual acts. God ordained marriage **(Gen. 2)**, but He did not order it **(1 Cor. 7)**; He desires that sexual intercourse and reproduction take place within the marriage union **(1 Cor. 7)**; and He forbids homosexual acts **(Rom. 1)**.

d. God has made us stewards (managers) of His creation. How do we do this? Students may mention ecology, physical exercise, avoidance of alcohol and other drugs, etc., in this connection.

3) a. God shows His care for us by giving us our marvelous bodies, caring for our physical needs, and by defending and protecting us. He showed His care for us in the strongest possible way by sending His Son to be our Savior.

b. **Ps. 136:13–16** mentions the marvels of the human body, including the fact that life begins with conception (thus showing that abortion involves the destruction of life). When we think of ourselves and others as God's creation, our entire outlook becomes one of managing—caring for—that creation.

c. **Ps. 8** tells us that our Creator God made everything, but that the crown of His creation is humankind. God has given human beings the rule over creation. For this even little children praise Him—and so should we! This tells each one of us that we are special and of great value, and we ought to praise Him always for His creation, and most especially for having created us.

Reply to My Father (Objective 3)

This is a creative activity. Students could express themselves in words, in drawings, in poetry—any way they wish.

Close by reading **Gen. 1** responsively, verse by verse.

Session 83: Jesus Is Lord

CENTRAL TRUTH

Jesus is Lord because He is our Redeemer. He has rescued us from the devil to bring us to God, from death to bring us into life, and now keeps us safe where He has brought us. The Second Article details what He did to accomplish this.

OBJECTIVE

By the grace of God students will
1. explain how Jesus rescued us from sin, death, and the devil;
2. list what Jesus went through to accomplish this;
3. confess Jesus Christ as their Lord and Savior.

BACKGROUND

The Second Article of the Apostles' Creed summarizes the central teachings of the Christian faith. It relates in simple yet precise words what God did when He sent His Son into the world.

Theologians have written volumes on this central article of our faith. It has been considered, weighed, and questioned from every angle. Here, however, Luther is wise enough to let the way of salvation by faith in Jesus Christ stand as a simple jewel. As **Rom. 5:6** puts it so beautifully, yet so simply: **"You see, at just the right time, when we were still powerless, Christ died for the ungodly."**

That is the heart of the matter.

GETTING INTO THE LESSON
(Objectives 1, 2, and 3)

Begin by asking students to tell what Jesus did for us and why this is important for our lives. Do not judge or contradict what anyone says. Without comment, move to the opening paragraphs in the Student Book. Emphasize that we do not deny the sovereignty of God. Rather, we emphasize His grace, because through this grace He made us His children. See session 15 of *Which Way Is the Right Way*, another course in this series, for futher discussion about sovereignty versus grace. Also recall the grace emphasis during the study of Romans in the first 45 sessions of the current course.

Jesus, the Redeemer (Objectives 1, 2, and 3)

1. Paul says that Jesus regained His lordship over us by dying for us even though we were completely alienated from Him. Now when God is angry with us because of our sin, in faith we can ask Jesus to intercede for us with His Father, and we will be saved from the eternal consequences of our sinfulness that causes the Father to be angry.

2) a. False. Jesus is fully God and fully a human being (both "true God and true man").

b. True. This is the doctrine or the virgin birth. Jesus was conceived by the Holy Spirit in a miraculous way we cannot understand.

c. True. Paul says that unless He did, our faith is useless **(1 Cor. 15:14).**

d. True, but not a complete answer. Jesus also sits at the right hand of the Father to intercede for us—

to remind His Father that all our sins have been paid for by His death on the cross.

e. False. He will come to earth again to judge the living and the dead.

3. This may seem like a repeat of 2 in some ways, but these central facts about our salvation are so important that we can never review them too much. Emphasize what it cost Jesus to bring us back under His lordship: the temporary abandonment of His place in heaven with His Father, a humble life on earth, suffering, and death on a cross. He risked everything—being forsaken of His Father, His very life itself—to bring us back under His rulership. That is why we proclaim so vigorously! "JESUS CHRIST IS LORD!"

The Heart of the Matter (Objective 3)

1. Give students a few moments to write their essays in class. These are not intended to be polished essays, but an expression of the student's understanding of one of the central teachings of Christianity.

Invite volunteers to share their essays with the class. Ask students to tell whether the essay catches the truth the teaching portrays. If any confusion arises about these teachings or student conclusions present wrong theology, be sure to clarify what the proper teaching is.

2. To help students get started thinking about this activity, invite (but don't press) volunteers to share some times when people feel alienated from God. If no one volunteers, provide examples for them—perhaps from your own life! Attempt to set a mood of quietness in the classroom before students begin meditating.

3. Before class, think of two or three people you know (perhaps former students) who reflect the love of Jesus. Share something about them to "prime the pump"—to get students started talking about people *they* know.

4. Make this activity as personal as possible. Think about "hurting" people in your school. If everyone knows about the hurt, name the person and the situation. Or mention a problem that may exist among several students. If necessary substitute those situations for the items listed in the Student Book. You might read **2 Cor. 5:14–15** to the class and ask, **How can we "live . . . for Him who died for [us] and was raised again"?**

Close by having students pray together the prayer in the Student Book. Then speak **John 3:16** together.

Session 84: The Holy-Maker

CENTRAL TRUTH

The work of the Holy Spirit is to make us holy. He does this in and through the community of saints. There the Word is preached, and the Holy Spirit, working through the Word, makes us holy through the forgiveness of sins. Here on earth that holiness must be restored daily, but when our bodies are resurrected, we will have life everlasting in perfect holiness.

OBJECTIVES

By the grace of God the students will
1. describe the person and work of the Holy Spirit;
2. explain the great importance of the Christian community;
3. affirm their belief in the resurrection of the body and the everlasting life of holiness that we have beyond the grave.

BACKGROUND

At one time theologians spoke about the Holy Spirit as the "forgotten person of the Trinity." Much had been written and much was being said about the Father and the Son, but little was being written or said about the Holy Spirit.

That is no longer true today. Today we hear much about the Holy Spirit and how He works in people's lives. Conflicting theories abound about how He carries out His work today.

Luther stays away from all of this. His theology of the Holy Spirit as expressed here in his explanation of the Third Article of the Apostles Creed is basically a simple one; one the "plain folks" for whom Luther wrote his catechism could certainly understand. He said simply that it is the Holy Spirit who makes us holy. He does this when the Word is preached and the Sacraments are administered in the Christian community. Through these means of grace we are prepared for that glorious day when our resurrected bodies shall live with our Lord in the perfect holiness of everlasting life.

GETTING INTO THE LESSON (Objective 1)

Have students look at the statements in their books that introduce this session and choose the one they believe to be most correct. Talk about these statements, but do not push for any conclusions at this time.

If misconceptions have arisen, come back to these statements at the end of the session. Numbers 1, 2, and 4 are correct, given the proper explanation:

1. I am holy because God has made me holy through faith in Jesus. He has forgiven all my sins.

2. God has offered His forgiveness to all, but most have rejected it, therefore I am holier than most people. Of course, I am no more or less holy than other members of God's church, and my own works certainly do not make me holy!

3. By God's grace I am holy (forgiven) *all* the time.

4. Through my own efforts I am not holy at all. This was the struggle Luther battled with during the

early part of his life—the attempt to *do* enough to become holy. Through God's forgiveness, however, I am completely holy.

How the Holy Spirit Works (Objectives 1 and 2)

1. The community of saints is the assembly of believers. It is not a denomination, but the local congregation. It consists of those who gather around Word and Sacraments. Through Word and Sacraments the Holy Spirit comes to us. Through those means of grace we receive the results of Christ's death on the cross—the forgiveness of sins. The Christian community is such an important place because through it God speaks all his Word and does all His work.

Students who have been taught again and again that "the Holy Sprit works through the means of grace," may be jolted by Luther's statement that the Holy Spirit works through the community of saints. Point out that Luther follows such words with a discussion of the community using God's Word (e.g., last sentence in last full paragraph on p. 89 in Janzow). Thus, Luther attributes the power to the Word; the communion of saints is the vehicle through which the Word is sent forth.

2. The Holy Spirit connects us to Christ and His atoning work. We can only acknowledge Christ's lordship by the work and power of the Holy Spirit.

3. The Holy Spirit's task of making us holy includes changing our sinful nature so that we do not indulge in sinful acts. Because we are sinful human beings, we never reach complete holiness. That is why we need the forgiveness of sins daily.

4. The unity of the Spirit is the oneness the Holy Spirit creates in Christ. This doesn't mean that everyone in the Christian community is the same but that all confess the same faith in the same Lord and Savior.

The Holy Spirit among Us Objectives 1 and 2)

The activities in this section are designed to "put flesh" onto the teachings Luther set forth in the Large Catechism. Select from them whatever experiences you think will best help members of your class live out their faith.

1. Have students write the paragraphs on their own. Invite (but don't require) them to turn in their papers. Then read their testimonies to the class anonomously. Allow listeners to comment about paragraphs they have heard.

2. Don't "push" this activity onto an unwilling class. If students are willing to proceed, however, this could become the beginning of a blessed ministry of building up one another in the faith. You could do this activity in small groups instead of a total class.

3. Ask students to turn in this assignment. Then read the sentences aloud, as you did with 1. Pray that God will enable your class (individually, in groups, or as a total class) to work together to enrich the spiritual atmosphere of your school.

4. Handle (a) in the same way as 3. Then provide the opportunity for students to help one another witness more effectively. You probably can help them by providing roleplay opportunities during class.

Beyond the Christian Community (Objective 3)

Have the students read the opening paragraph in this section. Then have them turn to **1 Thess. 4:13–18**. These words do not really give much specific information about what our life beyond the grave will be like except that "we will be with the Lord forever." That is comfort and hope enough for us. Come back to these words whenever death strikes—the death of a student in your school or of a parent or close friend of someone in your class.

Before you close the class, go back to the statements in the beginning of this session. See the discussion in that section of this guide.

Close by having someone read the prayer in the Student Book.

Session 85: Prayer Talk

CENTRAL TRUTH

God commands us to pray and promises to answer our prayers. As we pray, we honor God's name and use it purposefully. In the Lord's Prayer Jesus gives us the words and the pattern for how we ought to pray.

OBJECTIVES

By the grace of God students will
1. relate why and how we ought to pray and what we ought to pray for;
2. counteract excuses for not praying;
3. express a desire for a meaningful and rewarding prayer life.

BACKGROUND

Luther believed strongly in the importance of prayer. He believed that prayer was a powerful defense against the temptations of the devil. He also believed that we should come before God persistently in prayer, telling Him all our needs.

Prayer is important. As James wrote, **"The prayer of a righteous man is powerful and effective" (James 5:16b).** But, while we agree about the importance of prayer, too often we give short shrift to its place in our daily lives. We find it easy to pray in church or in other formal settings, but our personal prayer life is meager or does not really exist, except in times of trouble or special need.

We need to, therefore, be reminded of the importance of prayer in our daily lives. That is the focus of today's session.

GETTING INTO THE LESSON
(Objectives 1, 2, and 3)

Start by having someone read the introductory paragraphs in the Student Book. Then suggest that it would be fitting for a lesson about prayer to begin with a prayer. Say a short prayer asking God's blessing on today's class session.

Excuses, Excuses (Objectives 2 and 3)

1. This activity is designed to be a sharing and discussion session. There are really no right or wrong answers. Following are some suggestions.

a. God always has time for you. Time spent with Him is important for your life.

b. You don't have to "know how to pray." Ask God for what you want, and thank Him for what He gives. Any words or form are okay, or you may simply pray in your heart.

c. God may know what we need, but He commands us to pray, and as His children, we are to obey His command. God also promises to answer our prayers. He also says, **"You do not have, because you do not ask God" (James 4:2).**

d. No one is innately "good enough" to pray, but Jesus died for us and because of Him, we *are* good enough—we are His holy people—and we can come before Him in prayer.

e. If you have no physical, material, or spiritual needs, then pray for the needs of others and thank God for His goodness.

2. This is a private, personal activity. Allow students time to complete and reflect on their personal prayer inventory. If, however, some students desire to share, permit them to do so.

Why Pray? (Objectives 1 and 3)

1) a. The Second Commandment does not speak specifically about prayer. It forbids us from using God's name in wrong ways. Luther says that this means we should use God's name in the right way, and this includes calling on Him in prayer. See page 79 in Janzow.

b. The command in **Ps. 50:15** is "call upon Me." The promise is "I will deliver you."

c. The point of these verses is self-evident. We are to ask, seek, and knock. God will answer our prayers and meet our needs.

2. Do not force anyone to respond to this question. If your class works well in small groups, especially if they tend to speak more openly in such a setting, use that format here. Perhaps some students will share with the entire class after first sharing in small groups.

How to Pray (Objectives 1 and 3)

1. God rejects prayers that people speak to showcase themselves. He also rejects prayers that are mere babbling or mumbling with no intent or meaning. He accepts prayers when in faith we humbly bring before Him our needs and wants.

2) a. Here is one summary of the needs presented in the Lord's Prayer: to keep God's name holy, the coming of God's kingdom, doing God's will, material needs, forgiveness, deliverance from the devil.

b. This is a creative exercise to be done individually by students. They might spend a moment or two praying their prayers with one another.

3. Consider using small groups to discuss this question. Try to get every student to identify an environment in his or her life that is conducive to prayer. Some large-group sharing may help students get additional ideas for creating such an environment.

4. This question is designed primarily for reflection. Encourage sharing, but don't insist on it. Many people find prayer calendars (weekly or monthly) to be useful tools to remind them to pray for special people or needs. An acronym like ACTS (adoration, confession, thanksgiving, supplication) can help individuals plan their daily prayers.

Close by having one of the students pray the prayer he or she has written; or pray the Lord's Prayer in unison.

Session 86: Prayers of God's Family

CENTRAL TRUTH

We are to pray that God's name would be honored by us and that His kingdom would flourish among us. This happens when we speak, teach, and live according to His will. We pray also, therefore, for the Holy Spirit that we may speak, teach, and live as God's people. We may speak this prayer in confidence, trusting God's promise to answer our prayer.

OBJECTIVES

By the grace of God students will

1. pray that they will speak, teach, and live as God's children;
2. pray that the kingdom of God will take root in their lives that they may one day enter into God's eternal kingdom;
3. pray that God's will may be done in them so that they will be able to patiently endure the attacks of the devil and the world.

BACKGROUND

In the first three petitions of the Lord's Prayer, Jesus teaches us how we are to pray for our spiritual needs. In the First Petition we pray that we will acknowledge that the true God is truly God, and that we would praise and honor Him as we ought. In the Second Petition we pray that God would be the Lord of our life—the One we worship and serve above all others—because He purchased and won us by His innocent suffering and death for us. In this petition, we also pray that God's kingdom of glory would come to us—that by faith we who live with Him here by grace might live with Him in glory eternally.

In the Third Petition we pray that everything relevant to God's glory and our salvation might be accomplished. It is not a prayer that God would change His will to conform to ours, but that our will would be changed to conform to His. For it is we who must do the good and gracious will of our God. We also pray that God will move those around us to do His will.

In this session we want to encourage students to pray for spiritual gifts and graces. For as we pray for spiritual treasures, we have God's promise that He will add temporal blessings. **"Seek first His kingdom and His righteousness,"** our Lord tells us, **"and all these things will be given to you as well" (Matt. 6:33).**

GETTING STARTED (Objectives 1, 2, and 3)

Start today by having someone read the opening paragraphs in the Student Book. Continue immediately with the activity that follows.

Honoring the Family Name (Objective 1)

1. Either the words or the actions of a son or daughter can dishonor the family name. Recall Biblical or historical examples with which your students are familiar.

2. A member of God's family might dishonor God's name by false preaching and teaching, by speaking in God's name something false or misleading, or by living an openly wicked life. When the Father's name is dishonored, people's faith is shaken, and they may lose their respect for their heavenly Father. "If God's children act like that," some may say, "I have no use for their God."

3. When we pray, "Hallowed be Thy name," we are praying that God would give us His Spirit so that we would teach, speak, and act in a way that keeps God's name from being dishonored.

4. If students are reluctant to share examples, begin by sharing one from your own experience. Even though this activity looks for examples that show the positive side of people, students may prefer to keep those people anonymous. Permit this to happen.

5. Consider small groups for this activity, especially if students don't talk freely in the large group. Accent the joy God gives us through the forgiveness of sins.

Inheriting the Family Fortune (Objective 2)

1. The inheritance we have from our heavenly Father is His kingdom. That inheritance is ours on earth as we live in His kingdom of grace—that is, as by the power of the Holy Spirit we live each day in the forgiveness of sins and the love of God. That inheritance will be fully ours beyond this life when we will live in God's kingdom of glory forever.

2. We do not receive our inheritance simply by speaking God's name or even by doing good works in His name. We receive the inheritance by doing the Father's will. The essence of the Father's will is that we believe in Jesus as our Savior. Only then can we do good works in His name. Be sure to emphasize the role of the Holy Spirit in creating faith and thus empowering us to do the good works.

Doing the Family's Will (Objective 3)

1. Invite three or four volunteers to read their paraphrases to the class. Look for evidence that students recognize the battle we face against Satan and our need to rely upon God to grant us the victory in this battle.

2. God's will for us is "everything relative to God's glory and our salvation" (LC, pp. 103–4). His will is that we would believe in Jesus as our Savior and live our lives in a response of love to Him who loved us first and best.

3. God's will is done in the world without our prayers. We pray "Thy will be done" so that we might be moved both to do and to accept His will in our lives. Then, when troubles or temptations come, He causes us to be patient and to be willing to risk everything we have, if necessary, knowing that His will is being done. This means that we can be sure that God will take care of all our needs, for He has promised to do so. That is His good and gracious will.

4. Talk about the way angels carry out God's will and about actions of God that reveal His loving will. Relate God's actions to Luther's Small Catechism explanations of the First, Second, and Third Articles of the Apostles' Creed.

5. Note the attitude of love that causes God and His angels to carry out His will as you discussed it in the previous question. That love from God fills us with love. Ask students to describe the impact of that situation. **What happens when God's love moves us to show love? How does this action cause God's will to be done on earth?**

6. Close this session by having one or more students share their prayers with the class.

Session 87: Prayers for Deliverance

CENTRAL TRUTH

In the last four petitions of the Lord's Prayer, we pray for deliverance from the Evil One. Because of God's great love for us, we can confidently pray that God would deliver us from all bad things that would prevent us from obtaining material necessities, from guilt, and from all temptations and trials.

OBJECTIVES

By the grace of God students will
1. pray daily for deliverance from all the assaults of the Evil One;
2. live in the assurance that that deliverance will be theirs;
3. pray for that deliverance in faith, fully trusting that God will hear and answer their prayers.

BACKGROUND

In the first three petitions our Lord taught us to pray for spiritual gifts and graces. In the last four petitions He teaches us to pray for those things that affect our well-being in the world. In the Fourth Petition, we pray that God would care for our physical needs. Then in the Fifth, Sixth, and Seventh Petitions, we pray for gifts that provide spiritual and emotional stability.

These are, of course, rather arbitrary separations. For ultimately the Lord's Prayer is our Savior's model of a perfect prayer, for it is a prayer in which we ask God to meet all our needs—physical, emotional, and spiritual—as He has promised us that He will do. In this session we want to encourage students to bring all their needs before God, knowing that He has commanded us to do so and has promised to hear and answer our prayers.

GETTING STARTED

Begin with the opening paragraphs in the Student Book. Spend a few moments having students identify why the things listed might be classified as unexplainable terrors. Have them add to the list other unexplainable terrors they face today.

Give Us the Things We Need Here on Earth
(Objectives 1, 2, and 3)

1. When we pray for *daily* bread, we show that we trust God to fill our needs each day. Trusting in Him, we need not worry about whether there will be enough for tomorrow.

This does not mean that we should not plan for the future. It means only that we should not worry about it, but put it in the Lord's hands.

2. Answers will vary, but should include prayers that God would prevent bad weather, bad crops, bad government, bad chemical usage—anything that will stand in the way of our physical needs being met.

3. As you discuss people whom God has used to provide for us, cultivate a spirit of thankfulness—to God and to those He uses. Talk about ways to show our thankfulness, especially to our parents.

4. If possible, lead into some kind of service project, such as collecting food for needy families. Look for a project that can be completed rather quickly and that, as far as you can determine, is likely to succeed. Also discuss ways individuals can provide for long-term needs of others.

Deliver Us from Guilt (Objectives 1, 2, and 3)

1. We do not pray for forgiveness as a way of earning our forgiveness. We pray for forgiveness so that we will recognize and accept this free gift of God. Luther points out that our prayer is not for God, but for ourselves—that we would accept and acknowledge that God deals with our sins according to His grace, forgiving them because of Jesus' death for us on the cross.

2. God's forgiveness of us does not depend on our forgiveness of others. It is the other way around. Our forgiveness of others is a sign that we have been forgiven by God. Just as God forgives us, so we are to forgive others.

Our act of forgiving others does not earn God's forgiveness, nor does the mere act of failing to forgive others cause us to not receive God's forgiveness. Rather, an attitude of refusing to forgive others demonstrates that we are rejecting God's forgiveness and, therefore, do not receive it.

3. Our sins must be forgiven for us to live in a right relationship with God in this world and that we may have life in relationship with Him eternally. Forgiveness in this world also removes the burden of guilt that separates us from other people and creates psychological and emotional problems that prevent us from being all that we could be.

Deliver Us from Temptations

1. Temptations of the flesh are temptations to evil lusts. Temptations of the world are temptations to sinful words and deeds. Temptations of the devil are concentrated attacks on our faith by which he tries to get us to discard God's Word and works.

These categories as outlined by Luther cannot always be that clearly divided, however, since all are ultimately temptations of the Evil One. Temptations of the flesh might be temptations to sexual sins. Temptations of the world might include temptation to drunkenness or to do drugs. Temptations of the devil might include temptation to stay away from church and Bible class—never to be anywhere where God's Word might have a chance to work in one's heart.

2. In order to fight an enemy, we must recognize it. Encourage students to help one another identify ways temptations might approach them.

3. To ward off these temptations, you can pray daily these words of the Lord's Prayer. Of course, that act of prayer does not ward off the temptation; you are delivered through an action of the God to whom you pray.

Discuss some of the ways God works in the lives of the students to resist temptations. For example, talk about times God has helped individuals by leading them to spend their time with friends who also resist temptations; to avoid a party where they expect to find abuse of alcohol, other drugs, or sex; and to study for a test instead of relying upon cheating to come up with answers.

4. Luther says it is not sinful to feel temptation, since temptation comes without our inviting it. We sin when we do not resist temptation. This results in evil lust, and eventually in evil thoughts, words, and deeds. When this happens, we must return to God and His grace in Jesus Christ, praying once again, "Forgive us our trespasses."

Close by having the class pray together the Lord's Prayer, pausing between each petition to think about what they have discussed in the last two sessions.

Session 88: Living In/Out Your Baptism

CENTRAL TRUTH

God commands Baptism in His name. The Word of God connected to the water gives Baptism its power. God gives forgiveness of sins, life, and eternal salvation to those who receive it by faith.

OBJECTIVES

By the grace of God students will
1. affirm that Baptism is commanded by God and received by faith;
2. explain how God's Word gives the water of Baptism its power;
3. describe the change that Baptism works in people's lives;
4. daily remember their baptism to receive strength for daily living.

BACKGROUND

The Roman Catholic Church of Luther's day, as it does today, acknowledged seven sacraments. These sacraments were ways in which God communicated His grace to people. Luther accepted only two of these seven as valid sacraments—Baptism and the Lord's Supper—because only in these two sacraments, according to Scripture, is the Word of God connected to visible elements that convey God's grace to people.

Down through the years these two sacraments have been a leading cause of theological disagreements. Divisions have occurred among church bodies whose theologians have differed on whether or not infants should be baptized, whether or not immersion is the only correct form of Baptism, and even in one case whether those baptized by immersion should go into the water forward or backward.

Except for the question of infant baptism, Luther deals with none of these issues in the Large Catechism. He concentrates his attention instead on the true nature of Baptism and what God accomplishes through this sacrament. He wants us to see our baptism as that means through which God created faith in us, and as a way our faith is strengthened as we remember our baptism each day.

In this session students will learn what Baptism is, what it does, and how their baptism can strengthen them for daily living.

Before you begin, review the concepts of Baptism that were taught as you studied **Rom. 6:1–14** in session 15 of this course.

GETTING STARTED (Objective 4)

Talk briefly about students' baptismal birthdays. Ask whether any remember their baptismal day. If they do, ask them to tell briefly what that day was like.

Also talk about things people do to help them remember their baptism. Perhaps some of them burn (or at one time burned) a special baptismal candle on the anniversary of their baptism. Others may have seen framed baptismal certificates hanging on a bedroom wall, perhaps in a grandparent's home. Invite students to share any practice that helps them or others remember their baptism.

Practices like those mentioned above become hollow—empty—when we merely go through the motions. During this session students will have many opportunities to affirm the grace of God as it came to them through Baptism and comes to them again each day of their lives.

Baptism Is (Objectives 1, 2, 3, and 4)

Give students a few minutes to answer the questions in this section. Use their answers as the basis for class discussion.

Answers

1. (d)
2. (b) See **Matt. 28:19** and **Mark 16:16**.
3. (c) See **Mark 16:16**.
4. (b) Through Baptism God gives forgiveness and eternal life.
5. (c) Without the Word, water is simply water. The Word gives power to Baptism only as it is connected to the water.
6. (d)
7. (b) This is the best answer, although Baptism offers the things mentioned in (a), (c), and (d) also.
8. (b) This is Luther's answer. It is also true that little children can have faith, since faith is a gift of God through the Holy Spirit.

The Ins and Outs of Baptism
(Objectives 3 and 4)

1. When Jesus died and was buried, my old sinful self died and was buried with Him. I rose from the dead a new person to live a new life for Him.

2. Luther says the picture of **Rom. 6:4** appears in Baptism. Picture especially Baptism by immersion. Going under the water symbolizes my death and burial. The old person within me—that which I was—dies with Christ. I come out of the water a new person empowered by God to live a new life for my Lord. Luther says this should happen in my life every day, just as it happened once in Baptism. I should daily "drown" my old sinful self and become the new person Christ has made me by His death on the cross.

3. Paul mentions things that happen inside us (e.g., sin died, and we became alive to God) and outward effects of that change (e.g., we offer ourselves to God).

4. We have been freed from the mastery of sin. Invite students to share how God empowers them to live from day to day within the freed state.

5. Through Baptism God gives us the blessings Jesus earned through His sacrifice for our sins. We are His children for time and eternity.

6. You might look at the form for Holy Baptism on pages 199–204 in *Lutheran Worship*. Especially note where the pastor says, "Receive the sign of the holy cross both upon your forehead and upon your heart to mark you as one redeemed by Christ the crucified" (p. 199). This is more than a symbolic act.

   a. Notice the contrasts in **Col. 2:13–15**: We were dead; God made us alive. We were sinners; God forgave us. The written code condemned us; Jesus' death canceled it. Powers and authorities ruled over us; Jesus disarmed them.

   b. Answers may vary widely. You might ask students to identify aspects of **Col. 3:1–17** that get them excited. Perhaps their excitement will become contagious!

   c. Treat **2 Cor. 15–21** in a manner similar to your approach in the previous discussion.

7. As students share past experiences, seek discussion that will lead to enriched experiences in the future. What a blessing would occur if each of your students would be moved to tears of joy every time they witness a baptism—joy that brings tears because the students feel overwhelmed by the miracle that is taking place as a child who was dead in sin becomes alive in Christ!

8. Recall the discussions from the beginning of the session. Focus now on the salvation that we receive every day because of our faith in the sacrifice Jesus made for us.

9. **Be sure to allow time to discuss this question.**

Perhaps few topics contain as much emphasis on the Gospel as the topic of Baptism. Because of our sinful natures, however, we will feel condemnation when we discuss the changes that Baptism creates in us. We do have a new life, but the old life will continue to haunt us as long as we live here on earth. Emphasize that through the faith God created in us in Baptism, we receive His forgiveness for this sin, too. Also recall your discussion of the saint-sinner conflict from **Rom. 7** (session 18).

10. Luther says that we baptize children because God has commanded it (LC, p. 122). We would need no further reason. Nevertheless, Luther provides others. Take time to discuss a few of them, such as "the Lord sanctified and gave the Holy Spirit to many who were baptized as infants" (LC, pp. 120–21) and "even if infants did not believe (which, however, is not the case, as we have proved), yet their Baptism would be valid" (LC, p. 122).

Close with the prayer in the Student Book or another appropriate prayer.

Session 89: Bread and Wine Body and Blood

CENTRAL TRUTH

In the Lord's Supper we receive the body and blood of Christ in, with, and under the bread and wine. Those who receive this sacrament by faith, receive through it forgiveness of sins, strengthening of their faith, and eternal salvation.

OBJECTIVES

By the grace of God students will
1. express belief that with the bread and wine in the

Lord's Supper they receive the body and blood of Christ;
2. express belief that in the Lord's Supper they receive forgiveness of sins, strengthening of their faith, and eternal life;
3. indicate a desire to partake of the Lord's Supper regularly.

BACKGROUND

The Lord's Supper is a most precious gift of God. In this sacrament our Lord gives to us His body and blood. By faith we receive His very body and blood in, with, and under the bread and wine, the same body and blood that was given and shed for us for the remission of our sins.

How is this possible? No scientific data or logic can answer that question. The only answer comes by faith. Our Lord said it is so, and it is so. And as by faith we believe that the bread and wine are Christ's body and blood, so we also believe His words: "*Do this* in remembrance of Me." In obedience to His command, we are to come to the Lord's Table often to receive this precious gift of God.

The material in this session concentrates on the above truths. Christian church bodies, however, do not all agree. Therefore students may ask questions about other beliefs. In summary, the Roman Catholic Church believes in transubstantiation—that the bread and wine no longer exist but have been changed into Christ's body and blood. According to this teaching Christ is sacrificed again each time the Sacrament is celebrated. Many reformed denominations accept another false teaching—that the bread and wine *represent* Christ's body and blood. For further background on these teachings see sessions 7 and 17 in *The Church Takes Shape* and sessions 10–11 in *Which Way Is the Right Way?* the other 11th-grade courses in the Lutheran High School Religion Series.

GETTING STARTED (Objectives 1, 2, and 3)

If students know "Sons of God," you might open by singing it together. Talk about what the song says about what the Lord's Supper is (the Table of the Lord, the body and blood of Christ), who is to receive it (sons of God, that is, Christians), and what the benefits of receiving it are (you'll live forever—eternal life).

Invite students to tell about any special meaning the Lord's Supper has for them. Then proceed with today's session.

This Is . . . (Objectives 1 and 2)

1. Discuss the concept of *covenant*. Be sure to tie your discussion to the covenant God made with His Old Testament people.

   a. The content of the new covenant is the forgiveness of sins.

   b. The sign of the new covenant is the blood of Christ.

2. The words of Jesus tell us that the bread and wine *are* the body and blood of Christ. The bread and wine do not *become* the body and blood of Christ. There is no magical moment when they are transformed. When we receive the bread and wine in the Lord's Supper, we are receiving Christ's body and blood. This cannot be explained scientifically or rationally. It can only be accepted by faith.

   The benefits we receive from the Lord's Supper are forgiveness of sins, strengthening of faith, and eternal salvation. These benefits come when we receive the body and blood of Christ, given and shed for us for the remission of sins.

For You . . . (Objectives 1, 2, and 3)

The two lists made by students in this activity may vary considerably. The basic difference between the two lists, however, must be that those who should partake of the Lord's Supper are Christians who need forgiveness for their sins and who believe that that forgiveness is theirs through their Lord Jesus Christ. Here are two sample lists:

Should Partake of the Lord's Supper
1. Believers
2. Those who believe they receive Christ's body and blood in the Sacrament
3. Repentant sinners
4. Those at peace with their neighbors

Should Not Partake of the Lord's Supper
1. Unbelievers
2. Those who believe the bread and wine represent Christ's body and blood
3. Unrepentant sinners
4. Those who, because they do not forgive one another, are not at peace with their neighbors

Do This (Objectives 1, 2, and 3)

1. We should prepare ourselves for going to the Lord's Supper by examining ourselves—not to establish our worthiness, but to realize how unworthy we are and how much we need the forgiveness our Lord offers in this sacrament.

2. A person should go to the Lord's Supper as often as it is offered and as often as he or she feels the need for the forgiveness offered there.

3. A person should go to the Lord's Supper because Christ commands it and to receive the benefits offered there.

Another benefit of the Lord's Supper—one not mentioned by Luther—is identification with and strengthening of the Christian community. (The *Concordia Self-Study Bible* suggests two possible interpretations for the words, **"recognizing the body of the Lord"** in **1 Cor. 11:29.** Paul may be referring to the Lord's physical body, or he may be referring to the Christian community—the body of Christ that assembles at the Lord's Table.)

4. If a person feels no need for the Lord's Supper,

Luther says that person should do two things:
- Look inside himself/herself to see whether he or she is really a human being. For all human beings are by nature sinful and unclean, and in need of the Lord's Supper.
- Look around in the world and see how active the devil is. Then the person will realize how important it is that his or her faith be strengthened through the Lord's Supper.

Consider This

This is an application exercise. Answers may vary. The ultimate point is that if the student is truly repentant and wants forgiveness for his sins, he should go to the Lord's Table. The Lord's Supper is not for perfect people. It is for sinners— repentant sinners.

Ideally, as stated in 1 of the previous section, the student will prepare for the Sacrament by meditating upon his sinful condition and upon the forgiveness and strength God offers through the Lord's Supper; he will also apologize to his mother for his offense. We limit God's grace and focus too much upon a human act, however, if we state that adequate preparation cannot occur during the moment after the student looked up and saw the usher waiting for him to step toward the Lord's Table.

If a good reader is willing, ask him or her to read "On feeling worthy" with expression. Make the assignment ahead of time, so the student can prepare for the reading.

Close this session with a prayer that students would faithfully and regularly partake of the Lord's Supper and thank God for this most precious gift.

Session 90: "I'm Guilty, But . . ."

CENTRAL TRUTH

God, who for Jesus' sake freely forgives all the sins of all those who have faith in Him, calls us to voluntarily confess our sins to Him and our neighbors.

OBJECTIVES

By the grace of God students will
1. tell why it's desirable for them to voluntarily confess their sins before God and their fellow Christians;
2. confess their sins both publicly and privately;
3. describe what they will do when they feel a need for personal absolution;
4. express confidence that God does grant them forgiveness;
5. express a desire to confess their sins.

BACKGROUND

In Luther's day, private confession had become a mockery. People were required to go to confession and to confess before the priest every way they could remember that they had sinned against God. The priest then would assign duties—penance—that the confessing sinner must do in order to restore himself or herself to a right relationship with God.

Luther points out that that emphasis is all wrong. One ought to go to confession voluntarily, confessing those sins which trouble the conscience. Then the person should be sure of God's grace—that God fully and freely forgives our sins—not because we confess them or because we do something to atone for them, but because Christ has won forgiveness for all our sins by His death on the cross. When we believe that, we need do no more. For His sake and by His action for us, our sins are forgiven.

GETTING STARTED (Objective 1)

Have students individually read the opening paragraphs in the Student Book. Proceed with the activities.

The Three Confessions Objectives 1, 2, 3, and 4)

1. The three kinds of confession are confession before God, confession before your neighbor, and private confession before a Christian brother.

2. We should confess our sins before God to receive absolution, that is, the assurance of forgiveness by Him. Note that our action of confession does not earn forgiveness. God freely forgives, but our guilt at times causes us to feel estranged from Him. In a sense, we have moved away from Him; He has not moved away from us. When we hear the absolution, He moves us closer to Him, again.

3. We should confess our sins before another person so that person can also speak to us God's Word of forgiveness. If the person is someone we have wronged, we should confess to that person to receive his or her forgiveness, also.

4. The purpose of private confession is to bring before a Christian brother or sister sins that greatly trouble us so that person can assure us that those sins, too, are forgiven for Jesus' sake.

The Two Parts of Confession

(Objectives 1, 2, 3, and 4)

The correct answers are
1. Agree.
2. Disagree. The most important part of confession is receiving absolution from God.
3. Agree.
4. Disagree. The sole purpose for going to private confession is to receive God's absolution.
5. Agree. Only one who desires to be a Christian de-

sires the forgiveness of sins offered in the absolution part of confession.

Practically Speaking (Objective 5)

Emphasize again that we don't establish a good relationship with God; He establishes that relationship with us. When we have walked away from Him, He assures us (through the absolution that follows confession) that He has not walked away from us, and through that assurance He brings us closer to Him again.

The way students carry out the activities in this section is far less important than the action that follows. Attempt to build an atmosphere for sharing. (But don't require it. Remain faithful to the anonymity promised in the Student Book!)

REVIEW AND CONCLUSION

Use whatever time remains in this session for a free and open discussion of Luther's Large Catechism. Ask students whether studying the Large Catechism has increased their understanding of what they learned in Luther's Small Catechism during confirmation instruction classes. Ask them to share any insights they have gained from this unit or any questions they may have about any of the basic teachings of the Christian faith explained in Luther's Large Catechism.

If you must give a test, prepare a series of essay questions in which you ask the students to apply the teachings of Luther's Large Catechism to their lives.

Close by praying together the Lord's Prayer.

Printed in U.S.A.

www.ingramcontent.com/pod-product-compliance
Lightning Source LLC
Chambersburg PA
CBHW080548170426
43195CB00016B/2714